COLIN M. TURNBULL

The Mountain People

A TOUCHSTONE BOOK
Published by Simon & Schuster Inc.
New York London Toronto Sydney Tokyo Singapore

Copyright © 1972 by Colin M. Turnbull
All rights reserved
including the right of reproduction
in whole or in part in any form.
This Touchstone Edition, 1987
Published by Simon & Schuster, Inc.

Simon & Schuster Building
Rockefeller Center
1230 Avenue of the Americas
New York, NY 10020

TOUCHSTONE and colophon is a registered trademark
of Simon & Schuster, Inc.

Designed by Edith Fowler
Maps by Rafael Palacios
Manufactured in the United States of America

    12   13   14   15   16 Pbk.

Library of Congress Cataloging in Publication Data

ISBN 0-671-64098-4 Pbk.

For the Ik,
whom I learned not to hate;
and for Joe,
who helped me to learn.

Contents

Illustrations Follow Page 128

Preface

In what follows, there will be much to shock, and the reader will be tempted to say "how primitive . . . how savage . . . how disgusting" and, above all, "how inhuman." In living the experience I said all those things over and over again. The first judgments are typical of the kind of ethno- and ego centricism from which we can never quite escape, however much we try, and are little more than reaffirmations of standards that are different in circumstances that are different. But the latter judgment, "how inhuman," is of a different order, and supposes that there are certain standards common to all humanity, certain values inherent in humanity itself, from which the people described in this book seem to depart in a most drastic manner. In living the experience, however, and perhaps in reading it, one finds that it is oneself one is looking at and questioning; it is a voyage in quest of

the basic human and a discovery of his potential for inhumanity, a potential that lies within us all.

Most of us are unlikely to admit readily that we can sink
as low as the Ik, but many of us do, and with far less cause.
However, that is left for the reader to decide for himself;
this story concerns the Ik, the Mountain People, and their
struggle for survival. Although the experience was far from
pleasant, and involved both physical and mental suffering, I
am grateful for it. In spite of it all, and contrary to the first
tidal wave of disillusionment, it has added to my respect for
humanity and my hope that we who have been civilized into
such empty beliefs as the essential beauty and goodness of
humanity may discover ourselves before it is too late.

My thanks first and foremost are due to my friend and
colleague Joseph Towles, who shared much of the experience with me, at no small cost to himself, and who made
it more bearable. Together we discovered just how impossible it is, in certain circumstances, to be a beautiful human
being. He does not appear in these pages because he has his
own story to tell.

I am also most grateful to the Department of Anthropology of the American Museum of Natural History, which
financed the work, and to Professor Harry L. Shapiro and
other members of that Department for their help and constant letters of encouragement, appropriately if unbelievably
delivered to me in a forked stick. Jake Page, of *Natural History* magazine, helped by his constant interest and in many
subsequent discussions, as did my colleagues at Hofstra
University, and students who had a firsthand opportunity to
observe classical withdrawal symptoms. To Jerry Bernstein
thanks for transcribing many hours of tedious recorded
notes. Makerere University, in Kampala, and Dr. Raymond

Apthorpe offered a refuge to which I could flee, landslides permitting, and to Makerere I am also grateful not only for their traditional hospitality but for their very real and necessary help in securing the approval of the Uganda government for Mr. Towles and myself to work between 1964 and 1967, in a restricted area at a time when we could have been considerable embarrassment to them.

It is difficult to know how to thank the Ik; perhaps it should be for having treated me as one of themselves, which is about as badly as anyone can be treated. They did so with a curious elegance, even when dying, and they taught me much about myself. I fear I gave them little in return.

Epulu,
June 5, 1971

CHAPTER ONE

The World That Was

A NY DESCRIPTION of another people, another way of life, is to some extent bound to be subjective, especially when, as an anthropologist, one has shared that way of life. This is as it should be; but then the reader is entitled to know something of the aims, expectations, hopes and attitudes that the writer brought to the field with him, for these will surely influence not only how he sees things but even what he sees. At best his story will be only a partial one.

In this case there was all the advantage of an almost completely clean slate. Beyond the most superficial glimmerings, there was no way of knowing anything about the Ik, or the Teuso, as I thought they were called, for even their correct name was unknown. I could not have had a preconceived notion if I had tried. I neither knew anything nor, to tell the truth, did I particularly care. The Ik were, at best, a third choice, a last-ditch stand not to lose an opportunity to get into the field. So if I brought any attitudes with me, enthusiasm was not one of them; clinical observation was more like it.

For me this was something new. Until then I had been enthusiastic about almost everything I had done. India was my first enthusiasm, then colonial Africa, and then the Congo Pygmies. Up to this point I had made three field trips to the Pygmies, each with undiminished enthusiasm, but the nature of the work there was such that I was virtually excluded from village society. My major research objective for some time had been to return to the Ituri Forest and work among the villagers to complete the picture. When the opportunity for this time in the field came up, my first thought was of the Ituri, but continued disturbances in the northeastern Congo made it impossible.

A second project offered itself which was in some ways even more promising, and about which I felt no less enthusiastic. That was to return to India and work in the Andaman Islands, particularly the Little Andaman, among the Onge. Far removed from the Central African Pygmies, the Onge resembled them in a remarkable manner, both physically and culturally. They had never been adequately studied, and for years had been isolated on the Little Andaman Island, on which there were no foreign settlements of any kind, and which was accessible only by sea, and only during two months of the year, due to heavy surf. There were the usual rumors about their cannibalistic tendencies, almost certainly unfounded, and the very isolation that seemed uninviting to others seemed to me to offer ideal and almost unique opportunities for some very special and vital research. The project met with enthusiasm and support everywhere except in India. I should have recognized those vague responses for what they were, attempts to avoid the un-

pleasantness of having to say "no," but I refused to believe
that even the legacy of two centuries of British bureaucracy
could defeat such a worthwhile project, and I persisted up to
the last moment. I was finally persuaded to leave for India
regardless and argue it out there, when the polite corre-
spondence stopped abruptly, and I got the briefest and
simplest of notes refusing permission, with no stated reason.

There was little more than a month or two until I was due
to leave for the field, so I hurriedly drew up a triple project
to be carried out in East Africa, where there was the least
likelihood of any official refusal of permission. One possibility was to investigate the scattered groups of nomadic
hunters collectively known as Ndorobo (Wandorobo), still
to be found in Kenya, Tanzania and Uganda. Another possibility was to do some research among blacksmiths and iron
forgers. Work in both these areas was badly needed, and
either would have justified my time in the field. The third
possibility was a more detailed study of a small group of
hunters isolated in the mountains separating northern
Uganda, Sudan and Kenya. My attention had been drawn
to them by Elizabeth Marshall Thomas, who had run
across them while working with the Dodos, in northern
Karimoja. Rather like the Onge, this project offered some
opportunity for comparison between two very different
groups of hunters living in very different environments.
One of the objectives of anthropology is to discover basic
principles of social organization, and small-scale societies are
ideal for this purpose, the more isolated the better. Comparison between different societies is especially instructive, and
since I had no means of knowing what to expect of the
"Teuso," my attitude remained clinical rather than enthusiastic. But no amount of clinical interest could suppress the
disappointment at the failure of the two preferred projects.

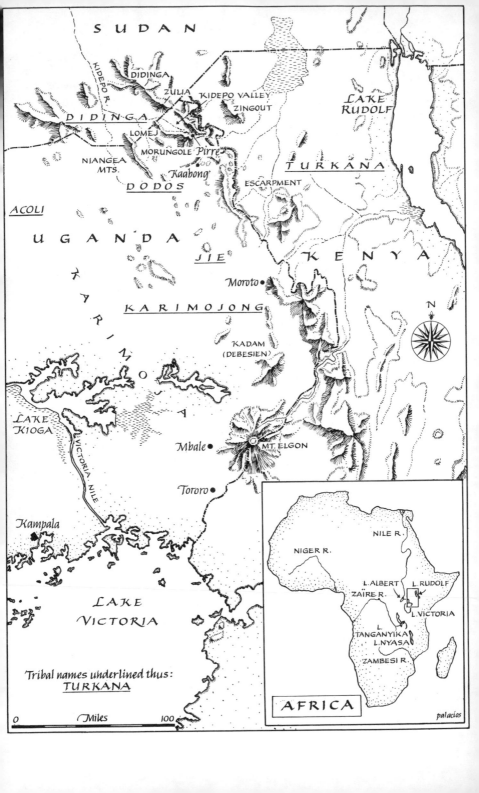

SUDAN

KIDEPO R.

DIDINGA

ZULIA

KIDEPO VALLEY

ZINGOUT

DIDINGA

LOMEJ

MORUNGOLE *Pirre*

NIANGEA
MTS.

Kaabong

LAKE
RUDOLF

TURKANA

ESCARPMENT

ACOLI

DODOS

UGANDA

JIE

KENYA

Moroto •

KARIMOJONG

KADAM
(DEBESIEN)

LAKE
KIOGA

Mbale •

MT. ELGON

Tororo •

Kampala •

LAKE
VICTORIA

Tribal names underlined thus:
TURKANA

0   Miles   100

N

AFRICA

NIGER R.

NILE R.

L. ALBERT   L. RUDOLF

ZAIRE R.

L. VICTORIA

L.
TANGANYIKA
L. NYASA

ZAMBESI R.

palacios

I make this point because one of the most delicate tasks of the field anthropologist is to establish a really satisfactory and amicable relationship with the people among whom he is going to live, and to regard them with a jaundiced eye is hardly the way to win favor. I might have forgotten the Ituri and the Onge by the time I reached northern Uganda if all had gone well from this point, but it did not. A stopover in Egypt was a near-disaster, and in Kenya I found that the Land Rover which had been specially ordered had not been delivered. When it did arrive in Mombasa, it did not conform to the given specifications, and on the first night out, near Kilimanjaro, a rainstorm showed how effectively the roof leaked, right over the beds. The idea was to drive through Tanzania and up through southern and western Uganda in search of Ndorobo and smiths, a brief initial survey before trying out the third part of the project. Both Ndorobo and the smiths were elusive, and the delay waiting for the Land Rover did not allow enough time for an adequate survey. Further, the Land Rover, painted fire-engine red, possessed the singular and by no means welcome ability to attract elephants, particularly male elephants very obviously in search of female company. This, like the leaky roof, remained a constant quality.

In Uganda there were rumblings of political discontent, for this was just before the coup in which Obote assumed dictatorial powers and attempted to assassinate the Kabaka, plunging Uganda into a prolonged and bitter period of hostility between north and south. This was not a happy omen for work to be done in the north while based on and supported by a university in the south, and, to make matters worse, most of the extreme north was sealed off due both to extensive cattle raiding and to the troubles in southern Sudan. However, the coup had not yet taken place, and

tentative permission was given, through the university, for
me to undertake research among the "Teuso," as we all still
thought the Ik were called. Before leaving Makerere I did
whatever was possible to discover more about the region and
the people so that I could formulate some kind of plan of
attack.

It seemed that just before World War II the Teuso had all
been encouraged to settle in northern Uganda, in the mountainous northeast corner bordering on Kenya to the east and
Sudan to the north. Until then they had roamed in nomadic
bands, as hunters and gatherers, throughout a vast region in
all three countries. It was only with the advent of nation-
hood, following the war, that the boundaries became of
major significance, but the process of settlement had been
begun well before.

From what I was able to learn later, their way of life then
had been very different from what it was now. The area in
which they are now confined, between the Kenya-Uganda
escarpment and Mount Morungole, on the eastern edge of
what is now Kidepo National Park, used to be a temporary
resting place in the annual nomadic cycle. Kidepo Valley, below Morungole, formed their major hunting territory. It was
some thirty-five miles across, almost completely hemmed
in by Morungole to the south and east, the Didinga Mountains to the north, and the Niangea Mountains to the west.
The only opening was in the southwest corner. The valley
is full of game throughout the year, but when the heavy
rains come the valley floor tends to get sodden and the
large game, especially elephant, used to move out either
through the southwestern corridor or up into the Didinga
Mountains. At this point the hunters began moving, following the game, especially through the Didinga Mountains and
into the Sudan, hunting the game and gathering wild vege-

tables and roots and berries as they went, seldom staying in one place more than a few days. Then with the end of the rains the hunters came down into northern Kenya, west of Lake Rudolf, and made their way back toward the escarpment, collecting honey as they went, especially in the Zingout Mountains. They then climbed up the two-thousand-foot escarpment back into Uganda, over to Morungole and back down into Kidepo.

Kidepo was undoubtedly where they spent the best part of the year, but, like most hunters and gatherers, these depended as much on vegetable resources as they did on game, and vegetable supplies can be exhausted even more quickly and permanently than game if a band stays in one place too long. Mobility is essential to the hunting-and-gathering way of life, and nomadism is by no means the random, aimless meandering it is sometimes thought to be. At the same time, hunting and gathering, even in a marginal environment, are neither as hard nor as precarious as they may seem. The hunter and gatherer gives little thought for the morrow, getting his feed fresh, from day to day, with the ready assurance of someone who has come to terms with the world around him. And this is exactly what the hunter does. He knows the world he lives in as few others do, and he lives in sympathy with it rather than trying to dominate it. He is the best of conservationists, knowing exactly how much he can take from where at any given time. His nomadic pattern is geared to this knowledge, and what appears to others to be a precarious existence probably affords the hunter a much greater sense of security than is felt, say, by many farmers. For the farmer the results of a year's work may be destroyed overnight, whereas the most the hunter can lose is what he can replace tomorrow. Partly for this reason there tends to be little fear of supernatural malevolence

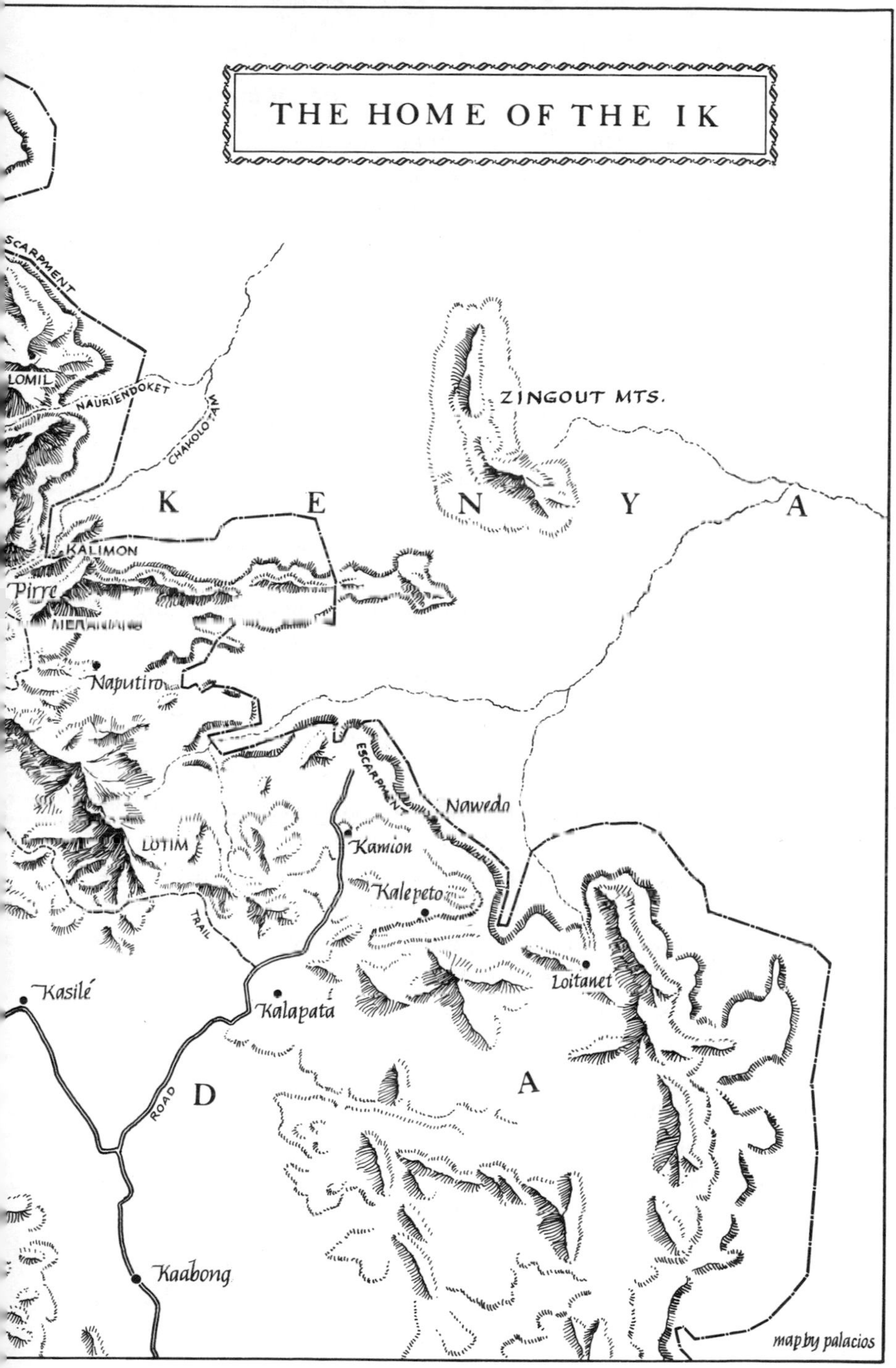

THE HOME OF THE IK
SCARPMENT
LOMIL
NAURIENDOKET
CHAKOLOTAM
ZINGOUT MTS.
K E N Y A
KALIMON
Pirre
Naputiro
ESCARPMENT
Nawedo
Kamion
LOTIM
Kalepeto
TRAIL
Loitanet
Kasilé
Kalapata
ROAD
D
A
Kaabong
map by palacios

among hunters; they live an open life untroubled by the various neuroses that accompany progress.

Before Kidepo was taken over as a National Park and the Ik were excluded, in this way, from their major hunting ground, they used to practice two kinds of hunting. In the open grasslands they hunted with nets, but when in hilly or mountainous terrain, which was most of the time, they used only spears and bows and arrows. Each technique of hunting called for the formation of different kinds of groups, but the essential was always cooperativeness. The net hunt, much as practiced by the neighboring Acoli peoples, calls for the cooperation of men, women and children. Virtually an entire band, perhaps of a hundred people, may set out with nets, long poles, spears, bows and arrows. The poles are stuck in the ground to form a wide arc, and the nets are hung on them, stretching fom one to another for as much as half a mile or more. This, at any rate, is the ideal, but even many fewer nets, if carefully placed, may be successful. The women and children act as beaters, driving the game into the waiting net. Sometimes the bush is fired to help, for beating in long grass can be both dangerous and ineffective. In the dry season there are frequent bush fires, and these used to be occasions when an entire band would start to life, grab the nets and poles and run to set them up in front of the advancing blaze. More frequently, however, fires can be observed for some time and their courses carefully plotted. At night it is particularly easy to see how predictable the course of a bush fire may be. At first you see the glow in the sky behind the silhouette of a mountain, then the first flames appear against the darkness along the crest and begin inching downward. It is rather like watching the molten lava flowing from the lip of a volcano, for the fire does not descend the mountainside in a straight line or cover it like a sheet; it flows downward, slowly but surely, in rivers of intensely bright orange, following the wooded ravines. The hunters study the progress of the fire with care, and plot their strategy. They may have time to set their nets up well in advance of the fire, where the ravines open out into the grasslands. Several ravines will be closed off in this way, and then a second, continuous line of nets set up farther back. In this case the women and children have little to do but wait in safety behind the last line of nets while the men stand guard with spears. With the first eddies of smoke the game comes out, sometimes cautiously, sometimes running blindly. Animals that escape the first net may fall into the second, and those that slip out to the side may still be caught by youths with bows and arrows. Such a hunt comes only once or twice in a season, and it is only a hunt like this that provides anything like a surplus worth drying and storing. The dried meat is carried around by men and women, in the hide pouches they often carry, for weeks, to serve as emergency rations when they are far away from camp, gathering honey or termites.

More often even the net hunt yields little more than can be consumed in a day or two, for once they have enough for their immediate needs the hunters return to camp. To over- hunt is considered one of the major crimes, in the nature of a sin against divine command, and it is done only before long treks through terrain where hunting may not be productive, or before the honey or termite seasons, when bands split up into tiny groups which are too small to hunt effectively and which may stay away for days or even weeks in the individual pursuit of these delicacies.

The spear hunt is much more arduous and still less productive, though perfectly adequate for daily needs. Although women and children are not used during the hunt,

which involves stalking rather than beating, their cooperation is still required. They are needed to carry the game back
to the camp as it is killed, so that the men can continue
unhindered. The women are always close at hand, and occupy themselves by gathering while the men are hunting. In this way they are even drawn into the evening
debates when it has to be decided where to hunt the next
day, since the vegetable foods gathered by the women are
every bit as important in the diet as meat. This is another
widespread characteristic of hunting-and-gathering societies, the cooperation and equality of importance between
men and women. Men generally are dominant only in so far
as the hunt is considered much more exciting and dangerous
(in more ways than one since it is thought to involve supernatural dangers as well as physical) and occupies the
thoughts of the people in a way that vegetable gathering
never could. It is, after all, rather difficult to get emotional
over the digging up of a root or the picking of a berry. None
the less, even though the vegetable supplies they bring in
daily are not greeted with the same enthusiasm as is meat,
the women have the satisfaction of knowing that their con-
tribution not only provides the bulk of the food, probably,
but that it is also the most reliable and predictable source of
nourishment. As they wander off each day, either with the
men or in small groups by themselves with one or two older
men to protect them, they note what will be ready for
gathering the next day, next week or next month. The men
can predict the movement of game with remarkable accu-
racy, but never with the same certainty.

Except when a large beat is planned, the ratio between
men and women on the hunt is not at all equal, so women
have plenty of opportunity for going off on their own foraging expeditions, which may take them even farther afield

than the hunt. This part of eastern Africa, bordering on the fringes of the Sahara, is by no means lush, and it is difficult country to traverse, gouged as it is by precipitous and rocky ravines. But for those who know it as intimately as do the Ik, there is always enough, provided they can continue to move from place to place. Even at the best of times women's gathering parties may be away for two or three days, roaming across to the far side of Kidepo Valley, into the foothills of Zulia Mountain, in the Sudan. Only when the annual movement of game begins and the Ik leave their relatively settled camps near Morungole do members of bands remain together continuously.

In the past even the semi-permanent houses were made of grass laid over an igloo-shaped frame of sticks. These can be put up quickly and simply and are as adequate for a stay of two or three months as they are for a stay of two or three days. There is no loss or hardship in abandoning them at a moment's notice, so they form a natural part of the highly mobile life of the hunters. This mobility serves more needs than the obvious economic need; it allows for a constant realignment of friendships and work units, and for the dissipation of latent disputes. It also allows for a constantly shifting locus of authority, and this is important to the essentially egalitarian hunter. Each time the band moves, the camp is reformed in a slightly different way; friends who have become less friendly build their houses farther away from each other, new alliances being created. Even in a fairly settled camp it is easy to abandon a house or, if you want to be dramatic, tear it down and build another elsewhere, to show your displeasure. If you want to be less demonstrative, you can simply let it fall down by pulling out one or two key sticks, and take this as an excuse to build in another part of the camp.

The concept of family is a broad one; what really counts most in everyday life is community of residence, and even within a camp those who live close to each other are likely to see each other as effectively related, whether there is any kinship bond or not. Full brothers, on the other hand, who live in different parts of the camp, let alone in different bands, may have little concern for each other. The needs of the moment are the needs that dominate the mind of the hunter, so that even the normally stable bonds of biological relationship become flexible, and the terms for parent or child, brother or sister, are used to indicate present lines of responsibility and friendship rather than anything else. Frequently the sociological relationship corresponds with the biological, but by no means always, and in the event of any difference biology takes second place.

It is not possible, then, to think of the family as a simple, basic unit, in biological terms or economic or any other. At best, the biological family—that is to say, a man, his wife and their children—provides a ready-made model for a cooperative social unit. The model may be extended, linking several families in a much wider unit, but this is much more typical of sedentary peoples than of nomadic hunters. With hunters a child is brought up to regard any adult living in the same camp as a parent, any age-mate as a brother or sister. These are the real and effective relationships, constantly shifting and changing as the composition of the band changes and the camps are abandoned and rebuilt. The Ik no less than any others had this essentially social attitude toward kinship, and it readily lent itself to the rapid and disastrous changes that took place following the restriction of their movement and hunting activities. The family simply ceased to exist.

In such a fluid society of hunters the environment invariably provides the central theme that holds them together, that gives them a sense of common identity; it is the hub around which their life revolves. It provides all the necessities such as food, shelter and clothing, and often some kind of spiritual existence of its own is attributed to it. Just as the Mbuti Pygmies in their lush tropical rain forest regard the forest as a benevolent deity, so do the Ik, in their rocky mountain stronghold, think of the mountains as being peculiarly and specially theirs. People and mountains belong to each other and are inseparable. It is not just that the Ik would not know how to live, to hunt or farm, in the flat, arid plateau below them, because they are as intelligent as any and a great deal sharper, quicker to learn and more adaptable than many. But with regard to the mountains it is different, and their adaptability seems to reach its limits. The Ik, without their mountains, would no longer be the Ik and similarly, they say, the mountains without the Ik would no longer be the same mountains, if indeed they continued to exist at all. In just the same way that there is something bewitching about the rain forest, so there is something intoxicating about high altitudes. There is a special quality to the air that can be felt and almost seen, for it colors vision with that same indefinable quality. One knows that things are not quite what they seem, neither as far nor as near, this color or that; the light is constantly changing and the shadows shifting. The mountains themselves seem to be, like the Ik, in a state of perpetual motion. And so the two live together, a part of each other.

Much of all this I was able to learn before I left Kampala, and much that I had to guess at was confirmed when I reached the mountains myself, though not quite in the way I

had expected. Still less were other expectations fulfilled,
such as to how I would settle among the people, how I
would live and what I would learn. If I had known what to
expect I would almost certainly not have gone, but as it was
I still had a few days of contented optimism left. I had no
very clear idea of how I would get up into the mountains,
but if the Land Rover failed to make it I was prepared to
walk as far as was necessary, and indeed I had begun preparing for a strenuous time while I was still in New York,
walking to and from work every day, from Twenty-first
Street to Seventy-seventh. It proved to be rather inadequate
preparation, excessive though it was by New York standards.
But I somehow visualized myself appearing up in the mountains and being welcomed by a warm, friendly people. I had
never had any experience other than this in Africa, and saw
no reason why the Ik should be different. The physical details of how they lived did not bother me at all, as I had
survived happily in the arctic as well as the tropics, the
desert as well as the forest. Nor did the prospect of high
altitude worry me overmuch, for I had spent some time up
in the Himalayas. Having lived with the Pygmies, who eat
almost anything that moves, I didn't give food a second
thought. In all, I was just about as unconcerned as if I had
been going upstate for a weekend.

As far as academic expectations went, I had neither any
specific hopes nor any specific fears, and this was as it
should be. It is too easy to go into a field situation expecting
or hoping to find this or that, for invariably you come out
having found what you wanted. Selectivity can do great
things in blinding one to a wider reality. I was interested
rather in a very general comparison between two hunting-
and-gathering societies (Pygmies and Ik) in totally different

environments; it was more of a fact-finding mission than the testing of some theoretical point of view; that could come later. It was unambitious, but practical and of solid worth.

It is a mistake to think of small-scale societies as "primitive" or "simple," however simple they may appear on the surface. Hunters and gatherers, most of all, appear deceptively simple and straightforward in terms of their social organization, yet that appearance is far from being true. What is true, perhaps, is that the result of a typical hunting-and-gathering social organization is a simple and effective system of human relationships, and this is what so strongly appeals to many of those who have worked with them. If we can learn about the nature of society from a study of small-scale societies, we can also learn about human relationships, and that seems fully as valuable and valid. The smaller the society, the less emphasis there is on the formal system, and the more there is on inter-personal and inter-group relations, to which the system is subordinated. Security is seen in terms of these relationships, and so is survival. The result, which appears so deceptively simple, is that hunters frequently display those characteristics that we find so admirable in man: kindness, generosity, consideration, affection, honesty, hospitality, compassion, charity and others. This sounds like a formidable list of virtues, and so it would be if they *were* virtues, but for the hunter they are not. For the hunter in his tiny, close-knit society, these are necessities for survival; without them society would collapse. It is a far cry from our society, in which anyone possessing even half these qualities would find it hard indeed to survive, yet we are given to thinking that somehow these are virtues inherent in man.

It was not foremost in my mind, I suppose, but, as with

the physical conditions, I took it for granted that the Ik would possess these same qualities. It was a shock to find myself wrong on almost all counts. The Teuso were not the Teuso, they were the Ik; they were not hunters, they were farmers, their mountain villages were far from livable, the food was uneatable because there was not any, and the people were as unfriendly, uncharitable, inhospitable and generally mean as any people can be. For those positive qualities we value so highly are no longer functional for the Ik; even more than in our own society they spell ruin and disaster. It seems that, far from being basic human qualities, they are superficial luxuries we can afford in times of plenty, or mere mechanisms for survival and security. Given the situation in which the Ik found themselves as I headed toward them, man has not time for such luxuries, and a much more basic man appears, using much more basic survival tactics. The much vaunted gap between man and the so-called "lesser" animals suddenly shrinks to nothingness, except that in this case most "lesser" animals come off rather well by comparison, displaying many more of those "human" qualities than the Ik did. Yet the relationship between cause and effect is so undeniable that one does not blame or criticize the Ik; if anything, one admires them for surviving in spite of themselves. It is rather like suddenly catching sight of oneself, in middle age, stripped naked in front of the bathroom mirror. One is forced to admit that the paunchy body is no longer as beautiful as it used to be, if indeed it ever was, and one hastens to don one's clothes to restore the illusion, for the greater ease of mind of others as well as one's own. The beautiful human, like the beautiful body, seems to be a myth perpetuated by the game of self-deceit, at which humans are so singularly adept. In fact, after even a few months with the Ik one is tempted to think that if there is such a thing as a basic human quality, self-deception it is.*

All this, however, was far from my mind as the fire-engine red, leaky, elephant-attracting Land Rover carried me north to the waiting jackals.

* After a few months among the Ik I had occasion to devote a chapter to them in *Tradition and Change in African Tribal Life* (World, 1966). It reads significantly differently from this chapter, and makes me question the validity of much field work, including my own. Admittedly it was a purely descriptive account, and an attempt to reconstruct the life of the Ik in an average year; but had I not arrived when I did, had I arrived when the famine had truly set in, I might well have never known that this side of the Ik, which I describe in that book, existed. I believe both accounts to be accurate, and the difference shows how shallow is man's potential for goodness, and how basic and deep-rooted his urge to survive. The Ik, like the rest of us, are kind and generous and light-hearted and jolly when they can afford to be. I saw the last vestiges of that in the first month or two, and I saw those vestiges replaced almost overnight, it seemed, by the basic survival instincts that lie in all of us.

CHAPTER TWO

Careless Rapture

On leaving Kampala, to reach Moroto you drive east to within a few miles of the Kenya border, through rich, rolling country. At Tororo the road heads north to Mbale. There I had to check with the police and get a permit to travel direct to Moroto along the watershed road; they said that I did so at my own risk, and cautioned me not to stop anywhere. They wished me good luck and said goodbye as though I were never coming back. But it was a gloriously fine, sunny day, still not too hot, and as I left the tarmac road just north of Mbale and plunged down a muddy stretch into the plains I could not have felt in better spirits.

Once down the hillside it was distinctly hotter, and the muddy road gave way to a dusty, bumpy track. The lush green countryside covered with rich banana plantations disappeared abruptly, and skirting the foot of Mount Elgon the landscape opened out into a vast flat plain, dry and brown,

34

with the huge jagged mass of Mount Debesien (or Kadam) reaching up into the hazy sky. There was one last police barrier to pass and then I seemed to have the whole world to myself. Even before the police were out of range of the rearview mirror I got the feeling of being incredibly and agreeably alone. Ahead there was not a sign of any living thing; the air was heavy and still; nothing seemed to move or be capable of movement; even the huge cloud of dust billowing along behind did not billow for long, it just hung suspended, gradually blending with the colorless sky. I passed the first herd of cattle, guarded by a tall, lanky youth leaning on a spear, without even really noticing them until they disappeared in the dust; they too seemed frozen still. Only when I was nearing Debesien were there evident signs of life, where quite a sizable village had grown up near some kind of prison settlement. There was an enormous crowd of about twenty or thirty people at a roadside market, and a dozen others ambling along to join them. All of a sudden the world seemed overpopulated. Yet with all this flurry of activity and people, there was still no impression of either movement or color. What movement there was took place in slow motion, and change in color was equally imperceptible, a slow fusion of gray and brown, rock and dust.

It sounds drab and lifeless, yet somehow it was neither. It was just an utterly different world living at an utterly different pace. Even the fact that most of the men wore nothing but a pair of sandals on the feet and a bit of cloth across one shoulder or bundled up on the head made no immediate impression, the naked bodies seeming to be a perfectly natural part of the gray-brown world around them. Perhaps it was just that, the naturalness of it all, that saved the scene from being one of desolation. I think I felt more relaxed than I had for years.

The dusty track became rocky shortly after this splash of life, and began to climb around the north side of Debesien and up onto the watershed. There was a settlement of Didinga refugees from the Sudan, trying hard to persuade some tired-looking crops to grow, but they too were evidently in slow motion: and after that, nothing. The road continued along the top of the watershed, with views far down to both east and west, and massive Debesien fading into the haze behind. I met more Karimojong with herds of several hundred head of cattle, scrawny, colorless and slow, like everything else, and I wondered that these were the people alleged to be such vicious fighters and raiders, about whom I had been warned. When I tried waving, the gesture met with not the slightest response, not even the faintest hint of interest at such a ridiculous expenditure of energy, just nonfriendly, non-hostile but somehow extraordinarily gentle looks.

By now my driving was more in keeping with the countryside, slow and leisurely, and the fire-engine red had long since been modified to the uniform brown of Karimoja. And when my hand waves were reduced to vague inclinations of the head, because I felt embarrassed that my open display of amity should be so studiously ignored, I began to notice gray-brown heads vaguely inclining a sober acknowledgment. I suppose it is part of the stage fright that many anthropologists feel each time they enter a new field. I feel it even when returning to one I have known well before: there is a sickening feeling in the pit of one's stomach that people are not going to like you or want you, that you are never going to be able to understand a word of their incomprehensible language and that they are not going to bother trying to understand yours. Every time I feel convinced the whole idea was a ghastly mistake, and react, I suppose, by doing my utmost to show what a nice, friendly kind of person I am. The reaction, invariably and properly, is one of utmost caution and reserve, which is not helpful to the situation. But here, in just one day's driving I seemed to have got over my stage fright and to have relearned that familiar lesson in a few hours instead of a few weeks. When I came to a bridge over what evidently was on occasion a river but now was a wide, grassy trough, and found it well and truly breached, I stopped to get out and see where I could best cross the dry bed. Out of the corner of my eye, however, I saw three men with spears approaching from behind, and I recollected the warnings and final farewell of the Mbale police. If I could have gone on I would have, with rapidity, but I was already almost up onto the bridge, and to go into reverse would have been to run directly into the three Karimojong, which as yet seemed uncalled for.

Then two of them were at one door and the third, around at the driver's side, put his head and shoulders through the open window, looked carefully around the inside of the Land Rover and only then looked at me. He opened his mouth in a great, toothy smile and closed it again, returning to impassivity. I felt encouraged enough to say something noncommittal, and, not knowing any Karimojong, said "Hi!" They responded with something I took to be equally non-committal and slowly walked off. The next I saw of them they were on the far side of the river, beckoning me to come across showing me the best way. They were gone even before I climbed up over the far bank.

When in the late afternoon I reached Moroto, then, it was no surprise to see these strangely reserved, tall, perfectly naked men ambling along the main street (a brief hundred-yard display of tarmac), occasionally stooping to enter a store and make some purchase, or sitting at a bar drinking.

The only thing that did surprise me was that when talking to anyone who was fully clothed, the Karimojong politely took their cloths and covered themselves, but since the cloths were inadequate as a total wraparound, they settled for half, covering the backside and continuing, naked as ever in front, their polite conversation. In no time at all it was the people with clothes on whom I noticed. They looked so hot and uncomfortable and even dirty, and decidedly ill at ease. I parked under a huge shady tree near the Rest House and prepared to begin to enjoy this field trip.

The Administrator was kind and welcoming, but he said he could not possibly let me go up into the mountains without direct approval from the central government, as there was fighting along the Sudan border and heavily intensified cattle raiding both within Uganda and between various groups of cattle herders in Uganda, Sudan and Kenya. It was bad at the best of times, he said, but particularly so in a drought year, and this was evidently very much of a drought year. In the end he allowed me to go as far as Kaabong, the last administrative outpost, and to await further permission there. He suggested I take an interpreter with me, and back under the shade tree, which was also headquarters for the geological survey teams working in the area, an Acoli youth named Martin offered his services, speaking both Karimojong and Swahili, though practically no English. He seemed ideal, as I had no idea of what relations were like between the "Teuso" and the Karimojong, and did not want to start off on the wrong foot by having a Karimojong interpreter. It so happened that any foot was the wrong foot.

The Administrator gave me final friendly warnings, and urged me not to go near the Sudan border without police escort when I did finally get into the mountains. He discussed freely many of his problems and said he would welcome any ideas that might come out of my researches. This is the kind of interest and cooperation that is all too often lacking, and it added to my growing enthusiasm. Armed with letters of introduction to the Assistant Administrator at Kaabong, and with a suddenly and peculiarly nervous Martin at my side, I drove the lurching Land Rover out of Moroto and headed still farther north, into the even dustier and flatter stretches of northern Karimoja.

On either side of the road was a great arid expanse of scrubland, studded with thorn bushes, hot and disagreeable. Within a few miles of leaving Moroto it was evident that Martin, who had claimed to know Kaabong well, was not even sure where it was. Then when we found and took the northward road and after an hour or two ran into an unusually large herd of cattle, whose herders fled into the bush as we approached, Martin showed signs of panic. Those were Turkana raiders, he said, from Kenya. The Turkana have a singularly unsavory reputation as one of the fiercest tribes of East Africa, and although I thought it odd that they should be returning from a raid in broad daylight so close to Moroto (which was also the headquarters of the Uganda Army), it was also odd that they should have fled so rapidly. Here and there we saw camels being herded together with the cattle, a sure sign of the proximity of the desert.

The dead flatness was relieved by an occasional conical hill rising like an island out of the sea, a barren, lifeless island. There was not a single village on the whole northward stretch. An occasional antelope bounded across the road, but the few herders we saw hid themselves long before we reached them, sometimes even flinging their spears down as they ran. While Martin worried about whether they were Turkana or Jie I worried more about what damage was being done to their private parts in their headlong flight through the thorn scrub. But my desire to be befriended had diminished, and I did not stop but drove on with growing disquiet, urged to greater and greater speed by Martin, who said we would both die if we did not reach Kaabong by dark.

Then the road curved sharply to the west and climbed a long slope on the far side of which was a breathtaking view of an enormous range of jagged, wildly irregular mountains stretching right across the northern horizon, or so it seemed. As we turned north and drew closer they seemed even wilder, reaching upward like gnarled, knotted fingers, a fantasy of what one used to think of as a lunar landscape. In the soft evening light it was specially beautiful, and after the heat and glare and dust of the day's drive it gave me a feeling of great relief to realize that these were the mountains in which I was to live. Then the road rose one final time and dipped gently down into Kaabong, an agreeable sprawl of a handful of small mud houses, a bar, a hospital and three or four Somali stores. Immediately beyond is a small hill crowded with the round tin huts of the police, and directly below it are the house of the Assistant Administrator and the Kaabong Rest House.

I had ignored the comforts of the Moroto Rest House, which I later found to be cheap, comfortable and well provisioned, but after that drive through northern Karimoja I was ready for some comfort and headed in the direction indicated by a neatly painted signpost. The dream was shattered by the sight of a low concrete building with corrugated iron roof and three metal doors standing open to display three bare concrete floors, empty but for cobwebs and spiders. It would have been even more shattered if I had known this was to seem a luxury haven during the months to come. As it was, I used one of the rooms to store some supplies and equipment in, and set the Land Rover up as office, kitchen and bedroom.

The Assistant Administrator made me as welcome as he could, and sent for two Teuso boys who had spent the previous year at the Catholic Mission school nearby. They arrived the next day, looking like models of Mission cleanliness, scrubbed and neatly dressed, and soon showed that although their English was not even basic, it was enough to give me a start on their language without the intervention of Martin's Karimojong, which turned out to be as doubtful as the boys' English. After two days in Kaabong Martin told me that he was not at all sure he wanted to stay in Karimoja, let alone go up into the mountains. He made a brief visit to the nearby village of Kasilé, where he had discovered a relative of his was teaching, and he said his relative was going to help him get to know some of the Teuso living there and then he would be able to let me know definitely whether he would stay on or not. That left me free to work with Peter and Thomas, who got permission from the school to take time off to teach me their language. The teacher made a special visit to confirm the story, because he had never heard of anyone wanting to learn to talk like the Teuso—not even the local Karimojong could understand them. But the two boys were regular visitors, and over countless cups of sugar and tea they quickly provided me with a fine four-hundred-word vocabulary, and together we worked out the basic essentials of the grammar. It was not easy going, and to the end many of the subtleties of pronunciation eluded me. They involved implosives and explosives following hot on each other's heels, and I never developed the sheer muscular control required. Many of the subtleties I did not even hear properly until Archie Tucker, the English linguist, accepted an invitation to come up and see just what this extraordinary

language was, for it certainly was not Sudanic or Bantu.
Archie finally pronounced, with no little satisfaction, that
the nearest language he could find to this one was classical
Middle-Kingdom Egyptian! But in total ignorance of the
historical importance of the language I was learning, I
struggled on and found, as might be expected, that the
further I got with it the more communicative Peter and
Thomas became. After a week they confided in me that
Teuso was not their proper tribal name at all, it was one of
several names applied by the various "foreign" tribes around
them. Their real name was Ik (pronounced as Eek), and the
language was Icietot (Eechietoht). I had begun to suspect
that Teuso was not their real name, but to my direct questions they had always answered that it was, until they decided to say the opposite. I found out that most Ik share this
habit. It is a kind of a game, to see how effectively you can lie
and fool someone. Then when you have proven your ability
you have the additional fun of telling your victim. Many a
time I was to hear them say, "You don't really believe what
we told you, do you?" But anthropologists have their own
ways of worming the truth out of reluctant informants, and I
learned to play the game the Icien way.

During the mornings I did my homework, then spent an
hour or two wandering around Kaabong and the surrounding countryside, getting to know some of the Dodos cattle
herders. They are one of the many Karimojong-speaking
peoples in this part of East Africa, and they used to stand
around and listen with open amusement as I tried out my
Icietot on them. Then they would tell me, in Swahili, that I
sounded something like an Ik, but that would do me no good
as nobody but the Ik could understand, and surely I didn't
want to talk to *them?* They spoke of them in much the same
terms as did the Assistant Administrator: troublesome, dis-

honest, elusive, tricky. However, the Dodos added that the Ik were also useful in helping them to raid their neighbors. Peter and Thomas, who always spoke in unison, denied this flatly, which added some weight to the Dodos story. One Dodos youth, Gabriel, was the best and kindest of guides. He took me to his home, showed me with pride the fields farmed by his progressive father, and spoke in favor of the government plan to reduce cattle herding and persuade more and more of the Karimojong peoples to take up farming. His own family had once possessed a large herd, he said, but a number of years back the Turkana had come and stolen it. Since then they had given up herding, and had become relatively prosperous farmers. Gabriel showed me his countryside, naming the various fantastic rocky outcrops with such graphic terms as penis, vulva, clitoris, rump, and other less interesting parts of the anatomy. It seemed nicely appropriate that the Mission should be dominated by "The Vulva," which had the alternative name of "The Gateway."

But all Gabriel's enthusiasm for the modern world of schools and farming suddenly evaporated when one day we stumbled across a collection of small stones lying in neat clusters on the ground. He immediately got down on the ground and started picking up the stones and talking to them. It was a child's game, he explained, representing a wealthy man's cattle *boma* with all his cattle. He reconstructed it for me, complete with calves' pen, milking table and enclosure for goats. He grouped the stones and then showed me how some of them had been chipped so that they represented the different shapes to which cattle horns are trained, each of which has a special name. The stones had also been chosen for their size and color, and for these too the Dodos have very detailed and specific terms, so that almost every stone had a slightly different combination of names, as do the cattle in real life. He told me of how he had had his own special calf, and how he used to sing to it. I had the distinct feeling that Gabriel felt great regret for all that progress had taken away from him, and would have given much to be less prosperous, less educated and more Dodos. Sometime in the second week I asked if I could have permission to drive up the old road that leads, or used to lead, to Kamion, a village long since deserted due to constant raids by Turkana. This road runs due north from Kaabong, parallel to the escarpment. As far as I could gather, most of the Ik lived along this escarpment, though the Assistant Administrator said there were some on Mount Morungole, a dark mass to the northwest, always hidden in haze. The boys were given a long weekend off, I was urged to be careful of the Turkana and we set off. I had been told of one village in particular, Kalepeto, and thought I would start there. I hoped to visit as many villages as possible to get a rough idea of the number and distribution of the Ik. It was already plain that the government had stopped them from hunting, which was a blow, but, knowing something of hunters, I could not believe they would give up that easily, and I expected to find quite a lot of illicit hunting still going on.

We reached a fork in the very rough, pitted track, and there, announced Peter and Thomas, was Kalepeto. There was a store and a school and half a dozen houses. It turned out to be Kalapata, and Peter and Thomas claimed to have misheard me. They now said, "Oh, Kalepeto, that's not this direction at all, it's way over on the escarpment." So we took an even less promising trail off to the east, and after nearly two hours' driving could go no farther. Peter and Thomas suggested we turn back, but I was beginning to feel that Peter and Thomas wanted to be the only Ik I ever saw. I insisted on going on, and we plodded on in the scorching sun for an hour. We were on no more than a foot trail winding along a high ridge when all at once two things happened. It was a ridge one moment, and the next I found myself almost on the edge of a great precipice falling sheer into a wooded valley. The other thing that happened was that between me and the precipice, a matter of a few feet, stood an ancient and tiny couple of what could only be Ik, as they were utterly unlike anyone else I had seen. They had their hands clasped and were jumping up and down in greeting, oblivious to the drop behind them. Peter and Thomas looked cross and said the old couple were nobody, just the parents of the Mkungu (the chief), who, they said, was back at Kasilé where Martin was. "That's where all the Ik are," they added. "There's nobody here."

They were almost right. After some argument the old couple were told I would like to see their village, and they took me a little over the ridge to a thorn enclosure with three grass huts in it. I said, "Kalepeto?" and learned, through gesture as much as by word, that it was nothing of the sort. Kalepeto was way back the way we had come. Peter and Thomas confirmed this, quite casually, and said that this was Loitanet. Well, it was my first Ik village—three huts and two people—and even though I had not been able to understand one word they said, none of which sounded like what Peter and Thomas had been teaching me, I felt I had made a beginning. I made a few small gifts, and as we trudged back to the car I started in again on Kalepeto. Peter and Thomas both pointed, as they spoke, in unison, and said that if they had known I wanted to go there we should have taken another trail, because it was on the other side of the gorge to the north of us. I remembered how suddenly the ridge had given way to a precipice, and since the gorge

looked almost as steep, I decided against the amused suggestion that I might like just to walk across and come back to
the car the next day.

We reached Kamion in the late afternoon. It consisted of
one half-collapsed church and a completely collapsed hut.
Peter and Thomas said it was too late to reach the nearest
village, and that if I would cook supper they would go and
spy out the land and make sure there were no Turkana
nearby. An hour later they were back, looking singularly
well fed but none the less ready for the meal I had prepared.
They had seen no Turkana, they said. We spoke to each
other in Icietot a good deal of the time, but often there were
long bouts of silence when they did not want to talk in any
language. It was like this when we set off early the next
morning for the nearest village, Nawedo, which they said
was just over an hour's walk away. After one hour the first
word was spoken. They both pointed to a hill we were skirting and said it was called "Thighbone of the Baboon." That
was the last they spoke for another hour. We were walking
at a brisk rate, over rough but relatively level ground, and
we passed several patches that had been cleared as fields but
had dried up and withered. Then the ground began to rise
and we veered off to the right, around a series of small
gulleys. The last of these we followed, keeping to the left-
hand side, until it suddenly opened out into the face of the
escarpment. It must have been a good fifteen-hundred-foot
drop right down into Kenya, and possibly two thousand.
Then Peter and Thomas were scrambling along a ledge, calling me to follow them. Nawedo was just around the corner.

Nawedo was around several corners. The path must have
cut across the face of the escarpment for the best part of a
mile, with anything from one to two hundred feet between it
and the top. Once started along it, there was no turning

back—it was all I could do to keep looking ahead. The thought of turning outward and facing that void never entered my head, and a brief experiment at turning the other way, with my backside hanging over the drop, was quickly abandoned. For the most part the trail was wide enough for two feet to be placed side by side, but in places one foot had to be carefully placed in front of the other, and my left leg was bruised and cut from scraping it along the rock face, to which I now unashamedly clung with both hands. Peter and Thomas looked back every now and then and said how glad they were I didn't mind heights, as the Ik were *kwarikik*, a "mountain people," and always traveled along paths like this, they were so much shorter. But it was my turn to play silent. I concentrated my attention on little tufts of grass at eye level a few inches away, and I remember a series of close-ups of the rock face, tiny cracks, nodules, changes in color, changes in texture. Even when the path was wide enough for each foot to follow its own trail without having to twist in front of the other, I kept my eyes on the rock face, and when at last it sloped away from me and the path broadened out to a full two feet in width I stumbled for the first time. I had been leaning against the rock face for so long that the left shoulder of my shirt was torn, and when there was nothing left to lean against I nearly fell over, my knees wobbling uncertainly. I really thought I was going to fall, but then I heard shrieks of merriment from Peter and Thomas, standing on level ground a short way ahead. There was no question about what they were laughing at, and rather than give them any additional pleasure I did not fall, but kept on and joined them, once more on the top of the escarpment, with the village of Nawedo clustered on a tiny spur a hundred yards ahead.

Nawedo was given its name because it is always in the

clouds, and so it was today. The ground was damp with
mist, yet ironically it was scorched brown. Nearby fields,
like those we had already passed a million miles back, it
seemed, were withered and fruitless. But there was the
village, a cluster of fifteen or so circular houses with mudded
walls and conical thatched roofs, surrounded by a huge
stockade. Some of the houses were no more than three feet
from the edge of the cliff, and there the stockade ended. I
wondered vaguely if Ik laughed, as had Peter and Thomas,
when their little children, inside the village, wandered near
the edge of that cliff. Thomas meanwhile had leaped like a
goat onto a tiny ledge, with nothing between him and
Kenya, way below. And there he squatted for half an hour,
playing a small musical instrument, the *sanza*, he had produced from inside his shirt. Peter said that Nawedo was
Thomas' home and he had not been back for two years. I
remembered how they had both talked of the fine views of
their homeland, how much better and more beautiful it was
than the flat grassland plateau of Karimoja, but when I suggested that Thomas was enjoying the view Peter disillu-
sioned me. Not at all, he said, "Thomas is looking for food." I
asked what game there was along the escarpment, and got
the curt reply: "Turkana and other Ik villages," with which
Peter turned and disappeared behind the stockade, crawling
on hands and knees through the low opening.

I met three people at Nawedo. Nearby there was a flat
rocky surface over which a rough shelter had been erected
to keep off the sun whenever it came through the clouds.
Two men sat there, looking at us without interest; neither
Peter nor Thomas had so far said a word to them. I went
over and greeted them with the traditional *"Ida piaji,"* and
was greeted in return with a simple *"Brinji lotop"* ("Give me
tobacco"). It seemed a little abrupt, but I gave them some

cigarettes and tried a brief conversation. They said everyone
was away from the village, but declined to say where. They
said all who were left were the two of them and Thomas'
mother, who was in her house, sick. It then struck me as
being odd that if Thomas had been away for two years he
should not have even inquired after his mother, but continued to perch over the edge of the escarpment, playing his
sanza, searching every inch of the country below and beside
him for signs of life. I said goodbye to the two men and got
up to leave, but as I did so a strange thing happened. I was
shaking hands with the older man and as I moved to take my
hand away he tightened his grip so that I found myself
actually pulling the old man off the ground. I don't think he
could have weighed more than sixty pounds. His haunches
were off the ground, and then his grip weakened and before
I could catch him his hand slipped out of mine and he fell
back and collapsed and lay on the ground, all skin and bone,
and he was laughing. He held out his hand, still laughing
breathlessly, for me to help him back to a sitting position.
He apologized for his behavior. "I haven't eaten for three
days," he said, "so it's difficult to stand up," whereupon he
and his companion dissolved into laughter again. I felt there
was going to be much I had to learn about Ik humor.

Thomas came over then and said it was time we were
going, as there was no food here. I mentioned his mother
and said she was sick, but he was uninterested. Peter
crawled out of the village entrance at that point and announced that he could find nothing. Thomas went around
the outside of the stockade, stopping to point to a section
that seemed to have an entrance of its own leading into a
sealed-off compound. "That's where we feed the Turkana,"
he said. Then he moved on and at another spot called
through the stockade to his sick mother a filial greeting,

"Brinji ngag," to which he received the reply, *"Bera ngag"* ("Give me food"—"There's no food"). This exchange of formalities was apparently all that was required after a two-year absence, and without further ado we set off, but not along the escarpment.

Peter and Thomas were now in an expansive mood. We had taken a long way around this morning, they said, because they had wanted to see how I liked the cliffside path. They would now take me back the direct way, and we would visit three more villages en route. We visited four, and the last of them was no more than twenty minutes away from the car and was plainly where the boys had eaten the night before. They were greeted by two young girls who were already outside the stockade when we arrived. The boys indicated that if I was interested in either or both, anything could be arranged for a small consideration. In particular they mentioned the large bag of sugar they had seen in the Land Rover. I suggested a suitable alternative arrangement, and we all sat down and discussed the kinship of this group of villages for half an hour. It all made sense, and more or less confirmed what little I had been able to learn at the other villages, but when I tried to find out just *where* all the people were whose names and relationships were given to me so freely, the old silence descended and I had had my bag of sugar's worth. Peter and Thomas dismissed the girls and led me back to Kamion. There they went into the church and said their prayers, very loudly, for five minutes, collected the bag of sugar and left. I saw them again early the next morning, patiently sitting outside the Land Rover waiting for me to wake up.

I decided to have one final try for Kalepeto, and this time it worked. I promised each of them a bag of sugar if we got

there, and took a bag of sugar and a bag of flour with me in
case of need on the way. It was about a two-hour walk from
where we left the car, across the usual open, dry, rocky hills
and then down a steep, wooded ravine. In places the descent
was so steep that I had to sit and inch my way down, but
Peter and Thomas leaped from stone to stone without falter-
ing, pausing a second only to look for the next firm place to
which they could jump. It was not just that the hillside
sloped down into the floor of the ravine, but the floor of the
ravine itself sloped almost as steeply down into Turkanaland, cutting through the escarpment. As we progressed
downward diagonally, we never seemed to get any closer to
the bottom. It was then that I began to realize how inadequate had been my ridiculous walks up and down Ninth and
Tenth Avenues, with a record time of forty-three minutes for
fifty-six blocks, including stops at traffic signals.

The last scramble down into the village itself was a slide
even for Peter and Thomas. From above we seemed to be
looking down directly onto the conical rooftops, and I got a
fine bird's-eye view of the village. It was itself divided by a
small gorge, with about half a dozen houses on each side.
Again, like all those except the ones at Loitanet, these were
in Karimojong style, with mud walls and thatched roof. But
what intrigued me was that from above I could see that
inside the village were other stockades, apparently as im-
penetrable as the outer stockade, dividing each compound
from its neighbor. Once we reached the level of the village,
it was impossible to see anything of this through the chinks
of the tightly bound barrier of poles and saplings; all I could
do was to peer into individual compounds, all deserted.
Peter and Thomas looked self-satisfied, and sat down waiting
for me to say something. Across the gorge I heard a brief

snatch of shouted conversation, and I asked if we could go
and meet whoever was shouting. The dual response came
back: "Of course, it's only a four- or five-hour walk." Looking down the ravine, I thought that this might well be so.
The boys volunteered that in any case the voices belonged to
men from Loitanet, not Kalepeto. I did not believe one word
of this and said so, and added a few other suspicions as to
the general unhelpfulness of my guides. Wounded, Peter left
Thomas and scrambled down a couple of hundred feet to a
rocky outcrop from where he could better shout across to
the other side. Then began the most ridiculous interrogation.
Peter remembered perfectly just how I had asked my various
questions, no matter how technical, about Icien kinship relations, and proceeded to direct these at the surprised men on
the far side. Even more amazingly, they began to respond,
giving quite useful and seemingly accurate information.
Thomas was not left out of the picture for long, for the man
answering from the other side interrupted to say, "If that is
you, Peter, where is Thomas?" and then Thomas scrambled
down and all four began shouting, and what had been a
peculiar but useful interview across the ravine degenerated
into a verbal brawl I could no longer follow. At this I decided to make my appearance and tumbled down to join
the two boys. As I appeared on the rocky outcrop, silence
descended on the other side of the valley. Then a voice said
with astonishment and, I thought, a trace of contempt,
"Who is *that*, wearing *clothes*?" Peter and Thomas were clad
only in very short shorts, yet even they were overdressed by
local standards. I suddenly realized not only how very much
more overdressed I was, but also how sensible it was to be at
least moderately undressed. My shirt and trousers, on the
left side, where they had endured so much contact with the
face of the escarpment, were torn. My trouser legs were full

of burs and tiny heads of grass that penetrated and jabbed into the skin below. I was hot and dirty and even to me I smelled.

I retreated up the slope to the village and was about to start the upward scramble when I heard a feeble but by now familiar greeting, "*Brinji lotop.*" From inside the stockade one scrawny arm reached out, and automatically I put some cigarettes into the waiting hand. Peter came running over and said angrily, "What are you doing? There's nobody there!" and snatched the cigarettes out of the hand, which withdrew from sight. I began to feel that the Mission had not done a very good job. The boy, sensing an impending flood of abuse, defended himself by explaining, in his most patient and really quite charming way, that I should not be upset, there really was *nobody* in the village, only that old man and his sick wife. The quavery voice from the other side of the stockade protested, "She's not sick, she died this morning. Help me dig a hole for her." "You see?" asked Thomas, coming to Peter's defense, as though it had been proven. "You shouldn't have wasted cigarettes in that way." He took them from Peter and handed them back to me, but the hopeful hand was gone. I felt a sudden surge of uncontrollable anger mixed with a feeling of utter hopelessness and helplessness. I picked up the bag of sugar and the bag of flour and, before the boys could stop me, threw them over the top of the stockade, but even as I was scratching my way up that slope, pulling on shoots and saplings to get myself up, I could swear I heard a quavery old voice saying: ". . . *lotop?*"

I took the boys back to the Mission, gave them all the sugar I had, overpaid them, but even so could not forestall that final "*Brinji lotop.*" Back at the Rest House I found two notes waiting for me; one was from Martin to say that I

should come and get him at once, that he was dying of
hunger at Kasilé, and the other was to say that I now had
permission to continue up into the mountains. I drove over
to Kasilé, where Martin, though not dying by any means,
was more than ready to leave; he said that he had indeed
met some Teuso, as he continued to call them, and that he
never wanted to meet any more, and would I please send
him back to Soroti. Even Moroto was too close for him! I
could sympathize with him, and rather wished I could join
him. Within three hours he was on his way.

While at Kasilé I met the Mkungu and told him I had met
his father at Loitanet. He was not particularly interested,
but invited me back the next day to discuss my plans,
promising to do whatever he could to help. He added, as an
afterthought, that he would offer me tea if I brought him
some tea and sugar. But my good humor was restored, and I
won the round by asking him if he did not want any tobacco.
At that he rocked with laughter and clasped both my hands
and called me Iciebam, "Friend of the Ik," and said, "Of
course, lots of tobacco."

I bought him a whole cake of it, looking rather like a large
cowpat and with a similar odor, with tea, sugar, flour, rice,
beans, four bottles of beer and a bottle of Uganda Waragi, or
banana gin. I thought it would be worthwhile finding out
just how much one could buy in this way from the Ik. It
seemed a successful bargain. For several days the Mkungu
went over the scanty information I had brought back from
the escarpment, and called in members of each village that I
had visited to fill in gaps and help build up the story. He
told me of a couple of villages I had not visited, but closed
right up when I asked him where everyone was. He indicated people standing around him and said that all the Ik
were in Kasilé with him. There probably were a good one

hundred, and that plainly was not all. He said that there were more up at Pirre, on Morungole, but he knew little about them. The Assistant Administrator told me that the government thought it wise that I should make my head-quarters at Pirre, to be near the Police Post, though I could go wherever I liked from there, so I pursued the idea.

The Mkungu told me that there were quite a number of villages on Morungole, even more than along the escarp-ment, and far bigger. He told me of the water hole at Pirre, under the shade of a huge sacred tree that gave its name to the site. He said that that was where I should live, to begin with, where I would be safe and well looked after until a house was built for me in one of the villages. He told me he would send ten people up to Pirre to start work at once building a house for me, that this would be his gift to me, and that anytime I needed help, just to send to him. Right then and there he called out ten men and paraded them in front of me, calling each by name: Longoli, Kauar, Loke-latom, Lomer, Yakuma, Lociam, Lokbo'ok and others. Like the Dodos, they were all naked, and several did not even have the cloth over the shoulders, but there the similarity stopped. The Dodos are a tall, large people, and the men wear headdresses that distinguish them even further. They carry themselves with a pride that is almost haughty and aggressive, although they are a gentle and friendly people. Their walk is the same slow, swinging gait that carries all these herders along so effortlessly over long distances. But the Ik are small, around five feet tall, and although their skin may be burned black from exposure, underneath you can see it is light red in color. They occasionally stick a tuft of animal fur in their hair as decoration, or a bird feather, but they do not wear the elaborate mud packs or head-dresses of their pastoral neighbors. They looked at me, as I inspected the task force assigned to me, with wide-open friendly expressions, smiling and cheerful as each greeted me in turn, and when they moved, it was with the quick, short steps that distinguish a mountain people from those of the plains. In contrast to the pleasant lethargy of the plains, these seemed a lively lot, and all too quickly I forgot about the escarpment.

The Mkungu brought me back to reality, however, by introducing me, last of all, to his assistant, to whom he gave the title Niampara, who would accompany me and look after me and see that everything was done the way I wanted it done. One look at the Niampara assured me that this would be anything but the full story. He too was stark naked, but this was accentuated by a tattered old raincoat he wore, almost down to his ankles. He did not share the open expression of the others, and when he made the usual demand of "*Brinji lotop*" there was a singularly unpleasant whine to it. Then when he began to announce all the members of his family that I was going to carry in the Land Rover, not failing to tell me what food supplies they would need from Kaabong, my feet touched firm land again.

I asked the Mkungu what I should bring to Pirre by way of gifts, and said I had heard that there was hunger there. He said yes, though there was much more hunger at Kasilé. He said that if I did bring food, I must be sure to give it all to the Niampara, who would see that it was properly distributed. Then in a moment of inspiration he said that he would come back to Kaabong with me himself and help me buy all the right things, so that I would not be cheated by those dreadful Somali thieves. Although it was already late afternoon, he told the work team to leave at once for Pirre, and to be ready to start in two days to build Iciebam the biggest and best house in Ikland. They all laughed their approval and agreement and without even a murmur of *"lotop"* they set off for the mountains, evidently not having a single possession to take with them.

The Mkungu and I went to Kaabong and bought a quantity of food, including an enormous sack of ground maize meal, sacks of salt, sugar, beans and rice, and while the Mkungu urged me to give him the money to pay the thieves, telling me the price in Icietot, the Somali traders wrote out a bill for nearly half the Mkungu's optimistic estimate and gave me final friendly warnings about the mountain road. Far from being thieves, these Somali traders were among the most honest and helpful people I was to meet in nearly two years. They found it funny to hear me doing my best with Icietot, and their parting farewell was an injunction to enjoy myself with my robbers. Evidently there was some mutual ill-feeling.

The Mkungu then suggested that it was too late to take him back to Kasilé, so he should stay and guard all the food until morning, but I outmaneuvered him into a truck heading for Kasilé, and returned to the Rest House to pack the Land Rover for an early start, only to remember that if I did that I would have nowhere to sleep. So after a compromise half-packing, I went to sleep surrounded by food and tobacco, as if in an Icien paradise, and wondering uneasily about the morrow.

CHAPTER THREE

The Disenchanted Tree

The Land Rover seemed grossly overloaded, and the luggage rack, well filled, made it top-heavy. When it skidded in the dust going around a corner on the way to Kasilé, the wheels on one side left the road, and no amount of rearrangement, at Kasilé, made it seem any better. However, it did give me an excuse to fill up the inside quite effectively, so that the Niampara was forced to admit that there was room only for himself and one other. He chose a younger brother who was strong enough, he said, to push us out of all the ditches and holes and riverbeds into which we were going to fall. Between the two of them they had a minute bundle tied up in a piece of cloth, and the younger brother's attire consisted of a skin pouch worn from a strap over one shoulder, used for carrying food and tobacco, as he took pains to tell me, showing how empty it was. In spite of the fact that I had arrived at Kasilé not long after sunrise, it was midmorning before we got the doors closed for the last time and drove off, to cheers and waves that temporarily boosted my flagging spirits.

Instead of driving back to Kaabong and up to Kalapata, we took a short-cut across country, and although it was over flat plain, it gave me the first taste of much worse to come. The apparently level ground was cut by deep, narrow gulleys where the rains, pouring off the mountains, had gouged out their paths to the arid grasslands. The gulleys were dry but thick with dust, and we averaged something under fifteen miles per hour. When we met the trail leading from Kalapata and turned left, Morungole was straight ahead and we started climbing a rough, stony track littered with boulders. It was not particularly dangerous, but it took a lot of handling since the Land Rover was still very top-heavy, and even to remain in the driving seat was hard work. Several times my head cracked against the roof, and I took to wearing a hat, on this road, for protection.

About a quarter of the way up, the road leveled out and became quite smooth as it ran around a low spur, and I was just relaxing and about to start a conversation when the Niampara pointed ahead and gave a delighted laugh while his brother, equally happy, gripped the edge of his seat and leaned forward expectantly. Guessing that this sudden good humor spelled trouble, I changed into low-reduction gear and, sure enough, around an innocent-looking corner, there began the roughest and steepest and most dangerous road I have ever seen. In first gear of low reduction we barely made it, but the grade was the least of the problems. The road had been cut by hand from the side of the mountain, and was by no means always level. For the most part it sloped downward away from the mountainside, toward the gorge below. The surface was of loose rock, all the looser wherever there

had been a recent landslide. Since the fall was seldom less
than a thousand feet, the constant slithering of the Land
Rover toward the edge drove any thought of conversation
from my head. Then we came to one hairpin bend that I
remember well. As you approach it an enormous boulder
jutting out of the mountainside forces you to the very edge
of the road and your inclination is to creep back in immediately afterward. But this places you in an impossible position for making the turn. I got used to it later, and stayed
near the edge, but this time I got halfway around and
realized I could not go farther without driving right over the
side, so I had to stop and slide back a few feet and try a
wider arc. But each time I put on the brakes the tires just
slid on the loose stones and I had to make another lunge
forward. It was a question of whether to go over the edge
backward or forward, it seemed, and I was ready to give the
order to jump out when I saw that my two passengers were
bouncing up and down in their seats, not with fright, but
with ecstasy; and it was me they were looking at, not the
road. I was so mad I just put my foot down and lurched
rapidly ahead, scraped around the corner and on upward. I
then tried to say something in Icietot, and not a word would
come to me. I tried to visualize my word list and grammar,
and nothing happened. Every time I thought of something
to say, it came to me not in Icietot but in Hindi, a language I
had not spoken for over twelve years! Even Swahili left me,
and the journey finished as it began, with hardly a word
having been exchanged. It was my first taste of real loneliness.

There were two long climbs of this kind, with equally
steep and treacherous descents, and I stopped only when we
reached the highest point. There I got out to rest and recover, while the Niampara and his brother remained in the

car, checking over the contents. It was early afternoon, but at about eight thousand feet the air was crisp and clear. To one side I could see the huge expanse of Kidepo Valley, though much of it was blocked out by the bulk of the summit of Morungole, still ahead. To the other side the ground fell away much less steeply, and a range of hills seemed to sweep north and then around to the west far behind where Pirre must lie. Not much farther on I saw Pirre, a cluster of the familiar shining corrugated-iron huts neatly arranged in rows, and just to the east of it I saw several villages which could only be the Ik villages, each perched on top of its own crag or hill. They were mostly about a thousand feet below me, and as I looked down they all seemed perfectly circular, surrounded by the invariable stockades. The scene looked idyllic, and I began to feel quite glad that the Ik were no longer hunters after all. In this kind of countryside a nomadic life would be particularly tough, and after the escarpment lesson I was not sure I was up to it. On the other hand, the prospect of setting up headquarters in one of these villages and enjoying all the conviviality of African village life, making visits to other villages in turn, was appealing. Meanwhile I was to be settled by the sacred Pirre tree, where, I imagined fondly, I would have a commanding view of Ik ritual life.

On the last part of the run we passed the Mkungu's work gang several times. On foot they took the direct route down, crossing the car track down which I was crawling, so that they kept appearing ahead of me. They waved and shouted noisily and disappeared into a wooded valley. Ik have a knack, either singly or in groups, for appearing and disappearing without your really being aware of what is happening—probably part of the hunter's ability to blend with the countryside around him. Only the two beside me refused to disappear, and they now looked rather glum with their Iciebam in control of both himself and the car. I tried once more to think of something to say, and formed sentences in English that I knew perfectly well I could translate, but still not one single word would come. Soon we were approaching Pirre; I could see the glint of the corrugated iron on the other side of a lush green valley, and as we descended into the valley I saw the gigantic Pirre tree, its uppermost branches standing above all the other trees, almost twice their height. It stood right at the edge of a water hole, in the middle of its own little forest. I parked the Land Rover nearby and walked up the last short stretch to the Police Post.

The police seemed as glad to see me as I was to see them, and commiserated with me for having to work with the Ik. They said there was no immediate danger of raiding, since there were no Dodos cattle nearby, so that I should be safe enough parked down by the Pirre tree. They were less certain about the idea of my eventually living in one of the Ik villages, some of which were many hours' walk away. They said they had been trying to get the Ik to come closer to the Police Post, not for protection but rather so that the police could keep an eye on them. They frequently poached game in the Kidepo Park, but that was the concern of the park officials, the police said. In fact, they rather sympathized with the Ik since originally it had been their land, and I later learned that the police were not above profiting from the results of the illicit chase. They wanted the Ik where they could keep some kind of track of their movements across into Sudan and down into Kenya, because such movements invariably coincided with an outbreak of cattle raiding and the police were sure that the Ik, although they had no cattle, had something to do with it all. They hungrily asked for news of Kaabong, as though it were the hub of the universe, and said that their radio had broken down and, as they had no transportation other than their legs, they were almost completely out of touch. Once every month or two a police Land Rover came up to Pirre with pay and a few provisions, but for the most part they were self-sufficient, with neat gardens stretching down the slope in front of the post. They had a bore hole and pump for water, to which they said I was welcome anytime I needed it, since the water holes used by the Ik were not fit for drinking, nor even for washing clothes or oneself. The police were not able to tell me much about the Ik, because every time they went to visit an Ik village there was nobody there. I asked if they had ever been inside a village, through the hole in the stockade, and they looked quite shocked and said that nobody but Ik ever went inside. Only in times of real hunger did they see much of the Ik, and even then only enough to know that they were hungry and to suspect that they would find some illegal way of rectifying the matter. They did not speak harshly of the Ik, although almost every comment was disparaging; they seemed to regard them more as unfortunate, ill-kept domestic pets, inclined at times to be treacherous.

With this I wandered back down to the water hole, where the Niampara was waiting for me, guarding all that food, as he said. His brother had disappeared. With him were two or three workers from the Police Post, who left as I came down the hill. What really caught my attention, however, was a little old man dressed neatly in shorts, shirt and woolen sweater, but barefoot, walking quite nimbly up from the valley immediately below the nearest Ik villages. He carried an ebony walking stick with a finely carved head and bound with metal rings, and his gray hair gave him an added air of authority. By the time I reached the car he was only twenty

yards or so away, and his face broke out into the loveliest of
smiles and a soft, gentle voice started greeting me, alternat-
ing Icietot with remarkably good Swahili. He said he had
heard the Land Rover ever since it reached the summit and
began its slow descent, and he had started walking down to
greet Iciebam, about whom he had heard from his brother
Yakuma a few hours earlier.

His name was Atum (another tantalizing connection with
ancient Egypt!) and he said that he was the senior of all the
Ik on Morungole. He said I could forget the Mkungu, who
was merely a government appointee and who made a lot of
noise without doing anything. I protested that the Mkungu
had been most helpful and had sent a team of workers to
help build a house for me. Atum gave a sweetly sinister
laugh of delight and said, "Oh yes, you will find out all
about them tomorrow." Then right in front of the Niampara,
who certainly understood a little Swahili since he had spent
some time in jail for stealing from a store in Kaabong, Atum
told me not to trust the Niampara with as much as a second
look since he would steal even my eyes if he could. Atum
said he would just check with the Police Post about what
was to be done for me, and, giving me another lovely open
smile, he went on up the road.

The Niampara wasted no time telling me that anyone who
spoke such good Swahili should not be trusted, and urged
me to let him help unload the food at once so that he could
take care of it. I asked how he would get it up to the villages
and he promptly told me that it would be quite impossible
to get to a village that day, it was far too late. It was only
about four o'clock, and the nearest villages could not have
been much more than a half hour away, but the Niampara
was adamant. It would not be a good thing to do at all, he
said, to arrive for the first time in the afternoon. He said this

in a conspiratorial manner, and I felt that perhaps there was some tradition behind the argument, so I accepted his offer to take me up in the morning, as soon as we had "settled matters" with the work gang. I could not keep all the food in the car, as I needed the space for sleeping and cooking and getting myself straight, and it looked as though it was going to rain, so I could not put it on top of the Land Rover where I felt it might be relatively safe. The Niampara put on his most piercing whine and implored me to hurry up before the rain came and let him take it to his house, which was nearby, and where he had servants who could be fetched in a minute. But then Atum came back and I asked him what we should do. He exchanged a few rapid words with the Niampara, which I could not understand, and then reminded me that he had warned me. "The only house he knows is the jail," he said, "he just wants to steal all that food for himself." But Atum too was quite definite about not taking it up to the villages that afternoon. That, he said, would be a most unfortunate thing to do. He said that he and the Niampara would take it up to the Police Post and keep it there for the night, where it would be dry and safe. I should stay and guard the car. Iciobam could not be allowed to carry anything or do any work, not on his first day anyway. He then snapped crossly at the Niampara and told him off roundly for being such a rogue, and in his most winning way indicated that I should open up Pandora's box. I did so, and Atum was inside in a flash, handing out things to the Niampara as I told him what was to go where. Then, as I rearranged my own things, they carted the food through the trees and up toward the Police Post, where I lost sight of them. In a couple of trips it was done, and Atum, with surprising strength, was helping me with the last of my own lifting and shifting. He dismissed the Niampara and told him to be at the water hole at dawn the next day with the Mkungu's workers, so that they could all start working for Iciebam. He had observed the cooking facilities in the rear of the Land Rover, and with a charming directness suggested that I make him some tea.

I did so gladly, and for myself as well, and we sat on the grass outside until it began to rain lightly, and then moved into the converted interior, which now boasted a spacious table with seats for four, as well as one bed, the other bed being sacrificed to have the table permanently set up. Atum told me there were seven villages at Pirre, and that I would see them all the next day and decide where I would like to live. He asked me how long I would be staying, and what it was I wanted to learn. He got far more information out of me than I got out of him, and he neatly deflected my inquiries as to where all the Ik were, why they were never to be found in their villages, and what on earth they did if they were not allowed to hunt and if the farming was as poor and unproductive as it seemed to be, from the few barren, withered fields I had seen. He just smiled and said, *"Itelida koroba jiig baraz, baraz"* ("You will see everything tomorrow, tomorrow"). He finished the tea and left, saying how happy he was to be working for me. I had a feeling I was acquiring an invisible payroll.

That evening the police came down, and a number of their porters, to say hello and talk, and to make sure I was comfortable and happy. I assured them I was comfortable. They too wanted to know more about the kind of work I was going to do, and seemed genuinely pleased that anyone should be so interested in the traditions and history of their country as to be willing to spend two years or so living out in the bush learning about it. Each of them suggested that really I would do far better by going to his particular part of

Uganda, even giving me the names of villages and relatives who would make me welcome there. When they saw that I was set on the Ik, they said that as far as they were concerned they would be happy to have me stay at Pirre, it was only me they were worried about. "But now you have met Atum you will know everything," they said. He had once worked as a police porter in Moroto, and was a person, not an animal. With which they left me to my first sleepless night at Pirre, mosquitoes and flies beginning the discomfort, which was continued by strange and disagreeable odors from the water hole which seemed to increase in intensity as the night wore on.

The next morning I rose early, but even though it was barely daylight by the time I had washed and dressed, the Ik were already outside. They had the Land Rover surrounded and were sitting there, on little neck-rests that also serve as seats, as naked as the day they were born. They were not talking to each other, they were just sitting silently, staring at the Land Rover impassively. I could tell nothing from their expressions, but somehow their impassivity, their sitting posture and their nakedness all combined to warn me that any breach in my defenses would be filled with a torrent of demands for food and tobacco. As impassive as they seemed, there was an air of expectancy, and I was reminded that these were, after all, hunters, and the likelihood was that I was their morning's prey. So, having taken a few exploratory peeps through the Land Rover curtains, I left them closed and as silently as possible prepared a frugal breakfast. I suffered from indigestion even so, and was going to suffer the same way for the next eighteen months. It was not that I wanted to eat alone, it was just that I wanted to eat, and I had the feeling that if one *brinji* (demand) broke through my armor I would be the meal, not the eater. And

wherever there is food there are Ik, wearing the same expectant, hungry, demanding look. What makes it worse is
that when you expect them to make a demand, they refuse
to give you the pleasure of being right. They just make it
silently, so that it is felt even through closed doors and
drawn curtains.

On this morning I did not see either Atum or the Niampara, and although I recognized some of the workers sent by
the Mkungu, yesterday's experience of a complete memory
blackout with the language made me feel too uncertain to
risk easing my mind, as I ate, by telling them I had brought
them plenty of food. In any case, I had a suspicion that
"plenty" was not a word they would use or recognize when
they were on the receiving end, only when demanding. So I
drank my tea in nervous haste and consumed some dry biscuits, the only possible substitute for bread. For two months
this was to be my prison, to which I would be driven, whenever I wanted to eat, by reproachful, sad brown eyes that
were still not the eyes of a truly hungry man. I came to know
those eyes only too well. And always there was the same
circle of impassive carnivores, waiting for some fatal slip—a
chink in a curtain, the too noisy crunch of a dry biscuit, an
expression of pain as I scalded my mouth with hot tea, a
momentary feeling of compassion. But Peter and Thomas
had taught me well. I wondered if the owner of the skinny
arm at Kalepeto was now as dead and cold as his wife, and if
both were still waiting for someone infinitely kind and
stupid to "dig a hole" for them. With that happy reflection I
munched my dry biscuits with a little more assurance, and
stepped out into the arena.

Atum was there, cap in hand quite literally. It was a
woolen cap, and everything about him seemed warm and
cuddly. He was smiling and his eyes shone with pleasure as

he greeted me in Icietot and asked if I had eaten well. I lied, but maneuvered and said I had slept well. He said that he had told all the Ik that Iciebam had arrived to live with them and they were all to stay home from work to greet me. They were waiting in the villages and as soon as I had discussed work with my workers (no longer the Mkungu's, it seemed) we could go and greet them. They were very hungry, he added, and many were dying. It was probably one of the few true statements he ever made, and I never even considered believing it—he and the work gang, which had somehow grown from ten to twenty, were far too well fed. They were not plump by any means, but lean and wiry, as one would expect of an active nomadic people. And starving people do not run and leap and jump and lift sacks and loads as I had seen these do. That reminded me of the food, so I said I would like to send some of the workers to get it so we could all go up to the villages and have our discussion there. The sweet little gray-haired old man, without changing his benign expression for an instant, said that unfortunately the Niampara had allowed all the *posho* (maize meal) to be stolen, but I had been warned and had left the Niampara in charge, so what could Atum do? But he had managed to save most of the other food, he said. Then before I could break in he forestalled me and said that he had personally attended to the distribution of that, and twenty Icien heads nodded agreement.

The Niampara was contrite, and said he had not known that the police would do such a dreadful thing as to steal Iciebam's food, and now what would all those poor starving people eat? He opened his dirty old raincoat and rubbed his bare belly. He said that he would personally repay me for the whole amount out of his wages, which, he reminded me, brought us to the impending discussion: How much was I

going to pay my workers? Personally, he would accept as
little as. . . . And before I could get back to the subject of
the missing food I was embroiled in a noisy dispute over
how much I was going to pay for my free gift from the
Mkungu. My Icietot was in no way capable of grappling
with the situation, and Atum stepped forward, still deferen-
tially holding his cap in both hands, stick tucked under one
arm, and proposed a masterly solution, in that it was to force
me to pay for what I had been promised free, provided me
with another ten workers that I suspected I did not need at
all, but offered me the bait of getting rid of the Niampara.
The only one to lose was the Niampara, and that did not
worry me too much, so I agreed. Atum then completed his
maneuver. He told everyone that I was truly Iciebam, for
despite the terrible loss of food for which he and the Niampara felt responsible—though of course it was not their
fault—I had made him headman, leaving all work under his
direction, and at a wage rate approximately four times the
government-approved minimum. Further, I had agreed to
pay the Niampara a full week's wages although he was leaving for Kasilé right away, and by way of celebration I had
given a day's holiday so that everyone could go home and
greet me in their villages. The Niampara held out his hand
for his week's wages, and grumbling that he accepted so
little only because of Atum and that I might at least give
him some tobacco and food, he left, his dirty old raincoat
flapping around him.

By then the others had also disappeared, and Atum suggested that we should eat before setting off for the villages,
as there was no food there, only hunger. His wife was particularly hungry, he said, because she was sick and could not
leave the house to gather food or work in the fields—perhaps
I would give him food and medicine for her? But on no

account was I to listen to the others; they would all demand food and medicine and they were not bad people but they were liars, and I was to consult him before I gave anyone anything. Atum helped me make the tea and countered my precaution of counting out four biscuits each by helping himself to nearly half a bowl of sugar in his first cup of tea. When there was no more to be had he stood up and without further ado set off at a brisk, short-stepped walk, swinging his stick to clear the path where the grass was long, which was only in the little valley beneath the rapidly rising series of hills on which the villages were perched.

There were seven of them in all, and since they were nameless I first came to know them by number, in the order in which I visited them that day, and then by the name of whoever became best known to me in each village. First we descended into the *oror a pirre'i,* the "Ravine of Pirre," a boulder-strewn ravine as deep as it was wide at the top, sometimes twenty feet, sometimes more than a hundred, and dry as a bone. It ran north/south, roughly, and as we climbed up the far side, scrambling to the first village, we were still in the morning's shadow since it was barely ten o'clock. Village Number One was built on a steep slope, and even the houses tilted at a crazy angle. Atum rapped on the outer stockade with his cane and shouted a greeting, but there was no response, just the annoying buzz of a swarm of flies that were devouring a pile of human feces near the entrance. A couple of them transferred themselves to a sore on Atum's right leg, and he watched them idly before he carefully scooped them into a cupped hand and crushed them. This was Giriko's village, he said, and he was one of my workers.

"But I thought you told them to go back to their villages?" I asked, rather pointlessly.

PIRRE VILLAGES
View of 1k villages from Pirre water hole

Field Shelter
Village

PIRRE OROR

C.M.T.'s Compound

TO POLICE POST

palacios

"Yes, but you gave them a holiday, so they are probably in their fields," answered Atum, looking me straight in the eye. "Let's try another village."

We crossed a small *oror* that ran into the ravine below, and edged our way up another hill to Village Number Two. Here there was indisputably someone inside, for I could hear loud, raucous singing, a rapid staccato of Icien vowels starting with an upward lift, then falling down to nothingness, a series of solitary wails. Atum did not enter, but again rapped on the stockade and called out, "*Ida, ida piaji.*" The singing went on, and we walked around the outside of the stockade until we came to a spot where spiders had woven a gigantic cobweb that almost covered the small compound inside. The singing stopped, a pair of hands gripped the stockade and a craggy head rose into view, two uneven rows of broken teeth giving me an undeniably welcoming smile. This was Lokeléa, actually not Ik at all, but a Topos who had fled from the Sudan and taken an Ik wife and settled among them. He was unlike the real Ik in that he had a few cattle which he had brought with him and managed to graze nearby. Atum introduced me, and Lokeléa encouraged me by saying how well I spoke Icietot, and at least he understood one of my questions. When I asked him what he had been singing about he answered simply, "Because I'm hungry." Atum caught me by the arm and lead me away, telling Lokeléa that I would come back later.

On the hill directly above Lokeléa lay Village Number Three, the smallest village of all, but with a surprisingly large *boma*, or cattle compound. It was even larger than Lokeléa's, and Atum had told me that Lokeléa was the only Ik (*Iciam*, to be grammatically correct), for he was fully accepted as such and spoke the language fluently, to have cattle. The small cattle compounds we saw in the other vil-

lages, he said, were to keep "stray" cattle the Ik might find
during their wanderings; they would keep them until
claimed by their owners, Dodos or Turkana. There was
nobody at home in Number Three, and Atum said that the
large *boma* was to accommodate cattle that Lomeja had
"won" from Dodos and Turkana by helping them, but nothing would make him divulge the nature of the "help." We
moved down the side of the hill to the top of the jagged little
oror than ran down into Pirre, and up the other side, passing
Village Number Four.

This was also a small village, rather more open than
others, and more sprawling. There were only eight huts, as
against the twelve or so in Lokeléa's village and eighteen in
Giriko's. Atum did not even need to rap on the stockade, for
looking down from the hill above, we had seen people
moving about inside. The outer stockade was broken in one
section, as though there had once been a *boma* that was no
longer needed, and we walked right in, with Atum shouting
to warn whoever was inside that we were coming. We
ducked through a low opening and entered a compound in
which a woman was making pottery. She kept on at her
work, but gave us a cheery welcome and laughed her head
off when I tried to speak in Icietot. She made me say her
name over and over again until I got the emphasis just right
on the third vowel, Losiké, and then asked Atum all about
me. She willingly showed me details of her work, and said I
could come with her when she went to cut more clay, if I
wanted, or to watch her firing the pots. She did not seem
unduly surprised at my interest, but she did keep on shaking
her head and laughing. She said that everyone else had left
for the fields, except old Nangoli, who, on hearing her name
mentioned, appeared at a hole in the stockade shutting off
the next compound. Nangoli looked as if she were a hundred

years old, but she was probably little over forty. She mumbled toothlessly at Losiké (who by contrast had an enormous and fine set of teeth that made her open smiles and laughs all the more infectious) and Losiké told Atum to give her some water. "That's the trouble of being a potter," she said, "everyone expects me to give them water." Atum had unhooked a large pear-shaped gourd from the stockade and filled a gourd cup that old Nangoli had passed through the gap. After a couple of refills Nangoli disappeared, and when we left we saw her cultivating a tiny field on the edge of the village, which is where old people have their fields, such as they are. Losiké told me to come back anytime and promised to tell me anything I wanted to know. "Everyone else will tell you lies, especially him," she laughed, throwing a lump of clay at Atum.

As we climbed up to his own village, Number Five, Atum said that Losiké was a witch, and that she made a lot of money out of her pottery and never gave anything away. Later I remembered that simple gift of water to Nangoli, and Losiké's unconcern when Atum helped himself to as much as he could decently put away. At the time I did not stop to think that in this country a gift of water could be a gift of life.

I could see from below that Atum's village was enormous—it had nearly fifty houses, each within its compound within the stout outer stockade. Atum did not invite me in, and in any case as we reached the entrance we also crested the top of the hill and a few yards farther on the ground dropped sharply away, opening up the huge vista of Kidepo Valley shimmering in a heat haze below. Right on the edge there was a small stony crest with a tree growing out of it, and climbing that, I looked across to the great mass of Mount Zulia and into the Sudan. Stretching toward it on the

right was Lomil, and a southern arm was formed by the dark
hump of Morungole. We were in a commanding position,
able to see anything that moved down in the valley or on
either of the neighboring mountain ranges, or, even more
important, in the Chakolotam Valley, which wound its way
up from Kenya, opening into Kidepo just between us and
Lomil but a thousand feet or so below. It was a magnificent
view, and Atum saw my pleasure and immediately said that
he would have my house built right there, near the entrance
to his village, with nothing between me and the view. That
is of course what he would have liked, and at the time I
agreed, thinking I would like it too; but long before the
house was completed I had learned the reason for those
stockades, and had shut out the view of Kidepo by a stockade of my own, even bigger and stronger than that of my
neighbors.

A hundred yards away, on another crest of the same hill,
stood Village Number Six. It was a long, narrow village,
conforming to the shape of the jagged ridge on which it
stood. It looked down over the top of Number One, Giriko's
village, and over to the Police Post, which, though it shone
brightly in the sun, looked tiny and insignificant. The
thought of the police in that handful of minute tin huts
trying to protect this whole vast border region was not a
comforting one when I remembered all the warnings I had
had, and in knowledge of the bitter fighting that was going
on just a few miles away in Sudan, on the other side of
Lomil. One solitary figure was sitting on a rocky slab on the
highest point just outside Number Six. He stood up as we
approached and I recognized him as one of the workers
assigned by the Mkungu back in Kasilé. His name was
Kauar, a great gangling youth who not once, to my memory,
even carried the shoulder cloth that most men carried or

wore. He had a smile like Losiké's, open and warm, and he said he had been waiting for me all morning, hurrying back so that he would be there to welcome me to his village. He offered us water to drink, and led us inside and showed me his own small compound and that of his mother, and from a rock within his compound he pointed out the rooftops of other members of his village, telling me about each of them in turn.

From Kauar's village we struck back north, across the hill-face just under Atum's village. We seemed to run from one patch of swarming flies to another, each patch accompanied by a rich odor of decaying feces, and it suddenly came to my mind that I had not so far seen any toilets, nor any reasonable cover for privacy, and determined that at least my compound would have a good deep toilet. With a pneumatic drill I suppose it might have been possible.

Number Seven Village was deserted, and we did not even bother to go right up to it, for we could see it as it lay slightly below us, down from Atum's village and to the northeast. Coming up from it, at quite a respectable speed, was a blind man, tapping the ground on each side of him as he picked his way nimbly along the uneven, narrow trail. This was Logwara, emaciated but alive and remarkably active. He had heard us and had come to greet me, he said, but he added the inevitable demand for tobacco in the same breath, and I was reminded that none of those we had met in the villages, Lokeléa, Losiké, Nangoli or Kauar, had even hinted at it. We returned together to the flat rocky strip between Atum's village and the large tree, and sat down in the open sunlight. There was a smaller tree nearby, and I suggested sitting in its shade, but Atum dismissed it as unworthy of sitting under. "It is only a rain tree," he said. But when I asked him what a rain tree was he just ignored me and talked to Logwara in his soft, gentle voice and I thought he had not heard me. The setting was so tranquil that for a brief moment I felt at peace. It even somehow seemed right to be sitting in the full glare of the sun; the heat bore down on me like an enormous weight, enveloping and smothering and making me one with the hot earth and rock around me. I lay back and dozed.

After a short time Atum said we should start back, and called over his shoulder to his village. A muffled sound came from within, and he said, "That's my wife, she is very sick— and hungry." I offered to go and see her, but he shook his head and explained the nature of the sickness, a pain in the right side, with such detail that I decided she must really be sick and became all the more concerned. He led me away, though, saying that he would bring food and medicine to her in the evening, after he had taken me back to the Land Rover. We then set off to scout for a suitable route by which I could get the Land Rover up to the house site, something Atum had determined as being absolutely necessary. He said we would build a *boma* for it, for it was my wealth, just as cattle was the wealth of the Dodos and Turkana. He knew what he was talking about, and we spent the afternoon slowly picking our way down the gentler slopes which led off to the west and north, until we reached a well-worn cattle trail coming up from Kidepo which we could follow with ease as it crossed the Pirre *oror* at a place where the ravine split into two relatively shallow gulleys that, with a bit of grading, the Land Rover might just be able to cross. We marked out a tentative trail, zigzagging in all directions but for the most part only in need of rough clearing and leveling, and decided to start work on it the very next day with half the team while the other half worked on the house. Back at the Land Rover I capitulated and gave Atum some

food and some aspirin, not knowing what else to give to help
his wife, and he reluctantly left, eyeing the food cupboard
speculatively. Then he set off at his brisk trot, and I was
reminded how dead tired I was and marveled at the energy
of this bouncy little old man. The police wandered down,
one by one, to ask how the day had gone and to see that I
had all I needed, then left me to the flies and nocturnal odors
emanating from the water hole at the base of the sacred
tree.

I was awakened well before dawn by the lowing of cattle
and the refreshingly different smell of fresh cattle dung as it
overcame the stale odors of old human offal. Some Dodos
had arrived to water their herd, water being short almost
everywhere else. As dawn broke I saw that they were not
only watering their herd at the edge of the muddy pool, they
were also washing themselves and their cloths, and evacuat-
ing their bladders and bowels all at approximately the same
time. I reflected that this was part of the anthropological
experience, and in self-defense took out my notebook and
told myself that it might all be of the utmost scientific value.

I am sure the psychologists would have something to say
about it, but the fact that my field notes are filled with reference to defecation is really no more than a reflection of my
zeal in recording everything that I noticed, and, customs
being what they were, the phenomenon was open, widespread and highly noticeable. I learned rather early to be
equally casual, for there was an old pit toilet nearby where a
game warden had once stayed for a few days, and on that
second morning, when I bashfully fought my way through a
thorn patch to use it and lowered my trousers, the keys to
the Land Rover, which I had locked, not knowing the Dodos
for the friendly, honest people they were, fell neatly into the
mire below. It took me half an hour of fishing with a long

branch with a forked twig tied to the end as a hook, lying on
my stomach with my legs outside the door of the little privy,
shining my flashlight down into the murky pit, to recover my
keys and make my way back through a cluster of wondering
Dodos to the Land Rover, now surrounded by my workers,
sitting patiently, pleased at having caught me before I had
eaten.

I made an extra pot of tea and let Atum distribute it, and
then we divided the workers up into two teams. Kauar was
to head the team working on the house, and Lokelatom,
Losiké's husband, a vicious wrist knife encircling his right
wrist, was to take charge of the road workers. The police
lent pickaxes, hoes and shovels for the road workers, and in
no time and with no further discussion everyone was at
work. I found that Atum, on his way back the night before,
had retraced our steps along the proposed route and had
staked it, making a few extra detours to avoid inclines that
would need too much grading or rocky patches that would
be difficult to clear by hand. And even then, as I followed
him and Lokelatom up to where the proposed route reached
the final crest between Kauar's village and the rocky outcrop that dominated it, it seemed unlikely that ten men with
simple tools could ever make a passable track, but they did.

It took a couple of months, with the house builders frequently being called on to help the road builders. To start
with, I spent much of my time helping and supervising, until
I found that both slowed activity down to a near-standstill.
Unlike other workers, the Ik worked furiously when unseen,
as I discovered when I took to hiding behind boulders and
sneaking around hilltops. But the moment a bystander
comes along, particularly one allegedly in authority, they
complain of aches and pains and even walk off the job,
saying they are too hungry to continue. The latter might at

times have been closer to the truth than I thought just
then. On occasions when I took a pick myself and set to
work, the others, taking advantage of my attention being
thus occupied, would gradually just drift away. More than
once I found myself working alone, and while sometimes I
would find the rest over a rise, lying asleep in the sun, at
other times they would simply have begun work on another
stretch of the road, leaving mine to me.

While they were working they were rather like birds—
their heads kept turning around as though they were expecting something to happen, someone to come. Then every now
and again one of them would stand up and peer into the
distance and, after saying a brief word to the others, would
take off into the bush and be gone for an hour or so. On one
such occasion, after the person—it was Lokelatom—had
been gone two hours, the others started drifting off one by
one, each in a different direction. But by then I knew them
better, and looking for a wisp of smoke, I found it and followed it to where the road team was sitting around cooking
a goat Lokelatom had managed to steal from a passing
Dodos herd. Smoke was a giveaway, though, so they econo-
mized on cooking and ate the food procured in this way
nearly raw. Once when I was out walking with Atum some
five or six miles from Pirre, he suddenly took off down the
mountainside as if a leopard were after him, holding his
stick high in the air and charging through thorn bushes and
all, to a wooded glen far below. I could not see the smoke
myself, but I guessed it was there, and followed almost as
rapidly as Atum. He was already eating when I arrived not
more than a half-minute behind, and the other three were
cramming food into their mouths as fast as they could so
that there would be none to offer me or anyone else who
might come. It is a curious hangover from what must once

have been a moral code that Ik will offer food if surprised in
the act of eating, though they go to enormous pains not to be
so surprised.

On this occasion an antelope had been killed by Lomeja, a
happy man in his late middle age, which is to say he was in
his early twenties. He had set off early in the morning alone,
and had picked up his bow and arrows where he had concealed them during the night so that nobody would see that
he was going hunting. But his half-sister, Niangar, was
already in her kitchen compound as he slipped out through
the gate to the side of the *boma,* and she promptly told her
husband, Lotibok, who tracked him, letting him do all the
work, as Lomeja bitterly complained, although he had his
own bow and arrows with him. The kill made, the beast
cleaned, Lotibok had appeared, claiming it was by chance,
and had offered to help cook the animal. They had been very
careful, carrying it into the thickly wooded glen to lessen the
chance of being seen, and they had not used much fire. Even
so, beady-eyed Lomongin had seen the telltale wisp of blue,
and so had Atum, his brother-in-law. When I arrived everyone ignored me and continued eating furiously, all except
Lomeja, who handed me a particularly good piece, despite
Atum's muffled protest. When I refused it, saying I had only
come to greet them, the others immediately offered me what
they had, outdoing each other in the extravagance of their
offers. It was not long before there was nothing left to offer.

I had come to know Lomeja fairly well since one morning
when I surprised him before dawn, sneaking out on a similar
mission. I was always up before dawn anyway, for the
Dodos continued watering more and more cattle by the
sacred tree as water holes elsewhere dried up, and since a lot
of enthusiastic flirting went on between the herdsmen and
the women who came to fill their water gourds at dawn,

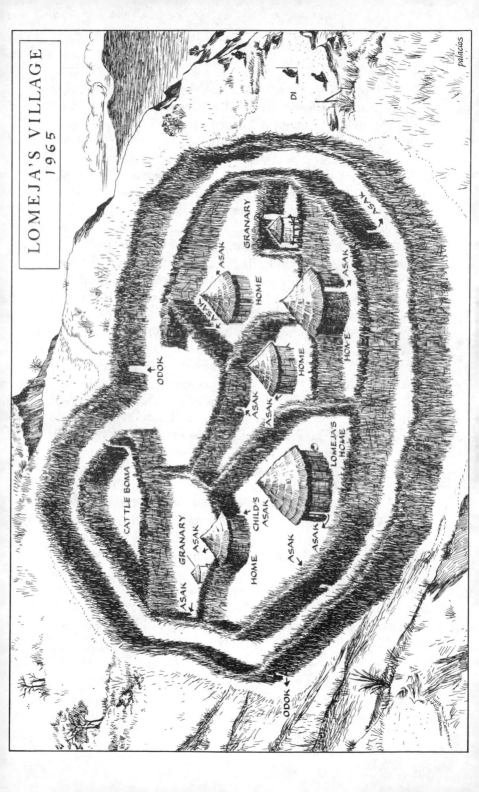

LOMEJA'S VILLAGE
1965

DI

ASAK

GRANARY

HOME

ASAK

ASAK

HOME

HOME

ODOK

ASAK

ASAK

CATTLE BOMA

GRANARY

ASAK

CHILD'S
ASAK

HOME

ASAK

ASAK

LOMEJA'S HOME

ODOK

palacios

sleep was impossible. But by the time I got up to the villages
they were always deserted, and I was always told that "they
are in the fields." I spent a lot of time surveying the fields,
with Atum and others as guides to tell me which field belonged to whom, and in any one day I never saw more than a
half-dozen people at work there. The reason was simple
enough: the fields were not worth working; the crops had
dried up and shriveled, and the earth had baked hard. The
occasional sprinkle of rain was little more than a mist and
helped nothing. But one morning I followed the little *oror*
up from *oror a pirre'i* while it was still quite dark, and I met
Lomeja on his way down. He motioned me to silence and
said to follow him, and so I went on my first illicit hunt in
Kidepo. Again he had concealed his bow and quiver of
arrows in a tree down the hillside, and he told me quite
frankly that if he got anything he would share it with me
because I was with him, and with anyone else who managed
to join us, but that he certainly was not going to take any
back to his family. He laughed heartily at that idea. "What
do you think they are doing?" he asked. "Each one of them is
out seeing what he can get for himself, and do you think
they will bring any back for me?"

He even spoke proudly of his eldest son, Ajurokingomoi,
and said he had caught him once, with a whole cob roasting,
ten miles out in Kidepo. Otherwise he would have got none
of it; Ajurokingomoi would have eaten his fill, dried some
and taken some to sell to the Police Post, which is what any
sensible person would do. I asked him about the womenfolk,
since they do not hunt. He said they set traps and caught
slow game, but they knew how to gather better than men,
and they similarly cooked their food away from home so
they would not have to share it. The children, he said,
learned from the baboons—whatever that meant.

Lomeja was one of the very few Ik who seemed glad to volunteer information and to enjoy talking. He helped me with the language, and in turn got me to teach him a few words of English. He never asked me for anything and, unlike many of the others, did not get up and leave as I approached. At first I had thought this latter trait had something to do with me, but in fact it did not. Many Ik just seemed to like to be by themselves, or, if together, not to talk to each other, and they all knew that I liked to talk. I am not so sure about "liking" it, under those circumstances, but it was difficult to see how I could do my work if I joined them as just another silent hermit. Anyway, I quickly learned not to force a conversation, nor even to try to stimulate one with offers of food or tobacco, for in that case the food or tobacco was demanded before talk began, and as soon as it was given, silence was resumed. So I was particularly glad for someone like Lomeja who talked freely, though he too could turn silent for hours on end.

Apart from him I spent most of my time, those days, with Losiké the potter, sitting with her while she worked in her compound. Lokelatom, head of the road team, was her husband, but he seldom was seen with her unless it was to get water. The old lady in the adjoining compound, Nangoli, was often home, and Losiké told me that Nangoli and her husband, Amuarkuar, were rather peculiar. It seemed that they helped each other get food and water, and that they brought it back to their compound to cook and eat together. Amuarkuar was all skin and bone, even more so than Nangoli, but he was remarkably sprightly and could be seen climbing up and down hills as nimbly as ever. I still do not know how much real hunger there was at that time, for most of the younger people were fairly well fed, it seemed, and the few skinny old people seemed none the less healthy and

active. But my laboriously extracted genealogies showed
that there were quite a number of old people still alive and
allegedly in these villages, though they were never to be
seen. The old ritual priest, Lolim, was the only other old
man I saw at that time. I wondered where they all were; and
why the children who were meant to be guarding the fields
were never there, and seldom seen except in the late afternoon when they reappeared on the edges of the villages.
Then Atum's wife died.

Atum told me nothing about it, but had stepped up his
demands for food and medicine and I felt that if she was
really critically sick I should try to get her to the hospital in
Kaabong. He refused the offer and said she was not *that* sick.
Then after a while, when I still had not once seen her, his
brother-in-law, the beady-eyed Lomongin, sidled up to me
and said that he supposed I knew that Atum was selling the
medicine I was giving him for his wife. I was not unduly
surprised, and merely remarked that that was too bad for his
wife. "Oh no," said Lomongin, enjoying the joke enormously,
"she has been dead for weeks. He buried her inside the
compound so you wouldn't know." No wonder he did not
want her to go to the hospital; she was worth far more to
him dead than alive.

Atum did not show the slightest embarrassment when I
told him I knew of his wife's death; he merely said he had
forgotten to tell me, and changed the subject. But his sweet
little old face never looked quite as sweet again, and his
gentle voice, though it sounded the same, seemed less gentle.
I had been barely two months in the field and if I could have
got out at that moment I probably would have done so, but
there had been a slide and the road was blocked. It must
have been then that I began to notice other things that I
suppose I had chosen to ignore before, for I am sure they

were nothing new. Only a very few, like Lomeja and Kauar, the tall, lanky youth working on the house, helped me with the language. Others would understand when it suited them, and pretend they did not understand when they did not want to listen. An alternative measure, if they were talking when I came on the scene, was to switch into Toposa or Didinga so that I would not be able to join in or understand what they were saying. With a year and a half yet to go, I began to be forced into a similar isolationist attitude myself, and although I cannot say I enjoyed it, it did make life much easier. There was a relief at no longer having to fight the stubborn wall of opposition to any form of communication, and I even began to enjoy, in a peculiar way, the company of the silent Ik. I still did not understand it, but it seemed less and less wrong. And the more I accepted it, the less often people got up and left as I approached. I used to come across little groups of them sitting silently on their *di*, the sitting place that each village had on a rocky spur or ledge with a commanding view. I assumed at first that, like me, they were content just to sit and enjoy the view, but then I realized that it was because they had nothing else to do, and that in fact they were keeping their eyes open, without much hope, for some sign of death. A vulture circling around would bring them all to their feet in an instant, however far away, and they would be off to seize what they could of the rotten flesh of some dead animal. On one occasion I sat on the *di* by Atum's rain tree for three days with a group of Ik, and for three days not one word was exchanged. People just came and went, silently, each one on his own.

The work teams were more lively, but only while working. On returning to the villages in the afternoons they fell in with the mood of everyone else. Kauar was the most talkative, and he used to sing as he worked, rather as Lokeléa had sung that first day I met him. It was also more of a lament than a song, and he too told me it was a song of hunger. I looked at him and wondered. He was always so very cheerful, and if he was thin, so was everyone else, and I took this to be the natural build of the people. But sometimes, when he was working on the roof of the house and I would catch him silhouetted against the sky, his private parts dangling like some monstrous but useless appendage (Did they ever have sex? I began to wonder. I seldom saw any flirtation or even mild sexual interest), his ribs did seem rather bare of flesh, and his limbs excessively bony. Once when he jumped down from the roof he fell over. I thought he had slipped; I did not guess it could be weakness.

Kauar was always careful to play and joke with children, though he had only one of his own, when they came back in the afternoons from their foraging expeditions. I even saw him give them some meat he had bought with his wages and dried. It is difficult to remember many other acts of kindness during the time, nearly two years, I spent with the Ik. Lomeja, as much as I liked him, was not a kindly person; for one thing, he was always on his own and so had nobody to be kind to, and that is how it was with most of them; you can hardly say they were unkind. So Kauar was exceptional, and he used to volunteer to make the long two-day walk into Kaabong and the even more tiring two-day climb back to get mail for me, or buy a few things for others. He was always pleased with himself when he came back, and asked if he had made the trip more quickly than the last time. He would come running up the last gentle incline, his long legs moving easily, it seemed, his underparts swinging wildly, and the cleft stick holding the mail held high above him like a banner. Then he used to sit and watch while I read the mail, studying the expression on my face to see if all was well.

When we drank tea together he always took exactly the same number of teaspoons of sugar that I took, and helped himself to exactly the same number of biscuits, never more, never less. The biscuits he often kept for the children, who used to snatch them from him and run away laughing at him for the fool he was.

Then one day Kauar went to Kaabong and did not come back. He was found the day after he should have returned, high up on the last peak of the trail before it descends to Pirre, cold and dead. Then you could see how thin he was, or so I was told, for those who found him just took the things he had been carrying, pushed his body into the bush and left it. "Why bother carrying him back? He was dead!" they said as they distributed the goods. Kauar's wife came out to see what she could get for herself, his son was playing with other children and paid no attention, only his mother sat and just stared, and who knows what she was thinking about? I still see his open, laughing face, see him giving precious tidbits to the children, comforting some child who was crying, and watching me read the letters he carried so lovingly for me. And I still think of him probably running up that viciously steep mountainside so that he could break his time record, and falling dead in his pathetic prime because he was starving.

CHAPTER FOUR

Warriors at Peace

I<small>F THE</small> sacred tree became less and less enchanting as my stay down by the water hole drew on, it did not lack in interest. I noticed that the only Ik who came there to get water were the oldest ones, and I was told there was another water hole farther down the Pirre *oror*, which I had not yet fully explored. I later found out there was yet another one a bare mile farther up from Pirre that actually fed the dirty hole by the tree, but it was almost never used by anyone, Ik or Dodos, since it was much frequented by leopards. I visited it several times and never found anyone there, though the water was clean and fresh. Our water hole at Pirre had dwindled in size until it was a bare six feet across, and the surface of the water had sunk to three or four feet below ground level. To water the cattle, youths stood in the muddy pool and baled out gourds of water with which rough-hewn troughs, above, were filled. People coming to get drinking water also had to

climb into the pool, and scooping the scum of the surface
with a backhanded motion, they then brought their gourds
forward to fill quickly before the scum could return. In this
way the drinking water was a relatively pure brown color,
without lumps of green and yellow matter.

The Dodos used to take cattle dung and throw it at the
sacred tree, so that its huge trunk, for as high as eight feet,
was plastered with splattered cowpats. This, I was assured,
would keep the cattle safe and bring rain. It was the only
form of ritual activity I ever saw, and the Ik never took part
in it. It was not notably effective, for the rain never came
and the Turkana stole the cattle. The Dodos consulted
Lolim, the Ik ritual priest, and Lolim went out, hobbling
painfully along the stony trail, carrying his sandals (used
only for divination) in his hand, his baboon-skin cape on his
hunched old back. He cut some vine, and supervised its erec-
tion across the trail from tree to tree. The trail led up from
the Chakolotam Valley, and Lolim said this would stop the
Turkana. He collected a fee for this, and Atum collected a
fee for the use of his rain tree, around which the Dodos
made offerings of food and milk. These of course were de-
voured by Atum and others as soon as the Dodos left, and
the Ik, in rare good humor, told me the Dodos were convinced that the mountain people had knowledge of supernatural medicines and could cure anything from a cut foot to
a stolen herd of cattle or a drought.

It was shortly after Lolim had erected his anti-Turkana
medicine across the Chakolotam trail that, one day, the
Dodos all turned and fled. The next morning the cattle were,
as usual, being watered at the water hole, plus a lot more,
and a number of camels. The herders seemed taller and more
slender than the Dodos, and more graceful in their movements. They wore colored mud packs matted into their hair,

accentuating their clean features. Most of them wore a wrist knife, its blade nearly two inches wide all around, encircling one wrist, and some had a finger knife worn as a ring. They carried spears and had knives in their belts, and a dozen or so stood in a silent circle around the Land Rover.

Lolim's anti-Turkana medicine had, of course, served as an indication to Turkana spies that there was a herd worth protecting nearby, and I was later told that Atum had sent down to the Turkana to tell them that this would be a good time to come. They came, in no small numbers, and they told me in Swahili that they had come to stay for as long as the drought lasted. Their first question to me was whether I had any guns in the Land Rover. I said no, and left it open so that they could look if they wanted to, but they just nodded and said they had heard as much. Since I had no guns or cattle, they said seriously, I was not worth killing. Would I like some milk and blood? It was a change to be offered something, so I said yes to the milk, and from then onward there was a gift of milk every morning, and nothing was asked in return. After the first exchange of a few words with their Swahili-speaking spokesman, a wall-eyed man named Athuroi with a huge ivory lip-plug, I felt more at ease than I had for a long time. Talking through Athuroi, the others were intensely curious about my work, and at first a little disbelieving. It was only when they heard me talking to the Ik in Icietot that they were convinced. They shook their heads and laughed and said they would teach me to talk like a Turkana, in a real language.

I thought that if I wandered up to the Police Post, it might be taken as an indication of hostility or renew their suspicions that I was really some kind of government official. But I was concerned as to what had happened, although I had heard no shooting, and was relieved when the police,

soon after daylight, came down to see how I was. They said
the Turkana had come during the night, and had said that
they intended to stay for as long as necessary and did not
want to fight and would steal no more cattle while they were
there. The police, heavily outnumbered, sensibly told the
Turkana they were welcome. I asked about the administration, but they said their radio had broken down. The Turkana told me they had dismantled it. Either way, the
administration did not get to hear of it until the invasion was
a fact. By then there were several hundred Turkana either
up at Pirre or down in Kidepo, and some twenty thousand
head of cattle, boldly grazed right across the park.

True to their word, the Turkana bothered no one and
refrained from raiding. They said that down in northern
Kenya there was no grazing and no water, and the cattle and
people were dying, so they had come up the Chakolotam
Valley, knowing they would find both pasture and water in
Kidepo, though it too was pretty arid by now. The administration, when it did hear about the invasion, reacted reasonably. They sent up a veterinary officer to check the cattle
and to arrange for inoculation, and the game warden asked
them to stay out of the park. But all across the park were
spirals of smoke where Turkana had set up camp and were
grazing their cattle, with supreme disdain for fatuous rules
that were designed to preserve animals while humans, in
consequence, starved and died. It was something the Ik were
curious about too, with the same lack of resentment, for the
administration had told them not to hunt in the park but to
farm, and when their mountainside fields proved useless and
they started farming on the slopes leading into the park they
were told not to farm there, that it was for animals only.

But whereas there was little or nothing the Ik could do
about it, beyond illicit hunting, the Turkana were trained

and ready to fight, and knew how scared everyone was of them. With good reason too, for when they got to know me better and took me down to their cattle camps in Kidepo they used to point out what I had taken to be the long beehives the Ik make out of tree trunks, slung up in trees, others in bushes. They contained rifles and ammunition, and I had no doubt that the Turkana meant it when they said that if Uganda wanted to make a fight of it they would fight. They got me to write a note to that effect to the local administration down in Kaabong, but for a while all was peaceful and nobody suggested they should leave. The myth was politely maintained that they simply were not there. Both the Ik and I were delighted, and we both prospered in our own ways. I watched all sorts of comings and goings between our seven villages and the Turkana cattle camps down in Kidepo, and there was a lot of activity all of a sudden in the fields, making charcoal. Meanwhile Turkana women toiled up the hillside bringing gifts of milk and blood to the Ik, and Lomeja's cattle *boma* began to fill with goats. There were fewer complaints about hunger, and work on the road and house suddenly spurted ahead and I was finally able to make the attempt to reach the house site by the trail we had cut.

As much as I had come to like the Turkana, I was glad to leave the water hole. It had become even more filthy, the doors of the Land Rover were always thick with flies waiting to get in, the smell was too much even for an anthropologist, and the watering became an almost continuous process, beginning at three A.M. and not finishing until near midnight, with a midday lull. Besides, more interesting things were going on up in the villages, and my house was ready, with a fine, heavy stockade all around it, the inside compound being divided so as to leave a special area, a sort of *boma*, for the car, with its own entrance. The car made it all right, with a bit of pushing here and there, though it nearly toppled over twice due to the sideways slant of the track. When I breasted that last ridge up by Kauar's village and drove down to where my *boma* stood waiting for me, I felt that now everything was going to be all right. I drove in and they closed the wide entrance after me, piling thorn scrub up against it so that it was as impregnable as any other part of the stockade. I could not see the view, of course, but then neither could I see the Ik, and even though they were the people I was meant to be studying and I had been there only three months or less, the privacy gave me intense pleasure.

Of course Atum was there, woolly and cuddly, cap held in front of him in both hands, stick under his right arm. But he had kept the others out, for this, he explained, was *our* house, nobody else's. He said that later on he would join it onto the village by enlarging the outer stockade, but happily that never came to pass. There was only five yards between our stockades, and that was near enough for me. The Turkana were there too, but outside, and simply to welcome me to the new home. Whereas the stockade was constantly being pried apart by little Icien hands so that they could peep through and see what I was doing, what I was cooking and eating, the Turkana showed no interest or concern. The constant rustling and cracking of twigs as the priers pried got so much on my nerves that I gave up eating outside or doing anything else in the courtyard, and used to shut myself up in the Land Rover again to cook my meals and eat them there. But here on the hilltop fresh breezes blew, and there was that glorious view over Kidepo which I could have by stepping outside the stockade, or by using one of the peepholes left by an inquisitive visitor. In the evenings the sun set behind Morungole and a cool stillness descended

that was so infinitely peaceful that I believed I must just be
getting old and crotchety, to be in such a bad humor all day
long with my friends, for despite that bad humor, which
manifested itself more openly as my vocabulary of Icien
swear words and knowledge of locally insulting gestures increased, the Ik continued to greet me warmly, if they
greeted me at all, and to call me Iciebam.

I quickly discovered what all the activity was about, and
the use for all the charcoal, for the seven villages became a
miniature Detroit with puffs of smoke and the clanging of
metal on metal announcing that the Ik were busy building
up the Turkana armory of spears and fighting knives, to
replace those lost in battle or confiscated by the government.
Ik children found a new occupation, helping the Turkana
herd their goats and graze them on the mountainside, feeding themselves on the goats' milk directly from the udder.
Youths and men even began to dress rather like Turkana,
sewing shin guards of hide around their legs and a few of
them attempting mud packs. The Ik had always said that of
all the herders they knew, they liked the Turkana the best,
and certainly Ik and Turkana seemed much more closely
tied to each other on a familial basis than was the case with
the Dodos. When Dodos came it was a purely individual
matter, one Dodos dealing with one Ik. They often seemed
not even to know each other's names. But with these Turkana it was different. As fresh Turkana arrived from Kenya
they were greeted as old friends, and immediately attached
themselves to "their" Ik family. But never did they go inside
even the outer stockade, let alone into individual family
compounds.

I told them that I had been to Nawedo and had seen a
special compound there used for "feeding the Turkana," and
they laughed and said that it was true, they often took

refuge there when they had been on a raid, or when they
were on a trading expedition to get tobacco, which the escarpment Ik in particular grew, or honey. They talked freely
about their raiding activities, and said that they did not particularly enjoy raiding, let alone killing or being killed, but
there was nothing else they could do when their cattle began
to fall off in number. It was then that people, through lack of
a steady diet of milk and blood, began to sicken and die. It
was a vicious circle, because if you took more blood than a
certain amount from the cattle, they too sickened. And this
was such a time, for the drought in Kenya was just as severe
as in northern Uganda, and Turkanaland was even drier and
more burned up than Karimoja. They said that other Turkana were fighting farther south, to replenish their dwin-
dling herds, particularly with the Dodos, and that many
were being killed. "But if we did not fight for cattle we
would die anyway," Athuroi said, and shrugged it off as a
regrettable necessity.

In the evenings I used to sit under the tree on the rocky
spur above Atum's *di* and listen to the herders in the valley
below or on the mountainside as they drove their herds back
to their *boma*. They sang—to themselves or to their cattle, I
don't know, perhaps it was all one and the same thing—and
unlike the mournful hunger songs of Lokeléa and poor
Kauar, these were lyrical and full of contentment. During
the daytime I often came across the older men lying in the
shade of a thorn tree, heads propped up on their neck-rests,
listening appreciatively to some youth singing of his love for
the world around him. It was another world apart, one in
which the Ik somehow just did not belong. Yet they were
there, up in their mountain villages, plotting and planning,
complaining about hunger even as they stuffed their mouths
full of food brought to them by the Turkana. The Ik were

never at rest either. Even when lying down, their heads or
their eyes were flicking back and forth to catch sight of some
sign that would lead them to food, even if they were so full
they could hardly walk. I thought I had better get out and
see a third, smaller group of Ik that I heard about accidentally, on the foot trail to Kamion but not more than a few
hours' walk away. I had of course asked if there were any
other villages, and everyone said no. I do not know whether
he did it on purpose or whether he really forgot that I could
understand Icietot, at least if it was spoken reasonably
slowly; but Lomeja the hunter, who was always more
friendly than anyone else, once mentioned in front of me,
but talking to others, that he was going over to Naputiro to
see what was going on there. There were hidden looks and
glances, and the others switched into Toposa and, I gather,
chided him for having given away something they wanted to
keep secret.

It took several attempts before I managed to get there.
The first time Atum simply did not turn up and nobody else
could be found to take me. He had an urgent message, he
said, that baboons were eating up his field on the other side
of Meraniang, the great mountain that loomed above us. The
second time we were met on the way by youths I am sure
Atum had sent ahead, but who were allegedly coming from
Naputiro, and who said that nobody was there and so it was
not worth my while going. I think the third time I called it
off myself, probably just to show that I too could be difficult.
Anyway, the fourth time I made the trip without event, with
Atum and his son-in-law, Lojieri.

I had scrambled up Meraniang and down into Kidepo and
knew the going could be rough, but I had thought that a
cross-country hike over what was relatively level ground
with no overall change in height, would be easier. Far from

it, and Atum and Lojieri could easily have left me far behind
had they wished. Atum went first, beating grass and small
thorn bushes aside with his stick, scorning what seemed to
me to be well-used trails going in the same direction, always
preferring to go in a straight line regardless of obstacles.
Several times he scared snakes out of our path. Lojieri,
carrying a spear at the ready, brought up the rear. I had
already seen one Ik with his face smashed in, kicked in the
jaw by an antelope he had not even been hunting but had
stumbled across as it was sleeping, and I knew it was not
only the leopards and occasional lion that were dangerous.
What I did not know was that the countryside itself was
dangerous, and that what seemed like level ground was anything but. Your goal might be only a few hundred yards
ahead, but between you and it could be one or even two
ravines several hundred feet in depth, and with almost sheer
sides. In fact, I would say that one hundred yards was just
about the maximum one could expect to walk on level
ground without such an obstacle. On occasions even Atum
and Lojieri had to slide down, though for the most part they
leaped nimbly from place to place, taking tufts of grass as
indication of relatively firm ground. If I tried to leap I usually missed, and I found it safer to sit on my haunches and
slide, rather as I do when I am skiing and the going gets
rough. There was no question of stopping or even going slow
on the descent, and once when I tried to stop and stand up I
nearly plunged over headfirst. Atum and Lojieri kept side by
side so as not to be struck by rocks loosened by the one
behind, and even so it was possible to be struck by a rock
loosened in the course of your own descent.

Climbing up was easier and safer, but no less exhausting,
and it was four hours before I reached Naputiro the first
time. Naputiro is the name of the valley and the stream that

sometimes flows down it in light cascades; like Chakolotam, it leads from Uganda down into Turkanaland in Kenya, and, like Chakolotam, is one of the few routes by which one can pass fairly easily from one country to the other in this area, and therefore much frequented by Turkana and Dodos raiders. I saw at once the reason for the two Ik villages placed high up on ridges on either side of the head of the valley. Between the three groups of villages, the Ik had every possible access route, even for raiders without cattle, well covered. Each village here too had its *di* a short distance from the village, out in the open with a commanding view. The villages themselves were like impregnable fortresses, built on rocky crags approachable only with a scramble, and, climbing to a height above them, I could see the now familiar layout, the village shape conforming to the shape of the crag and the interior being divided into independently fortified compounds. I made my sketches of the interior layout as best I could, and then went to meet the villagers who could be seen moving about below.

By the time I got there one of the two villages, the farther one, was deserted and no amount of cajoling would persuade anyone to take me there. Atum made the usual series of excuses and apologies and introduced me to the headman, so styled, of the first village, another Lojieri. This Lojieri greeted me perfunctorily with *"Ida piaji brinji lotop"* all in one breath, and, having got the tobacco, walked off with his back to the others so that they would not see how much I had given him. When he had concealed the bulk of it in a tattered shirt tail which he tied around the tobacco in a knot and then tucked into his shorts, he turned back and divided the rest, saying that as headman it was his duty to divide all gifts among his people and keep nothing for himself, and he showed me, expressively, his empty hands. In the same

situation I would probably have attempted sleight of hand
to create a better illusion that I was really sharing all the
wealth, but not so the Ik; that would be Icien dishonesty
and in any case unnecessary. While they still retain the
quaint old-fashioned notion that man should share with his
fellows, they place the individual good above all else and
almost demand that each get away with as much as he can
without his fellows knowing. Lojieri could have kept it all
for himself, had he wished, but that would have been poor
politics, and so he kept as much as he thought proper,
privately, then appeared to publicly uphold the custom of
sharing by grandly divesting himself of all that he cared to
publicly display. What was not seen by the others did not
belong to them. I began to see why the Ik did not go in and
out of each other's compounds, and why these seemed even
more tightly shut off from each other than the village as a
whole was from the outside. In building these fortresses they
were defending themselves not from some outside enemy,
but from each other.

The headman, who wore clothes in token of his headman-
ship, was such because he was supervisor of the Ik who
worked for the government in maintaining the Land Rover
track from Kaabong to Pirre, now abandoned. He was one of
the few Ik I met who showed much interest in the outside
world, and he was making serious efforts to learn English,
for which he was derided by everyone else. But he was still
an Ik, and while he stubbornly refused to take me even near
the village on the far side of the gorge and pretended not to
know which house belonged to whom in his own village, he
led me of his own free will to where a group of smiths concealed behind a slight rise were busy forging spears and
knives. I am sure that there was nothing sinister to conceal
in either village; he refused my wishes simply because they

were my wishes, but, being a truly unpredictable Ik, he
made up for it by voluntarily showing me something I had
not expected and therefore had not wished to see, and which
was in fact much more worth seeing.

I asked him if these were for the Turkana. His answer was
revealing: "Oh no, *your* villages are making spears for the
Turkana, we are making them for the Dodos." Atum nodded
in agreement and explained that the Dodos actually had
much more need of them since the administration had made
it illegal for them to carry spears and had confiscated all it
could find. How the administration then expected them to
protect their cattle from lions and leopards I do not know,
but, like the colonial administration, this one assumed
wrongly that the prime use of spears was for raiding and
fighting. Lojieri added that there was, however, this special
need for them now, as these were fighting days and cattle
were dying both among the Dodos and among the Turkana,
so there would be lots of raiding. I gathered from his expression of pleasure that for the Ik this meant there would be
lots of eating.

The administration had hinted that the Ik were playing
political games and causing a lot of trouble between different groups of herders, apart from being unable to farm
properly or stay away from poaching. I had been asked to
see if they could not be persuaded to relocate elsewhere,
where they would be able to farm more successfully, and
where there would be less trouble for them to get into by
playing one neighbor against another. I later went with
three Ik to see the area the administration had in mind, a
small hilly range in the southwest corner of Kidepo, known
as Lomej. They were perfectly willing to go and have a look,
but they grew increasingly unhappy the farther they got
away from Pirre.

We drove along to the south of Morungole, out in open, flat grasslands. It was hot and airless, and I felt as regretful, probably, as the Ik. Then we came to Lomej, the promised land. It was an ugly, scrubby hill, insignificant and unappealing in every way. None the less, we drove as far as we could and then walked and climbed. The ground was littered with rocks and stones, and would have been as unproductive as agricultural land as the land at Pirre, if not more so. The Ik's home was hidden, directly behind the high peak of Morungole, and the foothills of Morungole, on the other side of the Taan Valley, obscured the view of Kidepo and Zulla, except from the very top.

A dry riverbed ran down Lokimait to the northwest and into the park, and though game could be seen grazing there, the Ik knew that it was forbidden to them. They refused to go to the top of Lomej, saying something about that also being forbidden to them, which I did not understand. They returned to the Land Rover and were there, anxious to be gone, when I got back two hours later. They hated the low, flat land and seemed genuinely ill. They said there was nothing to look at, though I suspect that what they meant was that there was nothing to look for. I could see no advantage that Lomej had over Pirre except that it was much farther from the Sudan and Kenya borders and would to some extent remove the Ik from the scene of international politics, but they would be all the nearer to the Dodos and Karimojong, and poaching would be all the easier.

Farther to the west were the Niangea Mountains, running down from the north. On the far side lived the Niangea, and on the near side, facing the park, were the Napore. Both were recognized by the Ik as *kwarikik*, mountain people, and there was a linguistic connection. But both the Niangea and Napore had taken to farming, especially the Napore, and

with considerable success. They were held by the administration as a model of what could be done with hunters, a
model that the Ik should follow. The argument was not
quite valid, the major reason being that nobody had "done
it" to the Niangea and Napore, they had made the change
themselves, gradually, and under favorable conditions. The
Niangea continued to hunt, and the Napore no longer found
it necessary, their fields being as productive as they were.

The villages were large and open, with no stockades, and
the houses were neat and well made, in contrast to those of
the Ik, which looked as though they were thrown up just as
quickly as possible. The roofs were raised on an outer circle
of poles stripped of bark, and did not touch the walls. In this
way not only could air circulate and the spacious interior get
some light, but termites could not get up into the roof,
whereas the roofs of Icien houses were alive, and not only
with termites. Here was a people that had truly taken to a
sedentary life and was enjoying its comforts. There were
schools and stores, and the fields catching the runoff from
the long mountain range were green and full, even though
the expanse of Karimoja at their feet was dry and barren.
Many of the Niangea and Napore maintained individual
relationships with Dodos herders, and I met several Dodos
there, quite casually, whom I had known up at Pirre. There
was nothing surprising in that, for they travel vast distances
with their herds, but I jokingly asked one of them I knew
well, Lemu, what "trickery" he was up to with the Napore.
Lemu did not take it as a joke, but reproved me for assuming,
as everyone in authority seemed to assume, that they were
always up to some kind of trickery. He said that he and the
Napore family he was visiting had known each other even in
his father's day and his grandfather's, and he was bringing
them milk and blood and some goats. In the old days the

Napore would have given game in return, and honey and tobacco. Now they gave maize and millet and sorghum.

Lemu's shoulders were covered with rows of weals left by cicatrization. These are cut to show the number of people you have killed, and are an indispensable prerequisite to marriage. Lemu could look pretty fierce, if all you looked at was the rows of scars, his powerful body proudly bare except for the cloak flying in the breeze, and a string of ivory beads. His ears were pierced and lined with colored seeds, though, and he often wore a tuft of antelope hair on top of his head, and his smile and his eyes were warm and gentle like those of the rest of his people. His spear was for the protection of his cattle and his family, and it was difficult to think of Lemu wishing harm to anyone. He probably wished no harm at all even to those he killed, but faced with the choice of the life of a Turkana or that of himself and perhaps those of his wife and children, he made the same choice that most of us would make, without trying to justify it in the noble terms with which we justify our essays at mass murder.

Up at Pirre Lemu always stayed with Lokolóa in his village and had an Ik wife, but since the Turkana arrival no Dodos had been seen within miles, even Lemu. Now it seemed that he had a Napore village equally his own, but without any "wife" to make the connection. It struck me that Icien women offer themselves as wives just as traders offer any commodity, with a very clear idea of what they are getting in return, which is by no means the conventional return most often involved in marriage. The Napore and Niangea, like many others, may also be said to regard women as commodities, the most valuable they have, but not as items for trade or barter. Among the Ik if you see a girl wearing a certain kind of necklace, you know that she is a

Dodos or Turkana "wife." I remembered that Naputiro girls
were almost choked by such necklaces, and all the way back
I thought of Lemu and his death scars, of necklaces, iron-
smiths and Naputiro.

I still was not sure why the Ik had not wanted me to go to
Naputiro, and maybe it was simply *because* I had wanted to
go, but I had a feeling there was something they were
anxious for me not to know about. I began to feel rather
sorry for the Turkana, who seemed genuinely friendly toward the Ik, and wondered if they knew what was going
on at Naputiro. The Turkana position grew increasingly
critical as more and more entered Uganda and brought their
cattle with them, sometimes diseased as well as hungry. In
protection of the park, but even more in protection of their
own campaign to immunize all Karimojong cattle, the
Uganda government had to do something. The Turkana
listened politely when they were told they must leave, then
just simply walked away and continued grazing and watering their cattle as before. They boldly drove goats and a few
cattle down to Kasilé and Kaabong for marketing, and asked
me to complain to the administrator that they had not been
given fair prices!

Then a note arrived for me saying that I was to leave Pirre
immediately and return to Moroto, that it would not be safe
for me to stay as there might be fighting. If the Turkana did
not move, the government was going to have to send in the
army. It was far from just being a local incident, for this was
the time of the overthrow and attempted murder of the
Kabaka, to whom the Kenya government was, on the whole,
sympathetic. Relations between Kenya and Uganda were at
the breaking point, and the "Turkana invasion," although
utterly non-political in intent, could easily be turned to
political advantage by either side. Helicopters flying VIP

politicians passed overhead, much to the amusement of the
Turkana, and I continued to plead for their being allowed to
remain so long as they agreed to have their cattle inoculated
and to continue their abstinence from raiding. They had, in
fact, been provoked twice by the Dodos, but had not retaliated.

When I heard about the Uganda Army, I went down to
Kidepo with Athuroi and he called a number of the senior
Turkana together. We sat outside his homestead, a rough
circle of thorny windbreaks with hides stretched over them
and a large *boma*, and I listened to them talk for two or
more hours. I had little to say except that I had been told to
leave, and that there was trouble coming if they did not do
likewise. I tried to tell them that their few rifles would be
little use against the Uganda Army with its heavy guns and
tanks. They shrugged and said that they would die anyway
if they went back to Kenya, since neither they nor their
cattle could survive there until the rains came and brought
up fresh grass and filled the parched water holes. From the
top of Meraniang I had looked down into Turkanaland, as I
had from Nawedo. In those two or three months it had
turned from a brown wasteland into a desert. The Turkana
laughed at the notion of famine relief. "Perhaps some of us
might get it, if we are near enough to Lodwar, but are they
going to give our cattle famine relief? They would be glad to
see them die, so that they could make us farm."

They said they knew about the army—their Jie friends
near Moroto had reported troop movements to them. If the
troops came around and entered Kidepo by the southwest,
there would be plenty of time to snipe at them; mechanized
transport across the park at that time would be painfully
slow, if possible at all. And if they came up the Pirre road,
the Turkana said, they already had that ambushed, and had

prepared landslides to topple any convoy over the edge. Nothing would persuade them, and indeed it was difficult to see any argument against their position. They dictated a letter for me to take to the administration at Moroto and, holding my hands Turkana style, walked back with me up to Pirre. They were there the next morning to say goodbye, but their normal high humor was gone, there was no laughter. They saluted me with their spears and cattle sticks, and standing behind them the half-dozen policemen, in their smart white-and-black uniforms, waved forlornly.

All the way down that hideous road I thought of Turkana perched high above me, waiting to pry a boulder and start the avalanche. I thought of the rifles concealed in trees and bushes. I thought of the warm, friendly, hand-holding, honest people who had merely asked me if I had a gun and had accepted my word that I had not, of those who had said that their *menyatta* (homestead) was my *menyatta,* of the milk they gave me every day, of the food they gave the Ik, of their consideration for and politeness to the police, to whom they also gave daily gifts of milk and blood. I thought of them lying in the shade of thorn trees listening to the song of the herders, the song of love for a world that was far from easy, yet was a world they could love wholly. I had not seen one violent act, nor did I among the Dodos or Karimojong in two years, though I knew violence took place when it was unavoidable. Then, between Kaabong and Moroto I met an army convoy heading north, with Obote's specially trained thugs in the lead, and in my pocket I carried that gentle note saying that all my friends wanted was to share the grass and water of Kidepo with the animals of Uganda.

CHAPTER FIVE

Family and Death

I DELIVERED the letter and a report of my own, without much conviction that either would carry any weight, and was told that it would be at least two weeks before I would be able to return, and what happened then would depend on the Turkana. I took advantage of the enforced exile to go to Kampala and stock up with fresh supplies, and by the time I was ready to return, the miracle had happened and the emergency was over. Rain had fallen in northern Kenya, the water holes had filled and the Turkana had left as peacefully as they had come. When I got to Pirre the water hole was deserted, the dung on the trunk of the sacred tree had dried and scaled off and only the most impoverished of flies bothered to frequent my old camping site. I felt quite sorry to see it bare, but was none the less refreshed by three weeks away from the Ik and felt quite cheerful as I turned off to the right and began plowing my way up the homemade track to the topmost villages.

I gathered that there was quite a lot of raiding going on now, as Turkana, Dodos, Didinga and Toposa (the latter two both in the Sudan) tried to rebuild their herds by steal-ing from each other. Actually, it was not such a bad sys-tem—the number of deaths was relatively low, most raids did not even involve any injuries, and the system of alliances was such that the cattle were kept moving around almost in a cycle so that everyone benefited from them in turn. Prob-ably the most serious aspect of the system was that it made pest control almost impossible. Although the Turkana were gone from Kidepo and the traffic in milk and blood coming up and young girls going down had come to an end, the Ik were still active. The forges were busy, especially at Atum's and Lokeléa's *di*, and there were nocturnal comings and goings that nobody would explain. Lomeja was as cheerful as ever and his *boma* had been enlarged and now included a sizable number of cattle as well as goats. He said he was keeping them for friends, but I never saw the friends and it seemed to me that most of the nocturnal comings and goings centered on Village Number Three.

I had recovered from my depression, and was once again moved by Atum's gentle voice and welcoming smile. The view from his *di* was as breathtakingly beautiful as ever, and I was able to fend off the inevitable *"Brinji lotop"* for a few days by giving out tobacco before it was asked for. I had also brought food to give out, and some other gifts or, rather, bribes. But the moment they were all gone everything re-verted to normal and the old demanding game began again, the prying and peering through my stockade, the switching from one language to another so that I would not under-stand what was being said, and a new phenomenon, laughter that quite obviously, from the sideways glances and even open looks, was at my expense. I gathered it had something to do with my intervention on behalf of the Turkana. Atum did try to explain once, wiping the tears from his eyes. He asked me if I knew that, to start with, the Turkana had thought I was a government official, and I said yes. That brought laughter. And did I know that when they first led me down to their cattle camps some of them had wanted to kill me? I said I did not think that was so, and this brought lots of laughter. Then he said that I had helped them a lot and talked to the government for them and written letters for them, and what had I got out of that? When I said "nothing" the group just split its sides. "That," said Atum, "is what we are laughing at." And his clear blue eyes sparkled with pleasure.

Now that I had settled down into my new home, I was able to work more effectively, and having recovered at least some of my anthropological detachment, I could take such pleasantries in my stride, and instead of getting all choked up inside when I heard that telltale rustling at my stockade, I merely threw a stone at it. Other things that had bothered me before no longer bothered me. I had been desperately looking for something that would warm me to these difficult people, some human trait that I could enjoy and share, and I had thought I had found one when I first started living in my house and I saw that every morning men and women spent a lot of time just over the edge of the descent into Kidepo, simply sitting and staring at that great and wonderful stretch of country as the sun came up behind Meraniang. I used to sit outside my stockade and enjoy the view with them until I found that all they were doing was combining their morning toilet with their first hopeful search for signs of food. Then I began noticing the odors, but I did not have the courage to say anything about it. At the same time, I was frustrated because here was one massive toilet on my doorstep, but because of an ancient prudery I had to go scrambling up Meraniang for half an hour or so to find the requisite privacy, and even then Ik were likely to pop out from behind a nearby boulder with a cheery *"Ida piaji,"* delighting in the knowledge that they had caused me much discomfort.

Now, however, refreshed by my brief absence, I took this all more easily and if when out walking I stumbled during a difficult descent and the Ik shrieked with laughter before putting on a most concerned expression and clucking sympathetically, I no longer even noticed it beyond a mild wonder at the clucking sound which I could never imitate. As for the morning toilet, I merely laid claim to the stretch of land beneath my own domain and forbade anyone to use it, and then went and used theirs. It was quite impossible, in that land, to dig any kind of sanitary latrine, and it seemed as good a time as any to enjoy the view. The constant demands no longer bothered me too much unless I was tired, and of course it was then that the Ik, seeing that they had maximum effect, would go to outrageous excesses, reminding me rather of those swarms of flies gathered hungrily over fresh feces. I think it was the laughter that disturbed me most, and an indefinable absence of something that should have been there, perhaps in its place. Sitting at a *di*, for instance, men would watch a child with eager anticipation as it crawled toward the fire, then burst into gay and happy laughter as it plunged a skinny hand into the coals. Such times were the few times when parental affection showed itself; a mother would glow with pleasure to hear such joy occasioned by her offspring, and pull it tenderly out of the fire.

Anyone falling down was good for a laugh too, particularly if he was old or weak, or blind like Logwara, but I
never saw anyone actually trip anyone else. As far as adults
were concerned, anyway, they were content to let things
happen and then just enjoy them; it was probably conserva-
tion of energy. The children, however, were much more
active and sought their pleasures with vigor. In the afternoons, late, when they returned from whatever it was they
did all day long (I still had not found this out) they used to
play near their villages. There were conventional games like
building houses and making mud pies, but whereas the
houses were built crudely and quickly, with lack of any care
at all, the mud pies were beautifully and laboriously made;
earth was ground on miniature grindstones to make "flour,"
and pebbles were selected to represent lumps of meat, or
else strips of bark. Boys and girls joined in either activity.
But when it came to the fun part, the destruction of each
other's games, it was only the houses that suffered; *ngag*, or
food, was sacred even in play and, provided you stuck by
your mud pie and sandy flour and bark meat and ate it
quickly, it was left to you. And if it was not eaten, it was just
left, and children smacked their lips as they walked past.

The best game of all, at this time, was teasing poor little
Adupa. She was not so little—in fact, she should have been
an adult, for she was nearly thirteen years old—but Adupa
was a little mad. Or you might say she was the only sane
one, depending on your point of view. Adupa did not go and
jump on other people's play houses, and she lavished enormous care on hers and would curl up inside it, her distended
stomach clasped in her sharp, bony arms. That of course
made it all the more jump-on-able, and Atum's nephew and
granddaughter, Lokwam and Nialetcha, used to fight to be
the first to jump. Lokwam was particularly vicious, and the

other children usually let him have his way, unless there were enough of them to beat him up. Then when Adupa pulled herself from the ruins of her house, crying, Lokwam became genial and let others join in as he beat her over the head and danced around her. Adupa was one of the few Ik I almost shed a tear over.

Nearly all the games concerned food, including the hunting of the smaller and weaker children with play spears and slingshots. House building was about the only non-food game I saw, and that was treated as I say, with some contempt. Sometimes Ik children imitated the cattle game of the Dodos, building little *boma* and filling them with stones and pebbles to represent cattle and calves, but, unlike Dodos children, they would put these stones and pebbles in their mouths, though unless the pebbles were carefully selected, they were not swallowed. I never once saw a parent feed a child, except when Kauar did so, or when the child was still under three years old. In fact, you rarely saw a parent with a child in any context, unless it was accidental or incidental. The fields would have provided some kind of meetingplace, but at this time, the fields were all pretty much abandoned.

I felt that, as is often the case, the key to family life, which must surely somehow be the basis of this strange and outwardly rather horrid society, might lie in the physical structure of the village, the disposition of the houses and compounds, their geographical relationship, and so forth. By climbing up Meraniang I was able to look down on all except the lower two, Lokeléa's and Giriko's villages, and I could get a bird's-eye view of them from other hills. In this way I was able to draw fairly accurately the network of stockades and compounds that made up the interior of each village, and plot the disposition of the houses and granaries, which from above just looked like small houses, though actually they were enormous baskets on stilts, with a thatch roof. But now I had to get inside the villages, despite the fact that this was obviously not the thing for strangers to do. By a simple statement of intention to do so, and an offer of payment in cash or kind for cooperation received, and with Atum as a kind of woolly battering ram, I eventually covered all seven villages of Pirre, the two at Naputiro, and about half of those along the escarpment, plus one runaway village in the Sudan. I started with Atum's own village—nominally also mine, though as yet the stockade had not been extended to include my compound.

The stated ideal, and one that pertained in the smaller villages, was a circular village divided by stockades radiat-ing from a point in the center, forming a series of com-pounds. Each compound then had its own *asak*, or gate, into a peripheral corridor bounded by the outer stockade sur-rounding the whole village. This latter was pierced by two or three gates only, known as *odok*, each of which was used by the cluster of compounds nearest to it. In this way every family had its own *asak*, the doorway to the family com-pound, but shared its *odok* through the outer stockade with several other families. This would have been a neat system if it had worked, and in itself would have revealed much about the role that kinship plays in Ik life. And it was revealing, but not quite in the way expected. The actuality represented an unhappy cross between what was probably the tradi-tional residential pattern of the Ik when they were still nomadic hunters and gatherers and a residential pattern more suited to the sedentary life and needs of a farming people, with some elements undoubtedly borrowed from the neighboring herders.

In most of the villages the outer stockade, although pres-ent, was of much less importance than the inner ones, and

hence the *odok* unit, the group of families sharing one outer
entrance, was of less importance than the *asak*, or individual
family. In fact, *odok* was rarely mentioned or invoked as an
indicator of mutual kinship or other bonds, and *asak*, far
from linking you to anyone else, achieved just the contrary,
setting each family apart from all others. However, in the
course of three years, which is the maximum life an Ik village can expect, internal groupings and subdivisions occur,
reflecting temporary alignments. Atum's village, by far the
most complicated, and the furthest from the ideal, none the
less represented better than any others the present reality,
and it typified the Pirre villages fairly well. Those of Naputiro, Nawedo and Kalepeto were closer to the ideal. This
does not mean that the Ik of Pirre were any more cooperative or communally inclined; far from it. The best one can
say is that the situation at Pirre differed from that at
Naputiro and along the escarpment; for one thing, at Pirre
seven villages were clustered more or less together, if on
their separate hills, and there was the presence nearby of
the Police Post, and each village made its own alliance with
the police and their attached porters. The overall unsociality
of the Ik was amply confirmed by my first visit to Atum's
village.

The outer stockade, which in some places stopped where
an old person's field ran from a compound down to a gulley,
was pierced by three *odok*, shoulder high, so that you had to
stoop uncomfortably to pass through. The inside corridor,
however, gave onto only six more gateways despite the fact
that there were nearly fifty compounds inside, so these too
were *odok*, the outer ones not counting for much. These
inner *odok* were lower still, but you could pass through at a
crouch. Each led either into a corridor or into a courtyard off
which lay the various family compounds, each with its own

asak. In the geographical center of the village was Atum's compound, backing onto but in no way connected with that of his brother-in-law, Lomongin, and this division virtually split the village in half, grouping three *odok* against the other three. Atum's *odok* boasted the largest number of *asak*, and the second largest was that of a kinsman. But I could see where one gateway had been closed up and a new one opened, indicating a change of alliance where Lomongin had persuaded a whole section of Atum's original *odok* to come over to his side, boosting his numbers to rival those of Atum. It was difficult to see what they were fighting about, for there was no visible political or economic advantage to belonging to one *odok* or another, as I found out when I tried to see if the disposition of fields, for instance, in any way related to the grouping of *asak* under *odok*. Members of any one *odok* were neither necessarily kin nor necessarily even on speaking terms. Later on, when I saw new villages being built, it was evident that friendship was the prime element in determining who shared the same *odok*, for those people cooperated in the building of stockades that were common to them and helped each other with house building too. They also cooperated in building that section of the outer stockade surrounding their *odok*. But such friendships were fragile and temporary, and when Atum's village was abandoned later, he and Yakuma combined in a single *odok* in the new village, excluding Atum's brother-in-law, Lomongin. In a matter of a couple of weeks, however, an old rift had appeared again, and since building was not far advanced, realignments were made, with Yakuma closing himself off from Atum and joining forces with Lomongin, his brother's rival.

Plainly, once a village this permanent is built, nothing much can be done, except by abandoning your house or, if

geography permits, closing one gate and opening up another. Neighbors who have once been friends and have
fallen out often become the very worst of enemies, and this
results in some of the less attractive peculiarities of the
internal construction of an Icien village. For instance,
whereas the *odok* are uncomfortably small, even the rather
small and lightly built Ik having to crouch to pass through,
the *asak* that give entry to private family compounds are
even smaller. Some of them I could barely wriggle through,
and I had to lie with my shoulders diagonal to the ground
since the passage was neither wide nor high enough to allow
me to pass through flat on my face or on my side. When
Atum said, "That is to give us time to put a spear through
your neck if we don't like you," I thought he was joking, but
I soon saw he was not. Some *odok* are false, leading into
blind corridors where an unwanted visitor can be easily
trapped by closing the small gate behind him. Others are
booby-trapped with twigs and branches to crack and give
warning as soon as anyone walks on them, long before he
reaches any *asak*. The closer you get to an *asak*, the higher
the hazards are likely to be, and Atum had to warn me
several times where concealed spears were cunningly thrust
through the stockade, camouflaged to invisibility, or in the
low overhanging thatch of houses, to catch the unwary and
unknowing, in either case the unwanted, in the side.

That first day in Atum's village, I did not see a single
person. Atum would not enter certain compounds under any
amount of persuasion, and, having seen what I had, I was
not going to enter alone. Consequently a number of visits to
each village were required, for even in the smaller villages
no one person could or would show me everything, or tell
me what I needed to know about the various clan member-
ships and marriages that each compound represented. Not

once did I see food being cooked, or any sign of what might be called domestic activity. Some compounds were roughly swept, most were not. Roofs were alive with insects, including a particularly unpleasant-looking white cockroach, and at night when sleeping skins were taken out and unrolled, it was easy to hear the hiss and rustle of the lice and roaches and heaven knows what else so disturbed.

The insides of the huts were raised into a kind of platform, so that when the hut was built on a slope the platform leveled the floor. Doors always faced downhill, so that when rain did come and washed violently over the baked surface, it seldom entered a hut and the sleeping platform was always dry, and to one side of this was the hearth, with three round stones on which to set pots. Not all houses had such hearths, and those that did gave no evidence that they were ever used for cooking. Fires for heating, at night, were generally lit in a more central position, or in front of the doorway. Some houses had a rack up in the roof for storing or smoking food, but few contained anything beyond a few empty gourds. Atum showed me how, on coming into the house with a spear, it was an automatic reflex to raise it and thrust it through the thatch over the doorway, its shaft resting on the rack, to welcome any nocturnal prowlers. I asked him if it would not be both easier and safer for all concerned to challenge any such prowler and then deal with him if he was indeed hostile. He said that nobody would visit who did not have evil intentions, which I could well believe, and added with a touch of propriety that in any case Ik would not want to *kill* anyone. If someone ran into a spear on his own, that, however, was his own fault. Atum gave a happy little chuckle and rubbed his hands. There was nothing more to be seen in the dark interior of these houses, except the dreadful crawling sleeping skins rolled against the far wall.

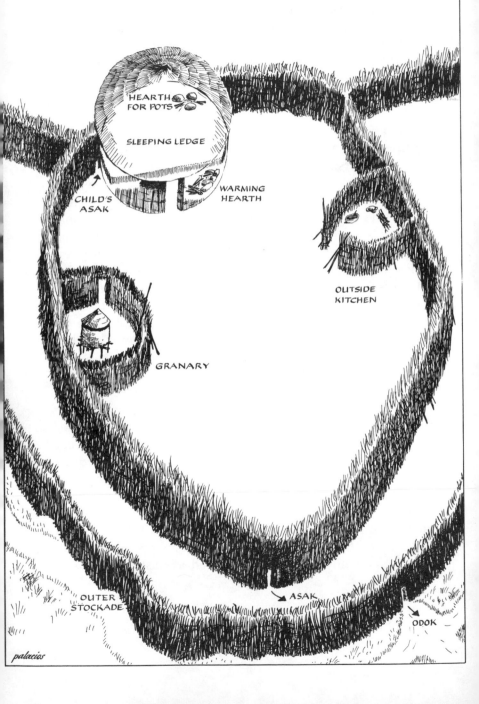

YAKUMA'S COMPOUND

HEARTH FOR POTS

SLEEPING LEDGE

WARMING HEARTH

CHILD'S ASAK

OUTSIDE KITCHEN

GRANARY

OUTER STOCKADE

ASAK

ODOK

palacios

The compound outside each house varies according to individual circumstances. Families with children have larger compounds, for children are not allowed to sleep in the house after they are "put out," which is at three years old, four at the latest. From then on they sleep in the open courtyard, taking what shelter they can by sleeping under the granary, if there is one, or against the stockade or the back wall of an adjoining house. The houses are windowless, so to economize on labor they are incorporated into the stockade wall, and almost every compound will have at least one house backing onto it in this way. There is usually no direct access, except in so far as sometimes a compound also serves as a corridor for the *odok*. But whereas adults are not supposed to pass from one family compound to another, in certain exceptionally friendly circumstances children may, and in that case a tiny gap on the ground is left between the house wall and where the stockade butts against it, above, so that only a small child could wriggle through. Children thus connected might jointly build a small shelter in the corner of one compound or the other, against rain. If caught without such a shelter, they may ask for permission to sit in the doorway of their parents' house, but may not lie down or sleep. "The same thing applies to old people," said Atum, "if they can't build a house of their own, and of course *if* their children let them stay in their compounds." He indicated by his tone that he disapproved of old people who could not look after themselves, and I wondered how he would feel about it himself in a few years.

The larger compounds boasted a kitchen section and a section for the granary, each a small enclosure of its own, private even from the rest of the main compound. Every granary I saw was empty but for a few bundles of personal belongings. They were enormous bulbous baskets, about

three or four feet high, raised on stilts, surmounted by a
conical thatched roof that, to give access, was simply hinged
back and rested on a long pole while someone climbed inside.
When milk and blood were available, these were mixed in
gourds and sometimes churned by hanging the gourd under
the granary while the owner sat and swung it back and
forth. At least, that is how Bila, Atum's syphilitic daughter,
Lojieri's wife, showed me that she would do it. But I never
saw her or anyone else invite such attention or take the risk
of wasting time in curdling milk. Any food received was
disposed of immediately and individually just as rapidly as
possible, regardless of whether one was hungry or not. Bila,
flicking some flies away from a suppurating breast sore,
laughingly agreed that this was so and delivered what might
have been an Icien proverb, had the Ik had any need for it.
"Milk uncurdled is milk unshared," she said, and gave the
empty gourd she was swinging for my benefit a swipe that
sent it flying.

Atum's family seemed more fly-ridden than most, although he and his brother Yakuma kept themselves reasonably clean and fly-free. Bila was always crawling with them,
as was her ill-tempered and mean little daughter, Nialetcha.
Nialetcha, being over three, no longer lived in the house,
however, so possibly had fewer lice. Yakuma's wife, Matsui,
I would probably have liked if I had been able to stand
either the sight or the smell. Poor Matsui had eye sores, and
the flies were constantly at them and had of course enlarged
them and had gradually, in this way, eaten away at the eye-
brows and eyelashes. Her eyes offered such a tempting meal
to the flies that there was never enough room, and they
crawled all over her face. Matsui never seemed to think of
brushing them away, and often when she opened her mouth
in a smile of welcome the flies would crawl in and explore

it. I do not think Matsui had the least idea that there was anything wrong with her. She was the mother of three sons and three daughters, two of whom were truly beautiful, all the more so, in my eyes, because they were the only people who seemed to share my opinion of their incredible younger brother, Lokwam, and who used to treat him much as he treated Adupa. It was one of the few real pleasures I had, listening to his shrieking and yelling when they caught him and did whatever they did (for it was always out of sight behind their stockade) and then watching for him to come flying out of the *odok* holding his head and streaming with tears, while Kinimei and Lotuköi laughed with happiness.

I saw a few old people, most of whom had taken over huts that had been abandoned, and who came crawling to the doorway to attract my attention. For the first time I realized that there really was starvation, and saw why I had never known it before: it was confined exclusively to the aged. I thought of Atum's wife, and wondered how many more had died in their huts and been hastily stuck in the ground inside the compound so there would be no fuss, for I was told this was the best thing to do with old people who died. A funeral, it was said, was a nuisance to everyone, and made everyone upset with all the crying and wailing. I would have given quite a lot to believe that the Ik were capable of crying and wailing, at that point. Down in Giriko's village the old ritual priest, Lolim, confidentially told me that he was sheltering an old man who had been refused shelter by his son and would have died of exposure if Lolim had not helped him. But Lolim did not have enough food for himself, let alone his guest; could I . . . ? I liked old Lolim, who not only knew about the past, but cared about it and was willing to talk about it when he had the strength. I also liked his daughter, Nangoli, who was almost as bald as he was, and who was on several occasions a true friend to me, though I never saw her much. So, not believing that Lolim had a visitor at all, I brought him a double ration that evening. There was a rustling in the back of the hut, as though the cockroaches had been disturbed, and Lolim helped ancient Lomeraniang to the entrance. They stood there laughing, supporting each other, looking like a couple of cadavers fresh from Belsen or Buchenwald. They shook with delight at the sight of the food, and told me to close the gate to their compound while they ate.

Lomeraniang's wife had died, and his son, who lived in Atum's village, had told the old man to clear out of the house the old couple had occupied because he wanted it for himself, to sell. He had promised to shelter the old man in his own compound, but, having sold the house, he denied any such promise, and said he had helped build the house and had the right to sell it. Nobody disputed him, and Lolim, a member of the same *odok*, had quietly taken the old man in. Lomeraniang had a sister in the same village, Koko, and she refused to have anything to do with her useless brother.

When the two old men had finished eating I left, and found a hungry-looking and disapproving little crowd clustered outside. They looked at the empty dish and muttered to each other about wasting food. From then on I brought food daily, but it did little good. In a very short time Lomeraniang was dead, and his son refused to come down from the village above to bury him; his sister hurried over and snatched his few belongings, leaving the corpse. Old Lolim scratched a hole, and covered the body with a pile of stones he carried himself, one by one. It was more than anyone was to do for him.

Village Number Four was virtually deserted by this time,

and Losiké, the talkative, laughing potter, turned up in Village Number Seven, where she had been grudgingly given shelter by her blind brother, Logwara. Her husband, Lokelatom, when he saw that the pottery business was no longer profitable and that Losiké was no longer able to feed them both and buy him tobacco, left her. Losiké was the victim of progress—she had progressed too far and become too specialized. The Ik had taken to farming, and had a need for pots in which to cook their favorite *posho,* a kind of porridge. Probably as hunters they had had little need for such utensils, which they would not have been able to carry about with them as they wandered from camp to camp. Most of their food would have been roasted on open fires, or steamed in leaves, or soaked and cooked in improvised containers of leaves or wood. But to cook cereals they needed pots, and Losiké did a thriving business. It was so thriving that neither she nor her husband needed to grow any food of their own, as they got food, even money, in exhange for her pots. She evidently loved Lokelatom very much, in which she sinned against a cardinal Icien maxim which is not to love anyone. She did all the work herself, carrying the water and cutting the right kinds of clay and chopping and carrying the wood for the firing. She bought Lokelatom whatever he wanted, which accounted for rare luxuries such as his Turkana wrist knife, a pair of shorts he sometimes wore and a store-bought pipe. All was fine and Losiké was happy and proud until the hunger set in and the fields withered. People reverted to hunting and gathering, and they had no need for Losiké's pots, and they had no need for Losiké, least of all Lokelatom.

So I found her in Logwara's village, where he had given her shelter in his compound. He had allowed her to stretch her infested skin in the shade of the disused granary, and

there she lay, day and night, skin and bone, but still trying
to flash those wonderful teeth in a smile. She also went on
the list for my daily food rounds. She asked me about the old
couple in her former village, Nangoli and her husband,
Amuarkuar; she knew it was useless to ask anyone else
because who was interested to know what happened to an
old couple? Her neighbors could not even tell Losiké where
her own husband was, or else they would not. He was a few
hundred yards away, in Kauar's village, living with some
Didinga refugees who had come in from the Sudan with a
few head of cattle, and who consequently had food. I told
her I had not seen much of Nangoli and Amuarkuar—the
village seemed abandoned and I thought they were mostly
down in the park, gathering what they could there. "Yes,"
she said, "we used to have lots of food there."

If this was all that marriage meant to the Ik, I wondered
whether they even bothered to formalize it with any ritual.
Up to that point there had been no marriages for me to
watch, and in fact there was only one during the whole
duration of my stay. The young seemed uninterested even in
sex, let alone marriage, and the old were as uninterested in
the young as their children were in them. But the older ones
told me stories of their marriages—Lolim, Lomeraniang,
Amuarkuar, Atum and others—and their account was confirmed even by the younger men, like my good friend
Lomeja. It was what is commonly thought to be a very early
form of marriage, marriage by capture, and I was sorry not
to witness it. The fact that it involves capture does not mean
that either the girl or her family are unaware of the impending marriage or opposed to it. The capture, as described by
the Ik, is very obviously a symbolic breaking of the link
between the girl and her family, the husband and his family
taking over all responsibility, the clan adopting her as a

daughter just as the husband adopts her as a wife. From
then on she assumes the clan membership of her husband,
with all its associated rituals and tabus, in so far as anyone
these days bothers to observe them. But Lolim and Lomeraniang assured me that this was a serious business in the
old days, and that while a wife could maintain her old tabus
if she wanted to, she *had* to adopt those of her husband's
clan.

In this way the lingering possessiveness of the girl's parents was largely countered, for the ritual of capture made
public their lack of power and lack of authority over their
daughter, and the subsequent rituals of gift exchange sym-
bolized their surrender of all responsibility. This led, invariably, to much happier future relations between the families
concerned, avoiding the rivalry and jealousy and uncertainty
so much associated with in-law relationships.

Lomeja said that when he was courting Losealim everyone knew about it; there was no secret at all. Her father,
Moding, liked Lomeja, and let it be known that a wedding
would please him. This made things easier, for otherwise the
battle of capture would have had to be more violent than it
was, and as it was, Lomeja lost his scalp, or a good part of it.
With some friends he decided on a certain day, and through
his sister, Kimat, he notified Losealim. Apparently from this
moment on it was considered better for the suitor not to see
or talk to his beloved. The time was invariably the evening,
to give the cover of darkness. The opportunity offered itself
when the girl to be captured left the outer stockade, after
dark, for a final defecation. This always took place, as I
could confirm, within a few yards of the stockade. At this
rather delicate moment she was seized and made off with,
and, depending upon her humor at the precise moment of
capture, she let out either a timid squeak of protest or else a

hearty shriek. In Lomeja's case, he said, she was angry with him for having kept to the convention and not spoken to her for more than a week, so, as much as she loved him, she let out a blood-curdling yell and brought her father and all the men of the village out to her rescue. Had she squeaked, only a few would have turned out and all would have been well, but her cry for help was such that they did not know if it was someone else trying to get her before Lomeja, which was sometimes done, or if she had changed her mind. In any case, they assumed that she wanted to be rescued, as she well knew they would, and gave battle. Had Lomeja's courtship been unfavorably received by Moding, they would have been ready for the attempted capture and armed specially. As it was, they were unprepared and had only their sticks and clubs: spears are never used in these battles, in which it is considered bad to open a wound with metal; some say it is bad to draw blood by any means. They came running out of their village with sticks flailing, and since Lomeja's team put up a strong fight Moding seized a huge pole from the outer stockade and began wielding that. He made for where his daughter was struggling with Lomeja, and struck his intended son-in-law across the head, taking a patch of scalp about four inches in diameter right off the top. Lomeja was knocked unconscious, but the battle continued, and eventually his friends made off with his inert body as well as with Losealim, and halfway between the two villages Moding gave up pursuit.

Nothing was made of the wounds—they were unusual, but in no way was anyone to be blamed. Lomeja, after a fitting delay of some weeks, during which time Losealim helped him build their new home, visited Moding and made him a present of some beer and some meat. The meat was cooked while the beer was drunk, and then Moding and

Peter and Thomas, whom I judged so harshly before I understood what "progress" had done to them.

A lone Ik hunter, poaching in the Sudan, sharpens his spear. Whatever he finds he will try to keep for himself; he knows that his wife and family will do the same.

Three Ik, with Atum's brother-in-law in the center, make fresh weapons for the Turkana, against all Government laws. Two others sit by listlessly, not even watching. In working iron the Ik still use stone tools, some of which can be seen here.

Lolim used to confer with Joseph Towles as one doctor confers with another. He carries his divining sandals, and wears his baboon-skin cape, a symbol of his high office. But no amount of doctoring could cure the basic ill, and Lolim died.

Lolim, the ritual priest, refused shelter by his son, staggers off to die on the barren, rocky mountainside. But he lay down to die so that the sun's first rays would strike his poor, dead eyes. He had hope, his son had none.

Blind Logwara...when he tried to reach a dead hyena for a share of the putrid meat, his fellow Ik trampled him underfoot. He thought it quite funny.

Loiangorok, in the house we gave him, with only just enough strength to put food in his mouth. We had to stand within arm's reach while he ate, to be sure that nobody would snatch the food from his mouth.

Loiangorok, after we had nourished him and given him the strength to stand for a few seconds at a time. But our attempt to help was a futile and, I believe, misguided attempt to interfere with a system that had to be, and which Loiangorok accepted with better grace than we.

Amuarkuar, where he lay down to die, after pleading for some water to drink. His wife was off trying to gather enough food to keep herself alive; he was not strong enough to make the trip. But he was old enough to remember to love, and he died while collecting grass to keep a home for when his wife would return.

A village in the making, the small thatched building in the back center is a granary, but the children suffer from gross malnutrition, and the granary is little more than a futile symbol, a forlorn expression of hope.

This small Ik village has an enclosure for keeping stolen cattle and sheltering the raiders, for which the village is handsomely paid. Their old economy taken away from them, agriculture virtually impossible, aiding and even encouraging cattle raids is now the major source of food for the Ik. It is also a major headache for a struggling new nation.

Above left: Kidepo Valley, with Morungole to the left. Once the major part of their extensive hunting territory and the center of their nomadic cycle, the valley is now forbidden to the Ik and is made to serve the nation as a whole, rather than a tiny segment of it.

Above right: At the *di* of Atum's village, near Pirre, men sit in clusters and gaze over their former hunting territory, now a national park, and wonder at those who ordain that animals shall be preserved while humans die.

Atum's village, "number five," was the largest and most complex. Even the innermost house had its own corridor to the outside so that any one villager had no need to see his fellow villagers or share any common ground with them.

Above left: The wall of an unfinished house, showing the sleeping ledge inside, and a forked stick from which gourds and other belongings can be hung. The owner of this house died before he could finish it; his wife, with good Icien sense, had already abandoned him.

Above right: The frame of a house roof, a design borrowed from their Karimojong neighbors but never made with the same art. Consequently the maximum life of a house, for the Ik, is three years.

The roof is well attached to the wall before either thatching or mudding, so that it can neither be blown off by gales nor lifted off, as mine was, by thieves.

A thatching party in progress at my new house site, overlooking Kidepo. What appears at first to be enthusiastic and altruistic helpfulness proves, invariably, to be a vital self-concern, as necessary as it is inevitable, and perhaps as basic to human nature.

Kauar and Lojieri help thatch the roof of my house. Kauar, exceptional in that he took such an enormous pleasure in being alive, died a month or two later, of exhaustion.

Left: Prostitution can be boring, say Ik girls, so when you are young and can attract healthy young herders capable of dealing with two girls at a time this makes for more amusement and creates fragile bonds between the girls.

Below left: Kokoi regarded her body as her greatest asset in the game of survival and used it wisely if not well. It helped fill her stomach with *ngag,* or food, which made her a good person. Eighteen months after this picture Kokoi fell ill and was unwanted. She lost her assets and died.

Below right: After eighteen years of age Icien women lose their ability to charm the cattle herders, and their fellow Ik have neither the energy nor the affection to spare. At eighteen a woman begins to enter the loneliness and isolation of old age.

Above left: Lokeléa's wife found it profitable to help her husband, and used to bring water back to his compound and prepare food there. But then Lokeléa was not really an Ik; he looked after and fed his wives.

Above right: Losiké in happier days, still active as potter. In a few months she was, like all useless things, to be abandoned to her fate.

Below left: Nangoli. Her husband, Amuarkuar, died of thirst and she fled to the Sudan with her sons and lived there in relative comfort. But something drew her back to Morungole, to die among the others.

Below right: Lo'ono, wife of old Lolim, the ritual priest who was turned out to die.

Above left: Adupa, in the unused kitchen area of her family compound, which was to become her grave. She made the mistake of thinking of it as a home. Her parents were unable to feed her, and when she persisted in her demands they shut her in. She was too weak to break her way out, and after a few days her dead body was unceremoniously thrown out.

Above right: Liza, younger brother of Murai, died, while his older brother thrived. Like Adupa, he made the mistake of expecting more of family than mere tolerance. Murai would eat while his brother, starving, watched. Yet he showed no malice or hatred, no regret, nothing. As Murai said, surely it is better that one lives than that both should die.

Hunger comes to animals and humans alike, and an Ik boy competes with a young kid for its mother's milk. This is his reward for helping the Dodos herd their goats.

Lomeja ate together, by which act all shred of responsibility passed from the father's hands. Two sons were born. The first Lomeja named Ajurokingomoi after his grandfather, and the second Losealim named Lokobirimoi because she liked the name. Lomeja was proud of them both, and in telling about the courtship and marriage he spoke fondly of his wife, yet I found it hard to detect any real emotion.

It was hard to detect emotion anywhere. In talking of marriage and its futility, Atum picked on his own daughter as the best example he could think of. She was dirty and lazy and was faithful to Lojieri only as long as Lojieri was in sight and looking. The idea that if there was any fault in her upbringing it might be Atum's did not seem to strike him. He spoke of her with contempt. But at other times when he thought that was what I wanted to hear, he spoke of her as though she were a jewel, pure and perfect. I think his attitude toward her changed, as it did toward his brother Yakuma, when circumstances changed. I began to suspect that Icien emotion is swayed in any direction, but only by the immediate moment, and with relation to one standard value, the good of self. I had seen no evidence of family life such as is found almost everywhere else in the world. I had seen no sign of love, with its willingness to sacrifice, its willingness to accept that we are not complete wholes by ourselves, but need to be joined to others. I had seen little that I could even call affection. I had seen things that made me want to cry, though as yet I had not cried, but I had never seen an Ik anywhere near tears of sorrow—only the children's tears of anger, malice and hate.

So it was with curious pleasure that I awoke one night to hear a distinct mournful wailing, such as heralds death. It came from Lomeja's village, and it continued, sobbing, until just before dawn. I got up feeling better than I had for a long time, hoping that I was right and that someone was actually crying over someone who had died. Outside I saw Lomeja sitting on a rock, motionless and stricken, and I knew it must be either his wife or one of his children. I was sorry that it had to be he, but still happy to have discovered that Ik can cry.

I was partly right, anyway. His favorite son, Ajurokingomoi, had died during the night. Losealim had suggested burying the body the next morning. Lomeja had said No, better bury it in the compound right away while it was dark, otherwise it would involve a funeral and, of all things, a feast. The boy was not worth it, he was only a boy. Losealim refused, so Lomeja beat her, and it was she whom I had heard crying, because she had been so badly beaten and, on top of it, made to dig the hole. And Lomeja was looking stricken because now everyone knew that Ajurokingomoi, named after his grandfather, had died, and they would expect him to give a feast.

I suppose one cannot blame him or Losealim too much. They had little enough to eat for themselves, and to try to provide for parasitical relatives because their son had died would only add injury to injury. What they did does not in any way indicate that they were incapable of love. What it does indicate, as did the whole lack of family life seen so far, was that there simply was not room, in the life of these people, for such luxuries as family and sentiment and love. So close to the verge of starvation, such luxuries could mean death, and is it not a singularly foolish luxury to die for someone already dead, or weak, or old? This seemed to strike hard at the assumption that there are such things as basic human values, at the very notion of virtue, of goodness even. I was not yet ready to accept that the hunger was as serious as all that, and if it was, I wished to ignore that it was being deliberately, consciously confined by the young and relatively healthy to the aged, left to be abandoned like Lomeraniang and Losiké, and now, it seemed, extended to the children. Yet biologically it made good sense. The children were as useless as the aged, or nearly so; as long as you keep the breeding group alive you can always get more children. So let the old go first, then the children. Anything else is racial suicide, and the Ik, I almost regret to say, are anything but suicidal.

Hunger was indeed more severe than I knew, and the children were the next to go. It was all quite impersonal—even to me, in most cases, since I had been immunized by the Ik themselves against sorrow on their behalf. But Adupa was an exception. Her stomach grew more and more distended, and her legs and arms more spindly. Her madness was such that she did not know just how vicious humans could be, particularly her playmates. She was older than they, and more tolerant. That too was a madness in an Icien world. Even worse, she thought that parents were for loving, for giving as well as receiving. Her parents were not given to fantasies, and they had two other children, a boy and a girl who were perfectly normal, so they ignored Adupa, except when she brought them food that she had scrounged from somewhere. They snatched that quickly enough. But when she came for shelter they drove her out, and when she came because she was hungry they laughed that Icien laugh, as if she had made them happy.

Partly through her madness, and partly because she was nearly dead anyway, her reactions became slower and slower. When she managed to find food—fruit peels, skins, bits of bone, half-eaten berries, whatever—she held it in her hand and looked at it with wonder and delight, savoring its taste before she ate it. Her playmates caught on quickly,

and used to watch her wandering around, and even put tidbits in her way, and watched her simple drawn little face
wrinkle in a smile as she looked at the food and savored it
while it was yet in her hand. Then as she raised her hand to
her mouth they set on her with cries of excitement, fun and
laughter, beat her savagely over the head and left her. But
that is not how she died. I took to feeding her, which is
probably the cruelest thing I could have done, a gross
selfishness on my part to try and salve and save, indeed, my
own rapidly disappearing conscience. I had to protect her,
physically, as I fed her. But the others would beat her
anyway, and Adupa cried, not because of the pain in her
body, but because of the pain she felt at that great, vast
empty wasteland where love should have been.

It was *that* that killed her. She demanded that her parents
love her. She kept going back to their compound, almost
next to Atum's and the closest to my own. Finally they took
her in, and Adupa was happy and stopped crying. She
stopped crying forever, because her parents went away and
closed the *asak* tight behind them, so tight that weak little
Adupa could never have moved it if she had tried. But I
doubt that she even thought of trying. She waited for them
to come back with the food they promised her. When they
came back she was still waiting for them. It was a week or
ten days later, and her body was already almost too far gone
to bury. In an Ik village who would notice the smell? And if
she had cried, who would have noticed that? Her parents
took what was left of her and threw it out, as one does the
riper garbage, a good distance away. They even pulled some
stones over it to stop the vultures and hyenas from scattering
bits and pieces of their daughter in Atum's field; that would
have been offensive, for they were good neighbors and
shared the same *odok*.

CHAPTER SIX

Self and Survival

T HE IK seem to tell us that the family is not such a funda-
mental unit as we usually suppose, that it is not an essential
prerequisite for social life except in the biological context.
The circumstances that have brought this about, for it certainly was not always so with the Ik, are admittedly extreme,
but they are circumstances into which we could all con-
ceivably fall, and the potential for what we might care to
call the inhumanity that we see in the Ik is within us all. It
manifests itself frequently enough everywhere, and with
much less justification, but seldom if ever has it attacked the
family in a similar way, except at an individual level. But in
the crisis of survival facing the Ik, the family was one of the
first institutions to go, and the Ik as a society have survived.
They still insist on living in villages even though the villages
have nothing that could be called a truly social structure, for
they encompass no social life, and despite the fact that mem-

bers of a village mistrust and fear each other more than any others, in direct proportion to their proximity and completely without regard to family and kinship. The mistrust begins even within the compound, between a man and his wife, and between each of them and their children.

It is here that we can see most clearly the reason for the collapse of those family values we like to cherish and hold to be basic. Under the circumstances that surround the Ik, the larger a family grows, the less security it can offer. The ideal family, economically speaking and within restricted temporal limitations, is a man and his wife and no children. Children are useless appendages, like old parents. Anyone who cannot take care of himself is a burden and a hazard to the survival of others. I found it difficult to see why they bother having children, the likelihood of their being able and willing to contribute to the family as a whole being as small as it is. There is always the chance of a good year in the fields during which the family proper—that is to say, parents with children—finds mutual advantage in cooperation, which is the only reason conceivable to the Ik. The family, otherwise, is for the insane, for it spells death, not life, as Adupa discovered. The other quality of life that we hold to be necessary for survival, love, the Ik also dismiss as idiotic and highly dangerous. But we need to see more of the Ik before their lovelessness becomes truly apparent.

Whether the villages and compounds can be called social units is questionable, though elements of social organization remain: *asak* and *odok* and a kinship terminology that defines the minimal familial relationships such as husband-wife, father-mother, parent-child, grandparent-grandchild and brother-sister. There is also a joking relationship called "friendship." But all this makes sense only in the strictest economic terms, in terms of survival, and individual survival

at that. If they achieve social survival it is purely accidental; there is no intent so to do.

In this curious society which seems to have bypassed
Karl Marx in economics, there is one common value, apart
from language, to which all Ik hold tenaciously. It is *ngag*,
"food." This is not a cynical quip—there is no room for
cynicism with the Ik. It is clearly stated by the Ik themselves in their daily conversation, in their rationale for action
and thought. It is the one standard by which they measure
right and wrong, goodness and badness. The very word for
"good," *marang*, is defined in terms of food. "Goodness,"
marangik, is defined simply as "food," or, if you press, this
will be clarified as "the possession of food," and still further
clarified as "*individual* possession of food." Then if you try
the word as an adjective and attempt to discover what their
concept is of a "good man," *iakw anamarang*, hoping that the
answer will be that a good man is a man who helps you fill
your own stomach, you get the truly Icien answer: a good
man is one who *has* a full stomach. There is goodness in
being, but none in doing, at least not in doing to others.

So we should not be surprised when the mother throws
her child out at three years old. She has breast-fed it, with
some ill humor, and cared for it in some manner for three
whole years, and now it is ready to make its own way. I
imagine the child must be rather relieved to be thrown out,
for in the process of being cared for he or she is carried
about in a hide sling wherever the mother goes, and since
the mother is not strong herself this is done grudgingly.
Whenever the mother finds a spot in which to gather, or if
she is at a water hole or in her fields, she loosens the sling
and lets the baby to the ground none too slowly, and of
course laughs if it is hurt. I have seen Bila and Matsui do
this many a time. Then she goes about her business, leaving

the child there, almost hoping that some predator will come along and carry it off. This happened once while I was there—once that I know of, anyway—and the mother was delighted. She was rid of the child and no longer had to carry it about and feed it, and still further this meant that a leopard was in the vicinity and would be sleeping the child off and thus be an easy kill. The men set off and found the leopard, which had consumed all of the child except part of the skull; they killed the leopard and cooked it and ate it, child and all. That is Icien economy, and it makes sense in its own way. It does not, however, endear children to their parents or parents to their children.

At the age of three a series of *rites de passage* begins. In this environment a child has no chance of survival on his own until he is about thirteen years old, so children divide themselves into two age levels and form age bands. The junior band consists of children between the ages of three and seven, the senior age band caters for the eight- to twelve-year-olds. I know of one girl who stayed in until she was nearly fourteen, but she offered certain enticements in return. Normally, thirteen is the maximum. Initiation into a band is as rough as the *rite de passage* by which you are moved out of it. Entering a band, you are the youngest, have the least to offer, and have the least physical resistance. You are no asset to the band, and are therefore not much more welcome than you were at home. But at least you will be in the band for four or five years, so it is known that if you survive you will eventually be of some use. Within the band each child seeks another close to him in age, for defense against the older children. These become "friends." There are usually only between half a dozen and a dozen children in a band, so each child is limited to one or two friends. These friendships are temporary, however, and inevitably there comes a time, the time of transition, when each turns on the one that up to then has been the closest to him; that is the *rite de passage*, the destruction of that fragile bond called friendship. When this has happened to you three or four times you are ready for the world, knowing friendship for the joke it is.

Early in the morning each village almost literally explodes. *Asak* and *odok* come down and the village reveals itself for what it is, a conglomeration of individuals of all ages, each going his own way in search of food and water, like a plague of locusts spreading over the land. There are, of course, some occasions on which adults move together, or even work together, but they are rare and relate to individual circumstances. The only fixed social groupings are the age bands, and usually each village will have only two such bands, one of each level, though Atum's village under Meraniang had four bands. Each age band moves as a whole, and lays claim to the territory through which it is moving at the moment. There are no fixed territories that "belong" to a band, but it does have certain rights by virtue of immediate occupation. The search is of course for food, and this usually takes the bands quite far from the village and they may well meet up with bands from other villages. In that case the right of occupation applies if the bands that meet are of the same age level. But if a senior band meets a junior band, even from its own village, and wishes to take the territory occupied by the junior band, it will do so by force. Force involves anything from fists to sticks and stones; I never heard of a child being killed in such a battle, just injured.

Any child on his own, like Adupa, is of course fair prey to all, and would *have* to be mad to be alone. But within the band there is such protection as is offered by numbers, not

only against other bands but also against the larger preda-
tors, lion and leopard. Within the band itself there is also
some protection; if a member of a band falls into one of the
rocky ravines, the others are likely to help him out unless he
is the oldest member, in which case they may well have been
the ones to push him in. But mostly the relationship between
band members is one of limited competition, each child
seeking his own food but not at the expense of others. That
is, he will gather only what he can eat, and will not try to
hoard anything.

Each band is on the move continuously, and once I knew
where to look for them, in the wooded *oror*, I used to try to
find a vantage point where I could follow their progress
from ravine to ravine. I could see that when two bands
approached each other they generally veered away so as to
avoid conflict; skirmishes occurred only when the junior band
was in a particularly productive *oror*. The food most sought
after was the fig, but the juniors were mostly too small to
climb the large trees and had to content themselves with
scavenging what lay on the ground. For the most part they
ate figs that had been partially eaten by baboons; there were
a few berries, certain bark was edible but sometimes made
them feel sick, and when really hungry they swallowed some
earth or even pebbles. The weakest were soon thinned out,
and the strongest survived to achieve leadership of the band.
But by then they were bigger than the others, and such a
leader would eventually be driven out, turned against by his
fellow band members including the next in line whom he
had befriended several years back, just as he himself had
turned and attacked the previous leader who had been *his*
"friend."

Then the process starts all over again; he is driven out and
forced to join the senior age band as its most junior member,

the weakest and most useless of its members. Here he will meet up again with the person or people who had befriended him in the previous band, and he may or may not turn to them again. Since in this band sexual interest plays more of a part, there are alternative ways of winning friends that are by no means adjacent in age. Bila's little Nialetcha needed no prompting to learn that her eight-year-old body held all sorts of possibilities for exploitation. She is one who will survive. But again the activity within the band, other than sexual, is primarily individual, as, indeed, is much sexual activity. Trees that were unclimbable before offer less and less difficulty now, and the senior age band also lays exclusive claim to the right to steal from fields. Any junior band found doing this will be severely beaten. There is usually not much to steal, except pumpkins. For the most part, however, the senior band continues to scavenge in the many ravines that scar the land, and they wander farther than ever away from the place that should have been home but was not, to them.

The final *rite de passage* is into manhood and womanhood, at the age of twelve or thirteen, depending on how long the candidate for adult status has been able to fight off the attacks of his competitors. By now he has learned the wisdom of acting on his own, for his own good, while acknowledging that on occasion it is profitable to associate temporarily with others. That such associations must be temporary he has had plenty of opportunity to observe as he has grown from junior member to senior member of each band, from the bullied and beaten to the bully and beater.

When fields are ripening, the senior band is utilized, or rather it is useful, in fending off the animals, birds and insects that are fully as hungry as the Ik in this difficult land. This is where adults see some point to having had children,

which is rather different from parents' seeing some point to
having a family. It is well known the young scavenge the
fields just as they scavenge the *oror*, but they do only a fraction of the harm done by grubs and caterpillars and birds
and baboons, all of which can destroy a crop before it is fit
for eating even according to Icien standards; so children and
adults alike have an interest in keeping it whole. If that can
be called cooperation, they cooperate. Towers are constructed from which the fields can be surveyed, and from
which someone armed with a long sapling can fling a projectile with deadly aim for quite a distance. Usually the
projectile is no more than a lump of clay that flies off the
pointed end of the sapling as from a slingshot. But that is
good only against birds and baboons, and only if they are in
small numbers. Otherwise it takes a whole gang of children,
the entire senior age band and sometimes the junior one too,
to be really effective. This is exhausting work, weakens the
weakest still further and thus contributes, by their decease,
to the welfare of the stronger.

For three years out of four the Ik can count on the possibility of the bare minimum amount of rain necessary to give
life to one or another of their widely scattered fields, and
accordingly will invest a judicious amount of energy in
slashing and burning, planting and hoeing. Never, however, do they count on a harvest, for the rainfall at best is
only minimal and is highly localized, which is why they
scatter their fields so widely. But one year in four they can
count on a complete drought, and that relieves them from
any investment of energy in the fields. Some do not even
wait for the drought to become manifest; they just divine it,
either by their own guesswork or intuition, or by consulting
a diviner. The latter is increasingly rare.

During drought years there is much more illicit hunting

than at other times, but it has to be done with care since the park *askari* are armed with rifles; and if the hunt takes them into the Sudan there are, or were at that time, additional dangers due to the war there and to the hostility of the Arab government troops toward the entire population of the south. So communal hunts, either by net or by beating, were ruled out, and hunting, like other activities, became an individual affair. It was common to hear and sometimes see men coming back after dark laden with meat that they could not consume on the spot, risking a brief night with it in or near the village, then off before dawn to sell it to the Police Post without as much as a bite for a wife or child. I remem ber that once Lomer, Yakuma's oldest son, came back from several weeks' absence hunting on and beyond Zulia. It was the height of the famine and Yakuma himself was away, scavenging for himself, but Matsui and the other children were there, all starving except Lokwam. The two beautiful girls had nobody to sell themselves to, Ngorok was ill, and little Naduié was the weakest member of the junior age band. Their oldest brother came back so fat, not just plump, that I hardly recognized him. His face was like a balloon, his arms and legs were fleshy and his stomach was obscene. He brought nothing with him except three gourds of honey, all of which he took straight to the Police Post for sale.

About this time it began to be apparent that there were going to be two consecutive years of famine, and nobody was in the fields except a brave few. Lokeléa, who had more energy than most because of his carefully guarded cattle, continued to work two of his plots, one on an east-facing slope of the *oror a pirre'i*, and the other on a violently steep west-facing slope of Meraniang, several hours away. The east-west orientation meant that the fields were kept in partial shadow for almost half the day, since in this location the sun rose behind Meraniang and set behind Morungole, thus shortening the day and adding to the time the ravines were shaded. Giriko kept one field going, lower down the Pirre *oror,* the one that also had the seventy-degree angle of Lokeléa's. To work such a field was not only exhausting but hazardous, as a slip could send you plunging to the rocky bed of the ravine below. Different kinds of hoes were used for different types of terrain and angles of slope, one being short and the other up to fifteen feet long, each with only a small, light iron blade at the end. The long hoe looked clumsy, but actually was simple and effective. It was held in both hands, dangling at arm's length, and a gentle swinging back and forth did all the work, providing just enough force, with the weight of the hoe, to scratch the poor soil to the right depth. Giriko worked hard at his field for two years, and for two years it yielded him nothing.

Longoli and Lociam both burned their fields early in the second year. Their field shelters were already collapsing through disuse, their watchtowers had fallen down, and a few sprinkles of rain had brought up only eager shoots to be burned dead by the sun. The Ik still use the fire-drill to make fire, twirling one stick rapidly between both hands as it rests in a notch on another stick held firm by one foot. In a matter of seconds the friction produces smoke, and a little dry tinder poured over the stick on the ground bursts into flame with one puff. Fires were lit like this everywhere, with no attempt to control them. Some of them spread up a heavily wooded section of Morungole, reducing it to ashes and destroying several beehives, but nobody seemed to think anything of it.

Men as well as women took to wandering off through the mountains or down in Kidepo, gathering what wild fruits and berries they could find, digging up roots with a stick, cutting grass that was going to seed, threshing it and eating the seed. Again the anxiety to eat before being eaten, so to speak, often caused additional suffering. I have seen women threshing the grass onto their skin capes, hurriedly pounding it with a stone from nearby and stuffing the gritty result into their mouths without even moistening it with water, let alone cooking it. The result could be a severe and dangerous stomach cramp, but both the need to eat hurriedly and secretly and the scarcity of water were real factors in the daily life of the Ik. For the seven villages of Pirre the nearest water hole was that by the sacred tree, but at times it became little more than scum and mud. The one higher up was avoided because of leopards. The only other one was off the *oror a pirre'i*, down toward Kidepo. This was the favorite hole, having the best water, but not everyone could take advantage of it, for access to it involved several minor descents and ascents, enough to make me barely puff but enough to kill any of the older Ik half my age, and then the final descent, a three-hundred-foot scramble down the rocky gorge face that required both strength and agility. For me, the first time, it also needed courage.

At the bottom was a pool studded with boulders, and except where water had become isolated in little pockets and stagnated, it was relatively clean. Owing to the steepness and narrowness of the gorge, the sun reached the pool only at midday for a brief hour or so, and it was a pleasant place to rest. There seemed to be a tacit understanding, another slender evidence of Icien sociality, that the women had the pool to themselves in the morning. They would try to gather something on the way, and if lucky they cooked and ate by

the water. But even there each woman took sanctuary behind a boulder of her own and huddled over her fire and her
food, gobbling it down in haste and alone. The trouble was
that food and water were by no means always to be found
together, or even close to each other. In times of plenty,
women carried water back to their compounds, to which
they also carried the products of their foraging, and they
cooked and ate there, or else, quite exceptionally, a woman
and her husband would divide the labor between them, the
one foraging, the other getting water. Since water might be
as much as five miles from a village in a drought, and given
the precipitous nature of the terrain, it was virtually a day's
expedition to fetch water. Such exceptions, even though they
never included cooperation between parents and children,
were rare, but they were important, for they lent much-
needed credibility to the notion of marriage.

More often, married couples separated at morning and
rejoined only at night, if then. Some individuals wandered
long distances, staying away days or weeks, searching first
for water, then food. Water could sometimes be found by
digging a hole in the ground, a foot or two deep. At the right
spot, often indicated by a cluster of butterflies gathered on
the earth above, such a hole would produce a cupful in the
morning and another cupful in the evening. Covering it with
a grass shelter, the owner of this hole could then wander
abroad in search of food, and return at night to another
drink. It was not enough for survival, but it helped and could
perhaps tide one over a critical period. Old Nangoli survived
like this. She made three such stops, regaining strength at
each one, to get her to the other side of Kidepo, where both
water and food were more plentiful. But she had to leave her
husband, Amuarkuar, behind. Neither he nor she was strong
enough to fetch water back from either water hole at Pirre,

and their three children had left their village, with their own
families, for the Sudan. The old couple alone could not survive, and Amuarkuar did not have enough strength even to
get down to Kidepo.

I did not know of this, though I knew that their village,
which lay just below my own compound but mostly hidden
by a hillock, had been abandoned. I did not even know that
Amuarkuar was still there, but one day he appeared at my
odok and asked for water. He was terribly emaciated, and I
gave him water and was going to get him some food when
Atum came storming over from the *di* and asked me what I
thought I was doing, wasting water like that. I told him it
was my water and I could do what I wanted with it, to
which Atum said the old man would drink like an elephant
and I would have none. I pointed out that I could get some
more, and looking around to offer Amuarkuar some food, I
found that in the midst of the dispute he had set the water
down and quietly left. He wandered over to the rocky outcrop above Kauar's old village and lay down there to rest, his
head propped up on his *karatz*, or neck-rest. Nearby was a
small bundle of grass that evidently he had cut and had been
dragging painfully to the ruins of his village to make a rough
shelter. To conserve energy, he had fouled inside his house,
which in any case had little roof left, and made it unlivable.
The grass was his supreme effort to keep a home going until
Nangoli returned. When I went over to him he continued
lying there exhausted, but looked up and smiled and said
that my water tasted good. He lay back and went to sleep
with a smile of utter contentment and happiness on his face.
He had been privileged to drink the clean water from the
police bore hole, water given him by the gracious anthropologist who had it brought to him every day, who did not
even go to get it himself. And that is how and where

Amuarkuar died, happily, his stomach full of my water. And that is how Nangoli survived.

There are other measures that can be taken for survival, involving the classical institutions of gift and sacrifice. These are not expressions of the foolish belief that altruism is both possible and desirable; they are weapons, sharp and aggressive, which can be put to divers uses. But the purpose for which the gift is designed can be thwarted by the non-acceptance of it, and much Icien ingenuity goes into thwarting the would-be thwarter. The object, of course, is to build up a whole series of obligations so that in times of crisis you have a number of debts you can recall, and with luck one of them may be repaid. To this end, in the circumstances of Ik life, considerable sacrifice would be justified, to the very limits of the minimal survival level. But a sacrifice that can be rejected is useless, and so you have the odd phenomenon of these otherwise singularly self-interested people going out of their way to "help" each other. In point of fact they are helping themselves, and their help may very well be resented in the extreme, but is done in such a way that it cannot be refused, for it has already been given. Someone, quite unasked, may hoe another's field in his absence, or rebuild his stockade, or join in the building of a house that could easily be done by the man and his wife alone. At one time I have seen so many men thatching a roof that the whole roof was in serious danger of collapsing, and the protests of the owner were of no avail. The work done was a debt incurred. It was another good reason for being wary of one's neighbors. Lokeléa always made himself unpopular by accepting such help and by paying for it on the spot with food (which the cunning old fox knew they could not resist), which immediately negated the debt.

The danger in this system was that the debtor might not

be around when collection was called for, and, by the same token, neither might the creditor. The future was too uncertain for this to be anything but one additional survival measure, though some developed it to quite a fine technique. A more acceptable measure was eating those who could not eat you back, and the troubles in the Sudan gave the Ik plenty of opportunity to play this game. At Pirre we had a steady trickle of refugees coming through Kidepo, mostly Didinga herders. Those who were at the end of their tether, ill or injured, and with no wealth, were sent on down to Kaabong, where, they were told, they would be helped if they could survive the final two-day walk. But those who had wealth of any kind were ushered with great protestations of friendship into a kind of refugee camp that the Ik thought up themselves. It was at the lower end of Kauar's long, narrow village, just across from me. The village even constructed a *boma* to contain the Didinga cattle and goats, but it was placed at the other end, away from the Didinga and convenient to the hungry Ik. Didinga who were thus welcomed never lasted long before they too joined the stream of refugees flowing on down to Kaabong, where in fact there was a generous and well-conceived working system for resettling them as farmers near Debesien. One or two who fell in league with the Ik remained to encourage others, and one or two intermarried. It was quite a profitable sideline, and involved little effort or energy—just sharp talk, at which the Ik excelled.

The manufacture of spears and knives was very important economically at this time, especially as the Uganda administration was confiscating spears whenever it found them. There were traces of cooperative effort to be found here, but only during the actual forging process; ownership and marketing were strictly individual matters. The forging never ceased to fascinate me, and I spent many hours either on Atum's *di* or Lokeléa's, watching small groups of Ik at work. The groups were never constant—men would get up from one *di* and join the group at the other, or just leave altogether. Villagers from Naputiro or Nawedo or even Loitanet were likely, if visiting, to sit down for a while, then quietly pick up a piece of metal that someone else had put down and continue working it. Even that would count for something in the underlying game of prestation and counterprestation. But what intrigued me most was that the Ik, with their ability to confuse and confound, seemed to have passed through the iron and stone ages in reverse sequence from everyone else, for they used stone tools to work and shape and cut the iron!

The work was done with great care and precision, and with no sense of haste at all. The customers, Dodos and Turkana, having selected their blade, usually asked the Ik to make the shaft for them, to their individual specifications. The Ik again showed what fine craftsmen they could be, straightening the shaft as they worked it, heating it and passing it through a special straightener. This required two people, the spear straightener being a stout length of hard wood with a hole in the center. One man had to hold the straightener as the other worked the shaft. It was typical of the Ik that they would get their customer to help with this, so that they would not incur a debt to one of their fellows.

Of major importance as a subsidiary economy—to the extent that it frequently became the prime economy—was the very special role the Ik played in relationships between the various herding peoples nearby. "Nearby" is perhaps misleading, for the Ik were involved with the Topos and Didinga in the Sudan, the Dodos and Jie in Uganda, and on

one occasion in my brief experience, at least, with the southern Karimojong, and in Kenya not only with the Turkana but
even with the Pokot, far southeast of Moroto. All these are
peoples who need to raid, in times of drought, to replenish
their stock of cattle. There are raids carried out at other
times, for ritual purposes or even simply to give the young
moran (young herders charged with the protection of the
cattle) some experience, and in this way it can be said that
raiding takes place at any time, varying only in intensity.
Regardless of the nature of the raid, the Ik can supply certain vital information, and, as well as acting as spies, they
also act as guides and help with the disposal of the stolen
cattle. At the time I did not know the full story, but at least I
knew that they virtually stage-managed many raids and
were almost a necessity to the herders in drought years
when lives depended on an adequate herd of cattle.

It seems the simplistic view taken by all administrations
—that raiding is bad and must therefore stop—is not shared
by the Ik any more than by the raiders. It would be impossible to predict the results of the cessation of raiding if the
administrators really were able to achieve it, but they *could*
be disastrous. Meanwhile the Ik hatch their plots and in
times of shortage keep the cattle circulating from group to
group. I have known them to plan with such skill that the
Turkana were led up the Chakolotam Valley to raid a Dodos
herd on Morungole while the Dodos were being led by other
Ik down the Naputiro Valley to raid the Turkana. Each
group found the other's defenses down and returned with an
easy catch, to find that the same had been done to them.
They recognize that Ik are not the most trustworthy of
companions, but they need them, and allow for such con-
tingencies. In turn, the Ik recognize that it is unwise to

spend capital and are reasonably fair in their dealings, and
their loyalty, although temporary, is generally reliable during any given arrangement.

Most Ik, when paid, consume their wealth immediately.
This is both a trait natural to hunters, who live from day to
day and to whom possessions are a burden, and a necessity
in their present condition. A meal in the mouth is worth two
in the granary would be an Ik adaptation of our proverb, or,
in this case, a cow in the stomach is worth ten in the *boma*.
The herders never slaughter their cattle for food except on
ritual occasions. These occasions occur frequently enough to
add to their diet in a welcome way, for they enjoy the meat,
but the notion of killing cattle for food is foreign to them.
Thus when Ik acquire cattle and kill them and eat them
immediately, the Turkana shudder at such barbarity, but
they can do nothing about it. When Ik keep cattle, however,
both Turkana and Dodos begin to notice, and plan to remove them to a place where they will be respected and not
eaten.

Lomeja's *boma* had been growing more and more full due
to a diversity of tricks that he was playing on both Turkana
and Dodos, and to the fact that as a hunter he was able to
offer them meat and demand livestock in return. I think he
was the only one who still spent most of his time hunting,
and for some reason he seldom sold to the Police Post. Then
one night, I had been sleeping soundly and so did not wake
up immediately; I heard a rumbling sound and felt the
ground shaking, and, running outside, I heard cattle being
driven at great speed past my compound and on up Meraniang. There was a lot of noise, and I was still not really aware
that it was a raid when the shooting began. Lomeja's village
was directly across a gulley, above the now abandoned
village of old Amuarkuar, and I saw flashes from there as

rifles were fired. Then there were more flashes from the side of Meraniang, and the fading sounds of the cattle as they disappeared were replaced by those of men shouting and yelling, sweeping past my compound in wake of the stolen herd. During the shooting I took cover under the Land Rover, with not much gallantry but some prudence. Now that it was over, however, I emerged and shouted through the stockade to find out what was going on. Only one person stopped to answer, and that was Atum, who told me to stay where I was, that I could do nothing and would only be in the way.

Shortly all was quiet except for the chattering of women-folk. I called to them and they told me that the Turkana had raided Lomeja and taken all the cattle, many of which were his own, but some of which belonged to Dodos friends who in turn had stolen them from the Turkana. I asked if all was well, and they replied yes and told me to go to sleep. I did so, and slept well until just after dawn, when I heard Lolim's bald-headed daughter calling to me through the stockade, beating on the *odok* with a stick. I asked her what was wrong, and she said, "Nothing, but do you know Lomeja is dead outside your *odok*?"

With the flat feeling that I was in for another lesson in Icien behavior, I pulled on some trousers and ran out. There, neatly curled up at the entrance to my compound, was Lomeja, in a pool of blood. He was dead only in an Icien sense—that is to say, he was no longer worth worrying about—and he managed a smile and asked me for some tea. I think he would have added a *"Brinji lotop"* if he had had the strength. I hardly knew what I was doing. What *do* you do when a man asks you for some tea and he is lying in a pool of blood? When he is about the only friend you have in a crazy world, when everyone else is passing by, unconcerned,

on the way to add to the pile of feces nearby? I tried to do
everything and did nothing, but I cried as I did it. Not with
pity or sorrow, just with blind anger at this world, a world
that made things as they were. I rushed inside and lit the
Primus stove and put on water to boil. I rushed outside to
look at Lomeja's wound. He had been shot twice in the
stomach, and the bullets had come out of the back near the
spine. He must have run straight into them. I ran back inside
and got some medicine and laughed at the stupidity: a
bottle of Dettol and some bandages and a bottle of aspirin
and another of anti-malarial tablets. Some ointment for
hemorrhoids. I wondered if Lomeja had hemorrhoids, or
malaria. The water boiled over. I tried to make the tea and
remembered that Lomeja was still outside, and that the flies
were finding him more interesting than the feces over the
hill. It should have been easy to ask someone to help, but
there was nobody, there were only the Ik. I tried to clean the
wounds and tied them up with bandages as though embalm-
ing the poor hopeless body. Lomeja grimaced and said again,
"*Brinji niechai*" ("Give me some tea"). At least the flies could
no longer get at the wounds—they might as well help themselves to the bloody pool. I made the tea, with about ten
spoonfuls of sugar. It was said to be full of energy—as
though that were of any use to Lomeja, but he liked sugar.

I filled a big new yellow enamel mug and carried it outside. His wife was there, bending over him. Dear, sweet
Losealim. I drove her off without even stopping to think
what she was doing; whatever an Ik does to a dying person,
it cannot be nice. She was furious and shrieked and cursed at
me. Why did I not leave him dead? She had folded him up
once before in the death position, and now I had straight-
ened him out again. She had been trying to refold him as I
came out, and Lomeja had found strength to resist. He

wanted that tea. I drove Losealim off, still shrieking, and I put the big yellow cup of hot, sweet tea down by Lomeja's head, where he could see and reach it. I asked him if he was strong enough to sip it himself, and he said yes and reached out. The aspirin were there too. I turned to inspect the bandaging to see if Losealim's struggle to refold her husband and make him dead again had reopened the wounds, but Lomeja had rolled in the pool of blood and everything was bloody.

Then I heard that familiar laugh of pleasure. Lomeja's sister, Kimat, had run up to see what all the shrieking was about, and seeing that lovely new bright yellow enamel mug of hot, sweet tea, had snatched it from her brother's face and made off with it, proud and joyful. She not only had the tea, she also had the mug. She drank as she ran, laughing and delighted with herself.

There was not much else to it. I had nothing left in me to give. All the tea and sugar in the world and the brightest of yellow enamel mugs could not have meant anything to Lomeja or me any longer. He was still alive and conscious, but something in both of us had died. It was not even hope; we both knew he was to die. Could it have been affection? What an idiotic thought; why should I care about him or he about me? There was a doctor in Kaabong who could get up in a day and a half if he walked fast. I scribbled a note and sent it to the Police Post and asked them to get on the radio and call for him. Oddly enough, the note was delivered and they radioed at once. And of course the doctor never even answered. Well, no matter; Lomeja was already getting cold as his surviving son was running down the hillside with the note. Not that the son cared, but I had promised him more yellow mugs like that nice one his aunt had.

The police came up in time to help me carry Lomeja to his

home, for that was his last request. Then they left me stok-
ing the fire beside him to try and make him feel less cold.
Someone else came in to watch, and another, and another. I
heard *"Brinji lotop,"* coming thick and fast, and it failed to
reach me, even to make me angry. Lomeja was so cold, yet
he still clung on, and his left hand clutched mine and his
eyes met mine for a brief moment. Then, true Ik, he let go of
my hand and just clutched at himself, and let his eyes rest on
a part of the hut where there was nobody, and he died alone.

CHAPTER SEVEN

Man Without Law

There seemed to be increasingly little among the Ik that could by any stretch of the imagination be called social life, let alone social organization. Yet such small-scale societies usually offer a shining example of how man can live sociably with his neighbors, often in the most difficult of circumstances. He even does this without the need for "law" as we know it, and without the physical coercion that accompanies it to force us to behave in the accepted manner. In such societies judgment as to what is right and wrong, good and bad, is based not so much on the nature of the action in question as on the circumstances in which the action took place, and on the sociality of the motivations.

The Congo Pygmies are only one example of this, for among them there is neither any law backed by the threat and possibility of physical coercion nor any centralized authority. The Mbuti Pygmies do not even have a council of elders, and anyone who has influence today may be without it tomorrow. Yet it is not hard to see what holds that society together, for they have all those things the Ik seemingly lack. They have a vital family life and a concept of family that can be expanded to include the band or even larger units. They have an economy that demands cooperation, cutting across differences of age and sex, involving the whole band. It reinforces and is reinforced by the familial ideal. This alone would seem to be enough, but beyond this they have a communal spirit that is difficult to define without either seeming like a woolly-minded romantic or reducing it to terms that are both unromantic and inadequate. It is, let us say, centered on a love for and devotion of their forest world, and results in their wholehearted, unquestioning identification with it. And what more powerful force toward social unity and cohesion can there be than such a deep-rooted sense of identity? All this the Ik lack, and more besides.

When the Pygmies, who are no angels, become involved in disputes, they manage to settle them without stigmatizing anyone as a criminal, without resort to punitive measures, without even passing judgment on the individuals concerned. Settlement is reached with one goal in mind, and that is the restoration of harmony within the band, for the good of the whole. If there is one thing that is surely wrong in their eyes, it is that the dispute should have taken place to begin with, and to this extent both disputants are to blame and are held in temporary disfavor. All this, too, the Ik lack, for while their disputes rarely reach the stage of physical violence, their violence is there, deep and smoldering, scarring each man and woman, making life even more disagreeable and dividing man against his neighbor even further.

There is simply no community of interest, familial or economic, social or spiritual.

With the Ik the family does not even hold itself together, much less serve as a model for a wider social brotherhood of Ik. Economic interest is centered on as many individual stomachs as there are people, and cooperation is merely a device for furthering an interest that is consciously selfish. We often do the same thing in our so-called "altruistic" practices, but we tell ourselves it is for the good of others; the Ik have dispensed with the myth of altruism, but they have also largely dispensed with acts that in reality served at least mutual interests. They too have no centralized leadership, nor the means of physical coercion, yet they do undeniably hold together with remarkable tenacity, and I had thought I might uncover something in the realm of law and custom, power and authority, that would offer the explanation. In some instances of transition from tribe to nation the central government supplants custom with law, and authority with power, by the use of the vast technology and armory at its disposal and by its sophisticated techniques of coercion. The Uganda government had the power, and it had supplied a law that was fair and equal to all, but it was unwilling to use the power to enforce the law in any but the most perfunctory manner, such as by shooting at hungry poachers or arresting starving farmers whose fields had barely encroached a mile into the park. To compel the Ik to accept any law or form of government that they did not want to accept would have been a vastly expensive project, and would have involved the open use of brute, and perhaps brutal, force. Coupled with understanding, this might not have been such a bad thing. But the Ik were of no concern to Obote and his government, who preferred to play inexpensive and less controversial games, such as confiscating spears from Ik and Karimojong alike (when they could) and trying to persuade them to behave in a more civilized way by wearing clothes, at a time when the "civilized" world was shedding them as fast as it could. Even had the government put into effect some efficient, comprehensive plan that had the welfare of the Ik at heart, the Ik simply could not have been influenced. Force would have been essential.

By no stretch of the imagination can it be said that the government exercised any cohesive influence over the Ik. One is tempted almost to suppose that they join together and sit in each other's presence on a common *di* without talking to each other, merely for the pleasure of ignoring each other. That might well be an appealing idea to the Ik, but hardly enough to justify in their eyes the considerable expenditure of energy involved. Sometimes men walk for over two hours simply to sit at a *di* that is not theirs. Yet, silent as they are on that *di,* they are there inescapably as a social unit. It is possible that they receive some comfort in the communal sharing of the pangs of hunger, in their lethargic but anxious quest for the telltale vulture, in their despair as they search the skies for rain, in their fear and mistrust of each other. This taking of comfort in a shared misery would at least help preserve the fragile sense of need for each other that is one of the bases of society. Even given the exceptional set of circumstances in which the Ik live, it seems that we are faced with a highly exceptional, and most would think exceptionable, mentality. However, few of us have really been hungry to the point of eating pebbles and earth; fewer still have starved and survived, or suffered the incredible pain of acute thirst. Ik reaction to authority and to dispute helps us to come perhaps a shade closer.

Positions of leadership are not much coveted by the Ik. They are backed by little power, and in so far as they confer any benefits (i.e., *ngag*, or food) upon the officeholder, that only serves to make him all the more edible. However, the possibility of using authority, and such power as goes with it, to fill their stomachs much as it is used elsewhere to fill pockets does not escape them. At the administrative level there is the appointed chief, the *mkungu*, through whom the administration attempts to exercise some control over all the Ik. But the Ik, some two thousand strong, not unwisely, are highly suspicious of anyone wanting or accepting a position of authority, all the more so if he is capable. The previous *mkungu* was capable; he was Lojieri, now headman of Napu tiro and head of the Ik working for the government on the Pirre road. The Ik complained about him and had him removed very quickly. Both Atum and his brother Yakuma had served terms as *mkungu*. The present *mkungu* was Longoli; he had no children, and he was popular because he was content to live with the Dodos in Kasilé and to leave his people as much alone as possible. He spent much of his time at the compound of the Dodos chief, or Jakite, and was always well fed. He took care not to amass too much, so that while he had enough to keep a number of friends around him he was never in danger of being completely consumed by Icien friendship. He maintained this precarious balance only with difficulty, and this made his position even more unenviable to other Ik. He depended on maintaining the goodwill of his "subjects" by implementing as few as possible of the government's attempts to exercise control. This meant placating the local administration and devising new reasons why this or that had not been done. Meanwhile he received a government salary and the hospitality of the

Jakite, who, although also a government appointee, was none the less interested in the *mkungu's* ability to predict the movement of Turkana and Jie cattle.

The *mkungu* himself appointed village *niampara*, or headmen. He chose, wherever possible, those who had some claim to respect in terms of age and lineage, so that they would be at least moderately effective. It was the *niampara* who always bore the blame for the implementation of government measures. It was necessary to change the *niampara* almost as frequently as they attempted to justify their existence. From their own point of view, their existence was almost impossible to justify, for such benefit as they could squeeze out of it derived on the one hand from enforcing action and on the other from avoiding it. As the *mkungu* always saw to it that the *niampara* took the blame, either the Ik or the administration were sure to demand their resignation the moment they even tried to do their job.

At the traditional level there was no office approaching that of tribal chief or elder, and even though the Ik were divided into clans and lineages with recognized elders, the largest effective political unit was the *ao*, or village. Every village was made up of members of various clans (*bonit*), that having the largest number of compounds being the dominant clan; the village might even be referred to on occasion by the name of the dominant clan. But although the descent of families from lineages and clans can be traced by the Ik, it is only for four or at the most five generations, rarely going beyond that. Common membership of a clan or lineage confers no special privileges, rights or responsibilities, though at one time it almost certainly did so. Nor are there any special behavioral patterns involved, except the avoidance of marriage within the clan. While brothers frequently have their compounds in the same village, that is as

far as lineage sentiment expressed itself; so it plainly is not a
very binding force. However, the oldest son of the oldest
son, traced in this way from the lineage founder, is the elder,
the *anazé*. He has no power, ritual or secular, but he has a
certain amount of influence within the lineage, though none
beyond it.

Of more influence in the village as a whole is another kind
of *anazé* who is descended from the founder of the village.
He need not be the most senior descendant, nor the oldest;
in fact, he is generally a younger person, and is elected by
the village as their leader. He too has no power, but he is
expected to settle disputes within the village, to mediate
with the elders of another village in the case of an inter-vil-
lage dispute, and to give the order when it is time to move
the village to another site. A village can be referred to, and
frequently is, by the name of this person. Slender as his
authority is, at least it derives from a traditional source, and
the *anazé* is much more respected than the *niumpara*, just as
his chances of cashing in on his authority are much less. It is
a temporary position, and he may be said to come up for
reelection each time the village moves, which is about once
every three years.

The importance of community of residence as different
from community of lineage or clan is well indicated by the
fact that villages are most frequently referred to by their
locality, several villages in the same locality sharing the
same name. Even when the villages move, they retain the
same name so long as they are rebuilt in the same locality.
This implies that community of residence involves, or should
ideally involve, community of interest and therefore community of behavior. With the Ik one has to be thankful even
to be able to trace an ideal; it would be foolhardy to expect
to find it manifest in action. But this ideal *is* a dynamic one,

as can be seen in the one important instance where it does
become translated into action. This, moreover, is at the
tribal level. It is implied in the term by which they differentiate themselves from some people, like the herders, and
associate themselves with others, like the Napore and
Niangea. The term is *kwarikik*, mountain people. They all
share common residence in the mountains, and it is this
sentiment that is the strongest stumbling block to any administrative attempt to relocate them. They prefer to die of
starvation and thirst rather than move out of their mountain
homeland.

There is one other bond, perhaps the strongest, though
also the most limited in immediate scope, for it binds only
individuals. It is the bond of *nyot*. It is established without
ritual or ceremony, simply by verbal agreement and an informal exchange of gifts. It is practiced between Ik, but at
the present its most significant form is when it creates links
between Ik and Turkana or Ik and Dodos, or any other herding people. By establishing this bond each individual vows
to aid the other, without any right of refusal, for the rest of
his life. The bond, once established, is indissoluble. It sometimes creates ill-will, since it may lead to Turkana and
Dodos each sitting on the same *di* with their respective *nyot,*
each negotiating a raid upon the other's *menyatta*. But it
does also offer a traditional avenue for effecting reconciliation, even for settling disputes at an inter-tribal level.

This is about all the Ik can be said to have by way of
government. For the settlement of disputes their organization is equally informal but by no means ineffective. In the
past their mobility not only led to their independence from
their powerful neighbors, it also made the informal settlement of disputes relatively easy and effective. If the dispute
between two individuals became serious, it was easy, during

the course of nomadic life, for one or the other litigant to join up with another hunting band, temporarily or permanently. There were frequent comings and goings in any case, for reasons other than dispute, so no loss of face would be involved. This situation still pertains to a large extent: although villages are more settled than hunting camps, they last no longer than three years, and in any case individuals are still highly mobile, having few familial or economic bonds to keep them in one place.

It is not surprising that in present circumstances they are highly disputatious and given to much acrimonious fighting. It is, however, nearly all verbal, though none the less vicious, and it is not uncommon for a fight to degenerate into a battle waged with clubs and sticks. Fist-fighting and wrestling are extremely rare, and the Ik say they never use spears in fights among themselves, which I believe to be true. While a stick fight is frightening, a verbal fight is no less dramatic. The fact that such fights are nearly always between villages indicates again that there is some cohesion to village life, some sense of village consciousness. Disputes within the village are generally settled quietly by the litigants themselves, or by the *anazé*. A fight between villages of different localities is most likely settled by arbitration between the respective *anazé*; the verbal fighting is primarily a means of resolving disputes within the locality. Each litigant stands at his *odok* and hurls abuse at the other so that all can hear and judge. A very common technique is for one adversary to be as aggressive and offensive as possible, while the other is quiet and almost obsequious, but persuasive. Nearly all those listening side with the aggressor. But after a while the two roles are reversed, so that everyone who was siding so bitterly with their champion on one side now find themselves equally bitterly supporting the other.

This is not difficult for an Ik, it is the bitterness that counts; it is sweet relief from hunger, and onlookers take time off to share a joke together before returning to the violence of participation.

Whereas ridicule is frequently used in small-scale societies to help settle internal disputes informally, the Ik use it only when the dispute involves outsiders. On one occasion there was a fight in Village Number Six between the Ik end and the end in which they kept their Didinga and Topos refugees. Kauar's mother, Lotuköi, stood at her *odok* and demanded that a Topos named Lokurei give her a cow because he had allowed his wife, Lotuköi's sister, to die. Lokurei retorted that the woman was weak and useless and not worth a goat, much less a cow. Lotuköi said her sister had borne him two sons and a daughter, and had died because of his ill-treatment. Lokurei was furious at this, and came running around to where Lotuköi was standing, screaming invective against the Ik, saying how much he had given them and now they wanted his last cow. Lotuköi faced him squarely and shouted no less loudly that she had not referred to his generosity but to his manner of having sexual intercourse, did he not realize that everyone knew he was an old donkey? Howls of laughter could be heard even from Lomeja's village across the hill, for the Ik find donkeys hilarious animals even to look at just standing still, and when mating they produce behavior among the Ik that is nearly hysterical. Lokurei saw he had fallen into a neat trap and tried to hit Lotuköi in the face, but she was ready for him and dodged back so that he missed and looked even more foolish. He gave her the cow and left shortly afterward.

In a similar dispute a Didinga who had paid an Ik a cow as bride wealth now demanded it back since his wife had borne him no children and had now left him, and since he had been stripped of all his wealth and was now as hungry as anyone else. The Ik replied that he had already eaten the cow and could not return it, but offered to discuss the matter. The Didinga said no, that he would go to the Dodos Jakite in Kasilé and get him to intervene and see that he was properly compensated. The Ik drove him out for thus threatening to take the dispute out of the locality and carrying it to the administration. You can be put in jail for getting the Jakite to settle a dispute, they said!

The only other open dispute of any magnitude with non-Ik involved the Police Post. One afternoon following a noisy night and much argument in the early morning, a huge fight broke out at the Police Post, and we all hurried over to see the fun. One of the police had been unwise enough to accept the advances of a daughter of Lokeléa; at the appropriate moment she screamed "rape" and was discovered by her husband, who just happened to be passing. He fell into a fit, so great was his horror at the outrage, and had to be locked up in the big corrugated-iron prisoner's cell. There he hammered on the metal walls, making a terrible noise, attracting still more attention, while his brother negotiated with the unfortunate victim, who by then was willing to pay almost anything to settle the matter. Lokeléa's first wife, a huge Dodos woman, went flying over to the Police Post and attacked the sergeant with a stick. By then every Ik within reach had gathered, and they were threatening to report the whole matter to the administrator in Moroto and tell how the police were locking up husbands while they raped innocent Icien women. The police settled the matter in the end by offering millet beer to the aggrieved family, which promptly grew enormously in size and solidarity. That, however, was not the end of it for the police, who knew very well that they had been made fools of. For days afterward

young girls, led by little nine-year-old Lokwimé, danced up
and down the road in front of the Police Post holding Coca-
Cola bottles in front of their beaded virgin's aprons, calling
out "*Butaanés, butaanés, butaanés!*" ("Copulation, copulation, copulation!") with appropriate gestures. The police
were made to give out more beer to stop the demonstrations.
They lined up with the Ik at the dispensary every day for
nearly a week to have the scars of battle treated. But by and
large such good nature and lighthearted fun was absent
from Icien disputes when they were purely internal.

One class of disputes was familial, for despite the break-
down of the family as a social unit, families still lived in
family compounds, or at least slept in them, and remem-
brance of past rules of conduct often gave rise to trouble.
For instance, in days when the internal divisions of a village
were less rigid, it was considered proper for a man to build
his compound stockade so as to separate himself from his in-
laws in the same village, but improper for him to so separate
himself from any of his mother's family who might be there.
However, since everyone stockaded against everyone else
these days, this never itself caused a dispute; it merely provided an ever ready excuse to pick a fight with almost
anyone. A husband would even accuse his wife of construct-
ing the internal stockade so as to exclude his mother's
family. This was as good an occasion as any for the splendid
pastime of wife beating, which, surprisingly, among the Ik
follows a formal procedure: one of their rare formalities, but
observed with diligence and exquisite pleasure.

Wives may be beaten for a wide variety of offenses, but
most of these no longer are considered offenses. It was law-
ful to beat a wife for cooking your food badly, or for not
having it ready on time, or for not fetching water for washing, or for not producing children. There was no provision

for the contingency of there being no food to cook either
well or badly, early or late; there was no provision for the
unavailability of water even for drinking, let alone washing.
And in these latter days the birth of children was received
with very mixed feelings. Consequently, wife beating was
rarer than it used to be, but when it occurred it still followed
the established formal procedure, and one form was, in
effect, equivalent to a legal separation that might or might
not terminate in divorce.

There were two ways in which to beat a wife. One was
with a light stick, and this was done if the offense was a
minor one. The wife, however, was entitled to defend herself
and if she could grab the stick she either broke it, which
ended the fight, or else she could in turn beat her husband,
which then led to his beating her again, using the second
technique. It was this second way of beating that served as a
preliminary to divorce, and I saw it take place several times.
The husband starts by declaiming against his wife in a loud
voice, listing all her faults. He does this at his *asak,* not at
the *odok,* for this concerns his immediate neighbors and
fellow villagers only, technically only those of the same
odok. However, if anyone else hears, all the better. The wife,
recognizing this opening formality, retires inside the house,
if she has any sense, and starts packing. Her husband then
goes out to search for the special thorny branches with
which he can beat her; he may use no others. Having gathered them, he must bind them at one end to make a switch.
This gives ample time for his wife to take to the hills, unless
she wants to stay and so force him to beat her, which would
involve drawing blood and is against the supreme Ik rule
which holds that one Ik must not draw the blood of another
by use of metal (spears), but implies that it is bad to draw
blood in any circumstances. So if the wife stays, having

prudently hidden her belongings a safe distance from the
village, and forces her husband to use the thorny switch, she
then places him at least partly in the wrong and she has
taken the second step toward divorce. If she flees before her
husband has finished making the switch, it indicates that a
reconciliation is possible. On his side, the husband can take
as long as he wants collecting the thorn branches, or else he
can have them already concealed in the outer stockade so
that there will be no escape for his wife. The severity of
feeling can be gauged on each side in this way. If the wife
escapes unbeaten she will take refuge either in another *odok*
where she has relatives and from which her husband will be
barred by the custom that prohibits visits from in-laws, or
else she will flee to another village. If she is beaten and the
thorny branches draw blood, no matter how lightly applied,
the blood restores the familial bonds which tie her to her
own parents and which were negated by the act of marriage.
Their home thus becomes hers again, and she can return
there.

The first formal move to reconciliation can come only
from the wife. She may, after a judicious interval, return and
cook food for her husband. If he eats it, the reconciliation is
complete, but if he refuses to eat, she has to leave again. If
the wife refuses to return to cook the peace offering, or if the
husband refuses to eat it, the divorce is considered to have
taken place. A wife could make a second attempt, or the
husband could let it be known he would like her to cook for
him again, but this is rare.

The advantage of the system is that it allows for the separation to take place without necessarily involving divorce,
and it does so very publicly so that all can judge the merits
of the case. In the case of the thorn-switch beating, nobody
interferes, however, whereas the stick beating may easily lead

to a large-scale battle between two kin groups. This is what happened when Lokelatom made the mistake of beating Losiké with a stick when he should have been patient and gone out to make a thorn switch. Losiké grabbed the stick and struck Lokelatom on the head, drawing blood. Lokelatom called on his friends and relatives and Losiké called on hers, thus bringing two more villages into the fight. It began in the middle of the night and lasted until nearly morning. It stopped when it did only because people were tired and hungry, and I was told that sometimes a whole village can be destroyed. As it was, the stockade around Losiké's village was uprooted and the sticks were used as weapons during the fight. Lokeléa's village was virtually destroyed in this way for no reason other than that one of his wives complained that his breath smelled. I heard her start shortly after dark, around 8:30 P.M. She continued for an hour, her voice gradually rising in pitch, until other women up in Lomeja's village started shouting down at her telling her to shut up, they wanted to sleep. By 10:00 P.M. women in Atum's village were shouting across to Lomeja's women, telling *them* to "close their teeth." They did so, and all was quiet for a short while until Koko started again, still complaining about Lokeléa's breath. This time, evidently, Lokeléa seized his stick and beat her with it and she fought back. Lokeléa's Dodos wife Kokoi then attacked Koko, and even from Atum's village we could hear the sound of splintering wood as the stockades were torn down and compounds smashed. Lokeléa had blamed his bad breath on the millet beer brewed by Kauar's village, perched just above the little *oror* that ran down into *oror a pirre'i,* and men from that village descended on Lokeléa and joined in the battle. The police finally had to intervene, and sent two Ik to Kaabong to spend three days in jail. Lokeléa had two enor-

mous welts on his head, and Koko was bruised under both
eyes. The village was in such bad shape that the police told
Lokeléa he would have to rebuild it on another site, closer to
the post and within sight, so that they could keep an eye on
him.

There was only one marriage during the whole of my stay,
and it had already broken down within a week of the
capture, so could hardly be called a marriage; more likely it
was simply an excuse for a fight to relieve the boredom of
hunger. A youth from Lomeja's village lay in wait outside
Atum's outer stockade with four friends, just after dark.
When young Lonipé came out to relieve herself the boys
grabbed her and carried her off to their village. The girl did
not even cry out once, but her father heard the mild scuffle
and gathered together friends to go and get Lonipé back. It
was not a proper marriage, he said. First of all, he should
have been consulted, and even if he had been he would not
have given approval, for the boy was useless and had no
food. Then they had obviously arranged it secretly with his
daughter, who had not made even the smallest cry of protest. It was just fortunate that he happened to be defecating
nearby when the capture took place and heard them all
moving off to Lomeja's village. So even though they had
reached the village, which would normally have concluded
the capture, he said he was entitled to take her back. With a
dozen men all armed with long staves he marched over to
Lomeja's village and demanded they return Lonipé. Much to
my surprise, they did so, the older men of that village not
wanting to fight the numerically much stronger village of
Atum. Loruyin grabbed Lonipé by the wrist and roughly
dragged her all the way back to his compound, and save for
some muttering and grumbling and muffled sobs from
Lonipé, all was quiet. Then just after midnight a tremendous

fight broke out, for the boys had gone around enlisting support from other villages, and about twenty of them broke
into Loruyin's compound and seized Lonipé once more. This
time the battle was inevitable, and raged between the two
villages, even though Lonipé was already settled once more
in her abductor's village. Loruyin finally gave up and con-
ceded defeat, saying that his daughter was not worth fighting all that much about anyway. He had hoped that one of
the Didinga refugees or one of the police would take her,
thus bringing him wealth and opportunity, but if she was
not going to cooperate he realized there was nothing he
could do. The cuts and bruises were all in vain, for in any
case Lonipé had retired from married life within a week,
saying she was hungry and her husband had given her
nothing.

Another class of disputes is economic, but whereas in
other hunting societies this might be quite a large class,
among the Ik the lack of food effectively removed much
cause of dispute, although food continued to play a central
role in argument. The only foods that were brought into the
villages and could therefore cause disputation were beer,
honey and *gomoi* berries. One dispute was a typical Icien
example of the way the gift works as a social institution, and
how far removed it can be from our notion of altruistic giving. Lemukal, from Lomeja's village, was a relative of
Lomongin, Atum's brother-in-law. When Lomongin and
Yakuma joined forces against Atum during the construction
of the new village, Lemukal lent the moral support of his
side of the family in return for some berries that Yakuma
gave him. Some months later Yakuma sent his son Lomer to
the Police Post to get some of the fermented millet which
the police threw out after making their beer, but from which
a very inferior beer could still be made. On the way back

Lomer was accosted by Lemukal, who demanded and took
the millet. I suspect that Lomer was given some inducement
to part with it so easily, but what was interesting was the
excuse which he gave Yakuma, and which Yakuma accepted,
however reluctantly. The excuse was that by having made a
gift of berries to Lemukal, Yakuma had established a bond
friendship, not as formal as *nyot* but binding to the extent
that until it was formally renounced either could make
demands upon the other. The fact that Lemukal was again
on the receiving end made no difference; having received
once, he was entitled to receive again. Needless to say,
Yakuma immediately renounced the bond, which he would
never have honored in the first place had Lemukal approached him and not Lomer.

Any dispute involving the theft of food is limited by the
knowledge that, once stolen, it will be impossible to recover.
This happened when Lokbo'ok, from Kauar's village, had
some honey stolen. He had brought it back to his compound
and hung the gourd container from a branch in his compound stockade, and someone had reached over from the
outside and taken it. He discovered this early in the morning
and we were all awakened by Lokbo'ok standing outside his
odok screaming in his high-pitched voice across to our village, accusing someone unnamed of having taken his honey.
He said he knew it was someone from Atum's village because they had a reputation for entering other people's
villages uninvited. Lokbo'ok hastened to add that he was not
accusing me, but someone else very close to me. Atum took
this as referring to him, and went to his *odok* and challenged
Lokbo'ok to name the person if he could prove it. Lokbo'ok
said that he was merely making this harangue so that everyone should know what thieves there were in Atum's village.
Atum said that Lokbo'ok was welcome to search for the

honey, to which Lokbo'ok replied that he would find it only by cutting open someone's belly, but that he had another way, he was going to go to old Lolim and get him to throw his sandals and divine who stole his honey. That shut Atum up completely, for everyone still feared Lolim's powers of divination, though he had no power to curse. Lokbo'ok did not get his honey back, but that night someone returned his gourd.

The only other case I know where partial restitution was made concerned some *gomoi* berries that Bila had collected from Kidepo and brought back to her compound. These are as hard as nuts and need a lot of work to prepare, but in season they are quite plentiful. In preparation they first of all have to be pounded to loosen the outer shell, then dried in the sun until the shell is cast off. This may mean leaving them exposed in a compound or on a rock in the open for several days. In the compound they are safer, but get less sun and so have to be left in the open for longer. Outside they may crack their shells off in one day, but you have to sit by them the whole time to prevent them from being stolen. Then they are put into a hole dug in the ground and filled with water. Here they have to be soaked for three days. Again, this can be done in the compound, but as water has to be constantly added and the berries stirred around, help is needed and this would mean admitting someone to your home. If the hole is dug on the outside, however, the berries have to be taken in at night, which delays the process and spoils the flavor. Finally the berries are boiled for one whole day.

Staying in Bila's compound was her husband's younger brother, Longoli, with whom Bila was on rather intimate terms. She got Longoli to help her with the *gomoi* preparation in return for favors given when Lojieri was off hunting or scavenging. However, Bila discovered that during the drying process about half her berries disappeared, and she did not know whom to accuse. She accused both brothers, saying they were in league against her and this was what came of sharing food and trusting your relatives.

The dispute proper began when Bila announced it outside her *odok* in the early morning. She accused both Lojieri and Longoli, and shrewdly said she was going to call on her father, Atum, as *anazé* to settle the matter. Atum's *di* began to fill up with interested spectators hoping for a fight. But Atum was too clever. He depended on Lojieri and Longoli for help with his main field on the far side of Meraniang, and Bila well knew the arrangement. It was also a place where Turkana took shelter in a cave when on a raid. Atum could not afford to alienate either of the brothers, so he named a third person, Lemukal, who was not related to any of them but was a member of the same *odok*. Atum said that Lemukal had confessed to him, but since he was a member of the same *odok* and shared the same field shelter he really had been entitled to some of the *gomoi*. He produced about half the number that had been stolen, miraculously, saying that Lemukal had taken only those, no more.

I heard later that it was Atum who had taken the berries, using his authority and influence over Longoli. He was useful to Longoli, so when Longoli himself was accused by Bila he did not name Atum, but left Atum to find a way out. Atum knew that Bila would settle for half the stolen *gomoi*, and also knew that he could name Lemukal as the culprit since Lemukal was both a member of the same *odok* and shared neighboring fields with both Atum and Lojieri, each factor alone giving him, in ordinary times, some privilege. Atum also knew that his own relative wealth made it unlikely that anyone would challenge him directly. It was a very minor dispute, but it showed how little familial bonds counted for, although they might be cited. It also showed how *odok*, even more than family, is ideally a cohesive bond, as are the proximity of fields and the sharing of common field shelters or watchtowers. Although none of these bonds, and least of all familial bonds, were strong enough to prevent theft or other forms of abuse, they still were of use in the resolution of disputes, and in times of less stress might well have been major cohesive factors in the life of the Ik.

Disputes of a political nature were rare, due largely to the highly uncentralized nature of Ik society and the informality of its political organization. Their relationships with neighboring tribes offered the greatest chance for disputes of a political nature, and if such had occurred they would theoretically have been settled through the offices of the *mkungu*. They occurred rarely, however, and were always settled at a local level. Whether it was an individual or a group of individuals who committed some offense against any of the neighboring peoples, the rest of the Ik turned on their own with a remarkable and rare show of unanimity, a measure of the great value placed on this inter-tribal relationship. The willingness of the herders to accept compromise settlements that seldom did them much good indicated that for them too the relationship was too important to prejudice by pursuit of an individual dispute. A good example was when one-eyed Jana was setting off across the hills, not far from Pirre, and came across a stray goat. He promptly killed it, took it to where he hoped he would escape notice, cut it up and cooked it. By the time the Dodos herdsman who was looking for the stray goat found him, he had been joined by Atum, Lokeléa, Kauar, Lokbo'ok, Lomer and a few others, and the goat had been all but eaten. The usual excuses—that it had been found already dead, nobody knew to whom it belonged, and so forth—were *not* made. As soon as the Dodos appeared, Lomer, who had been keeping watch, gave the alarm. Atum and the others sprang to their feet, swallowing the last morsels, and turned on Jana, chasing him and shouting, *"dzuuam, dzuuam, dzuuam!"* ("Thief, thief, thief!") They caught him and thrashed him soundly and then threw him at the feet of the Dodos, telling him to take Jana to the Police Post and have him sent to Kaabong to be tried. The Dodos demurred, and said he wanted a goat in exchange, and would let the matter drop since the Ik had given Jana such a thrashing (one of Jana's legs was badly gashed where he had been dragged across the stony ground, and it was nearly a month before he could walk properly again). The very next day Atum, in his role as *anazé*, produced a goat from somewhere, a scrawny little beast, and offered it to the Dodos, who reluctantly accepted it. The goat was then slaughtered and consumed by the Dodos, two friends he had brought with him, and seven Ik(!) to restore the friendship between them.

Of an internal political nature, the only dispute that I knew of was between Atum and Lomongin, the troublesome brother-in-law. They were both among those few Ik who sought positions of authority, believing they could manipulate such positions to their personal advantage. Atum had the edge on Lomongin, for he had already served as *mkungu*, he was the acknowledged *anazé* not just of his own village but of the entire Pirre locality of seven villages, and he had married one daughter into the police force in Moroto. For quite a time Lomongin was content to live in Atum's shadow, reaping divers benefits through his relationship. When it came time to move to another site and rebuild the village, however, he made his play. Atum chose the site and gave the word to move. Lomongin immediately counseled everyone not to move, since Atum had chosen badly, on a smallish rise with poor views, looked down upon by other villages. Atum could say little, for Lomongin was right. The site had been chosen for Atum's personal benefit. When he announced the site he had already staked out his new field boundaries, which ran from the site up to the lower extension of the police fields. Atum had his eye on the overflow irrigation water from the bore hole, and had been manipulating his daughter's marriage to try to get access to the bore hole itself. For a long time Lomongin held sway, and Atum, who had to make the first move, was stranded on his new site with nobody else there except his daughter Bila, his friend Lociam (father of Adupa), another member of his old *odok*, Lemukal, and finally Yakuma.

Lomongin saw that others were going to join Atum, so he went and quietly staked out his home site so as to be in the same *odok* as Atum. Atum promptly got Lojieri and Nakurongolé to build there, getting all the house poles in and the *odok* stockade completed in one day while Lomongin was off cutting his own poles. Atum's sister Lo'ono, Lomongin's wife, refused to be dissuaded by this offensive move, and insisted on Lomongin moving in immediately on the other side of Atum before the *odok* was closed. Atum waited until Lomongin had work well advanced on the three houses of his three wives. Lo'ono, the senior wife, herself helped the junior wife, building the roof taller than any other, at a sharper pitch and more smartly thatched. Atum loudly made the caustic remark that "that woman and her husband have aspirations . . . they are trying to build houses like the police." He accused Lomongin of "having ambitions." But Lomongin kept quiet, quieter than he had ever been, so that people began talking and saying how he had changed, whereas Atum was getting old and quarrelsome. At that

Atum played his master card, cut off part of his own compound and detached the stockade from where it abutted Lomongin's, and joined it up the other side so that Lomongin was effectively isolated not only from Atum's *odok* but from any *odok;* he was outside the village.

Lo'ono then went to her other brother, Yakuma, who had also been *mkungu,* and persuaded him that Atum was ruining the village and the good name of the family (!) by his selfish behavior. Yakuma took over the space vacated by Atum and changed his own stockade and so brought Lomongin into the village, creating a new *odok* shared between them, closing his stockade against Atum's *odok.*

Atum's final move was the smartest of all. As *anazé* of all Pirre, and as a former *mkungu,* he now publicly appointed Lomongin as *niampara* for that particular village. Technically it was a position of responsibility and authority, so nobody could now accuse him of monopolizing the authority or of deliberately excluding his brother-in-law. In fact, however, it was seldom that a *niampara* could use his position to much advantage, for he had too many people to please. But Lomongin was confident of his ability in the political field, and Atum knew this. By accepting the appointment, which he did, Lomongin virtually confirmed Atum's own position and authority, on the slender chance of being able to challenge him eventually from the lesser position. It was not long, however, before he fell into disrespect, as all *niampara* do, and he lost all the support he had begun to win.

Religious belief and practice relatively seldom were manifest in disputes. Under the stress to which this society was subject, all the trimmings were shed, everything that was not directly functional to the problem of survival was abandoned. Matsui tried to extract a fine from her husband once, for having broken one of the ritual tabus surrounding birth. After a woman has given birth to a child her husband may not enter the house for one week, but must stay with friends until the baby is ready for public display. Yakuma of course was having no nonsense of that sort, particularly since there were no relatives or friends who would give him shelter, so he continued sleeping in his house with his wife and the newborn child. Within the week the child became ill, and Matsui called Lolim, who provided some medicine, a plant to be grown near the door of the house so that it and the child could grow together in strength, and he confirmed Matsui's accusation that Yakuma had been to blame for the illness, brought on by his breaking the tabu. But Yakuma had not been mkungu for nothing, and he had his own share of the family skill at manipulation. He retorted that it was all Matsui's fault, and if anyone was to pay a fine it was she, for she had lain on her back and looked at the ceiling while pregnant, and everyone knows that this is forbidden and is likely to result in a child's being born blind. In this case his wife's infidelity to ritual had brought a curse on him, Yakuma, and made him blind to his own duty and led him to break a tabu. Lolim agreed with that too and, having exacted a payment from both of them, gave them his blessing, and the medicine, and left.

Accusations of witchcraft were sometimes raised, but more as forms of abuse than with any intent to make a case. One afternoon two women passed each other near my house, between the two villages of Atum and Kauar, in the little hollow where bald-headed Nangoli was planting a tobacco patch. Niangan greeted Nangoli, who simply walked on by without responding. As Niangan neared her odok she began hurling abuse over her shoulder, and Nangoli responded in kind, without looking around. Then as they reached their respective *odok*, timed to a second, each spun around as in a duel and shouted the accusation *"badiam!"* ("sorcerer!") But Nangoli, who was Lolim's daughter and so knew a thing or two about sorcery, followed up immediately with a long ululation, high and warbling and increasing in volume until Niangan cowered back as though the sound were piercing her. Atum came flying out and grabbed her and pulled her into the *odok* just as Nangoli completed the curse by putting her thumb to her lips and jerking it out at the fleeing Niangan with a final ululation. Nangoli caught me watching all this, and shook her bald head at me, laughing, and jokingly sucked her thumb at me too. Still laughing, she picked up the bundle of tobacco she had been carrying and ducked through her *odok*.

The weakness of ritual injunctions and sanctions can be seen in almost every aspect of life. Lolim and others of the older people told me, for instance, of how in the old days adultery had rated equal to incest as a crime, second only to the killing of a fellow Ik. Either act was meant to bring death, and was therefore a form of murder. The punishment was a particularly horrible one. The old men told me that they used to build a great pyre and set fire to it. Then when it was burning merrily they threw the offender on top. Atum described in detail watching it once when he was a child, and told how they waited as the victim writhed about, flapping his arms and beating his chest in the midst of the flames. Atum gave a lively imitation so that I could fully appreciate what a funny sight it had been. Then seeing that I was not laughing, he broke off and said shortly, "We usually pulled him off before he died. Then whether he lived or not didn't matter, he never committed adultery again." I am still not sure whether this was just a creation of Icien imagination, but since it was told by more than denied it, I

am inclined to believe that at least it was the *stated* punishment appropriate to adultery and incest. Whether it ever
took place, or whether Atum ever saw it, I do not know. I *do*
know that Atum enjoyed the vision as he conjured it up, and
would doubtless have been first in line to throw his daughter
on the fire had I suggested that the custom should be re-
vived. Bila probably qualified on both accounts, and, as far
as I could gather, both men and women were penalized in
this way. But when I mentioned Bila's flirtatious life to him
and asked if he was not afraid for her, he laughed and said
that the Ik had dropped all that kind of thing, now anyone
could sleep with anyone, there was nothing wrong with Bila
sleeping with her brother-in-law or anyone else. He hinted
that she had even slept with her uncle, Yakuma, his own
brother. He found that quite funny. Apart from being an
indication of the weakness of religious sanction, this was yet
another indication of how completely family values had
broken down, and it may well be that the almost universal
practicing of adultery was in a sense designed, or func-
tioned, to complete the destruction of that useless and non-
functional unit, the family.

The one bond that stood up in the midst of this almost
total collapse of society was the bond of individual *nyot*
friendship, significantly a secular bond created by a simple
exchange, with affirmation of mutual obligation, without any
ritual sanction or ceremony. I used to see these *nyot* relationships working almost every day. They could hardly be
said to be social, since they affected only pairs of individuals, but it was something, a sort of bedrock below which
even the Ik could not sink. They tried, halfheartedly, for
they never acceded to a *nyot*'s demands too willingly, but
they never demanded what could not be given. I never saw
the *nyot* relationship being invoked for food; it was gen-

erally restricted to tobacco and snuff. The Ik, rather like the herders, carried snuff in little boxes or tubes or stoppered antelope horns, slung around the neck and usually hanging down the back. This was the fashion among the youths, anyway; the older men concealed what snuff they had. A *nyot* coming across his fellow wearing a snuffbox, however, simply went up and unstoppered it behind the owner's back and helped himself without asking. The owner would often protest, saying he did not have much and his *nyot* should ask someone else, but this was always rejected by the others, "He's your *nyot*" having the same sense as "He's your lookout." But although I saw many a protest between *nyot*, not once did I see a refusal. Inter-personal relations, at the most minimal level, still retained some value and permanence.

This reduction of human relationships among the Ik to the individual level puts the Ik one step ahead of civilization, in some respects. Our society has become increasingly individualistic. We even place a high value on individualism and admire someone who "gets ahead in the world," tending to ignore the fact that this is usually at the expense of others. In our world, where the family has also lost much of its value as a social unit, and where religious belief and practice no longer bind us into communities of shared belief, we maintain order only through the existence of the coercive power that is ready to uphold a rigid law, and by an equally rigid penal system. The Ik, however, have learned to do without coercion, either spiritual or physical. It seems that they have come to a recognition of what they accept as man's basic selfishness, of his natural determination to survive as an individual before all else. This they consider to be man's basic right, and at least they have the decency to allow others to pursue that right to the best of their ability without recrimination and blame.

CHAPTER EIGHT

Retreat of the Icien God

It is certainly difficult, through a study of Icien behavior, to establish any rules of conduct that could be called social, the prime maxim of all Ik being that each man should do what he wants to do, that he should do anything else only if he is forced to. That the word for "want" (*bédés*) is the same as for "need" illustrates something of the practical outlook of the Ik; so when they say "I want to help you" it equally means "I need to help you," which would be a more accurate translation, probably, of "*Bedia ingaares abi.*" In other small-scale societies much the same is often true, but with a very different underlying sentiment. In such societies there is also a lack of law backed by any power of physical coercion, and people do what they "want" to do; but the nature of society is such that what they "want" to do is the socially acceptable thing. This is due partly to education, partly to the circum-

stances surrounding their daily life, and is almost wholly
supported by religious belief and practice.

In large-scale societies such as our own, where members
are individual beings rather than social beings, we rely on
law for order; we need, and therefore perhaps want, physical
coercion. The absence of both a common law and a common
belief would surely result in lack of any community of
behavior; yet Ik society is not anarchical, and given the
validity of that one maxim, there is a curious community of
behavior, however distasteful it might appear to those view-
ing it from afar. One might well expect religion, then, to
play a powerful role in Icien life, providing a source of
unity, of social responsibility, of community of action. In a
legalistic society religion does indeed become an opiate for
some, a nuisance or an inconvenience for others; but in small-
scale societies religion is a dynamic and cohesive force.
There is a powerful community of belief, manifest in community of ritual practice, which serves in a sense as a model
for community of secular behavior.

The Ik, as may be expected, do not run true to form.
However, when I arrived first, there were still three ritual
priests left alive, and although two of them died shortly
afterward, the other survived for nearly a year. From them,
and from the few other old people, I was able to learn
something of both Icien belief and practice as they had been
before the world of the Ik was so abruptly and terribly
changed for them. There had indeed been a powerful unity
of belief, in Didigwari—a sky god—and a body of ritual
practice reinforcing a community of secular behavior that
was truly social.

Didigwari himself is too remote to be of much practical
significance to the Ik. He created them and abandoned

them, and has retreated into his domain somewhere in the sky, unreachable and unreaching. The Ik have a very practical knowledge of the sky; they are aware of the movement of heavenly bodies, they divide the year into seasons marked by the movement of the setting sun from the head of Morungole to its foot; they even accused my watch of not keeping time with the sun. They laughed at the idea of God being in the sun or the moon, and when asked silly questions gave appropriate answers. Asked why these bodies moved across the sky, as they believe they do, they said it was like my Land Rover—there must be somebody there driving them. But they were simply not very interested as to whether there were people on the sun or the moon. However, old Lomeraniang, just before he died, said he had dreamed he was a star. "That means," he said, "that I shall soon be with the *abang anazé* looking down upon you all." The *abang*, or ancestors, are often likened to the stars; they are as numerous and as widely scattered, as ever changing and as quietly watchful. Every now and then one descends to earth again for some unknown purpose, but mostly, like Didigwari, they are remote and can be approached only by the great ritual priests.

God was originally a double person, part male, part female, and he gave birth to many who became Turkana, Dodos, Topos, Ik and others. The Icien ancestor divided and one part of him settled at Loitanet, another at Kalepeto, another at Niagum and another on Lomil. The clans were formed in this way, and the ancestors were reborn in their children. But now the ancestors are like stars in the sky, for when a man dies only his body dies; his soul, his *gor*, leaves and ascends to the stars and joins the *abang*. Didigwari never came down to earth, but the *abang* have all known life on earth, so it is only against them that one can sin, and only to them that one can turn for help, through the ritual priest. If the *abang* are angered they will punish: they can send hunger, they can kill.

During the creation God gave the Dodos and Turkana cattle, so they always have food. But he also gave them the spear, so they kill. God gave the Ik the *nakut*, or digging stick, and told them not to kill. But he also gave them *nyeg*, hunger. That is why, my saintly old informants never failed to tell me, it was the duty of everyone else to give the Ik cows, goats, sugar, tobacco and lots of money. The Turkana do this, they point out, and even the Dodos. But the Dodos are not so friendly toward the Ik. When they first met, the Ik were big and strong and healthy, but they did not have the power to kill and neither did they have the power to curse. When they met the Dodos an old Dodos woman cursed them, giving them illness and making them weak. The hunger God had given them never did that, it was merely a hunger that kept them moving every day in search of their food. This Dodos witch was evil. The Ik caught her and beat her, careful not to draw blood, but they beat and they beat and they beat her none the less. Finally she agreed to remove the curse, and to do this she poured water over some leaves and sprinkled the Ik with it. But she should have dipped the leaves in the water instead of wasting it by pouring. Now the Ik are still small, hungry and thirsty as well. Before the Ik met these other creations of God, including police and the white men, they never knew such bad things. In those days even hunger was not a bad thing.

The places of clan origin, at Loitanet, Kalepeto and others, may very well be points of origin of the clans as they presently exist, and there are stories of migrations between these places because of hunger that give this part of the creation tale a tone more historical than mythological. But

when it comes to the story of where and how the very first
man was set down, the flavor is different. The tale is not told
to young people, and, as far as I know, it is now no longer
told to anyone. Didigwari himself decided that the small
mountain of Lomej, at the foot of Morungole, was where he
would set the first Ik down. He lowered him on a long vine,
carefully and gently, and then when he saw that it was a
good place he lowered others, more and more. They were
big and healthy and strong. He gave them the digging stick
and told them not to kill other men, but to hunt and to live
by hunting and gathering. But the men hunted and got meat
and refused to give it to the women, so Didigwari became
angry and cut the vine so that man could not climb back up,
could never again reach him, and he went far off into the
sky. Since then, the Ik say, they never go to hunt or gather
near Lomej, which at least in part accounted for their lack of
enthusiasm at the administrative plan to settle them there.
Atum says that many years back he went on a hunt there,
but the hunters all got sick and many died, and those who
got back brought nothing with them.

While Morungole itself has no such legends attached to it
by the Ik, it none the less figures in their ideology and is in
some ways regarded by them as sacred. I had noticed this by
the almost reverential way in which they looked at it—none
of the shrewd cunning and cold appraisal with which they
regard the rest of the world, animate and inanimate. When
they talked about it too there was a different quality to their
voices, and I found this still to be so long after I had given
up expecting anything among the Ik comparable to our notions of what is good and beautiful and truthful. They seemed
incapable of talking about Morungole in any other way,
which is probably why they talked about it so very seldom.
Even that weasel Lomongin softened and became gentle the

one and only time he talked about it to me. It was not much
in quantity, what he said, but it was significant. He said, "If
Atum and I were there," indicating the mountain without
even looking at it, "we would not argue. It is a good place." I
asked if by "a good place" he meant that it was full of food.
He said yes. "Then why do Ik never go there?" "They do go
there." "But if hunting is good there, why not live there?"
"We don't hunt there, we just go there." "Why?" "I told you,
it is a good place." It did not get far as a conversation, but
what impressed me was Lomongin's attitude as he talked.
He did not look at Morungole once, yet somehow he seemed
to be seeing it while he spoke; his eyes were certainly not
seeing the piece of wood he was whittling. Although his
answers to my questions were invariably devious, this time
they were not. If I did not understand him, that was my
fault; for once he was doing his best to communicate something to me.

With others it was the same. A few said they occasionally
hunted, but only alone, not in groups. Others said they
gathered, and quite a large number said there was much
honey there. All agreed it was "a good place." From the *di*,
Morungole looked immense. I asked about going to the top,
and there was no objection, but I sensed that I had asked the
wrong question. Then Lemu, a Dodos *moran*, took his spear
and pointed to a dark, rich streak running almost vertically,
it seemed, up and down the side of the mountain. He said,
"That is a good place." The others just nodded. Lemu added,
"That is the Place of God." And again the others just
nodded.

I set off with Lemu and Atum early one morning. It was
just getting light, and as we scrambled down the hillside into
Kidepo we passed three old women and a man, armed with a

spear, going to gather wild berries. Lemu took the lead and, much to Atum's disapproval, chose a very roundabout way which did, however, keep us away from sharp inclines, leading us gradually but steadily upward, skirting under the mist-shrouded peaks, which now looked barren and uninteresting. At one point we had to cross a gorge, and from down below came a roaring sound, muffled but angry, and a wisp of smoke through the trees. Lemu gave Atum a look, and Atum nodded, and we started across the gorge. We reached the other side none too soon; the fire was already in sight when we were halfway across, and was above us as we made the last scramble. It evidently went exactly where Atum had thought it would go, and neither he nor Lemu was in any way perturbed.

We then came to a high and steep ravine, at the head of which were two enormous overhanging rocks, one on each side, almost meeting overhead. There was a pool of clear water, from which Atum and Lemu drank, solemnly rather than thirstily, but they denied that it had any ritual signifi-cance. Their faces showed something else, and Lemu raised his hands to his mouth and started to sing, in short, beautiful snatches, listening as the song was echoed back to him. He looked at me and said, "This is the Place of God," and con-tinued singing. Atum said nothing, but climbed slowly onto the top of the far overhang. He did not tell me to follow, but I did. He was standing there gazing across to Zulia, across the game-filled park to the Sudan, over the land that Didi-gwari had given the Ik as their hunting ground, and he said, "This is the Place of God." What either of them saw or meant I never discovered. I had little to do with the Dodos, and the Ik became increasingly uncommunicative. Never again would they take me near that place, or talk about it.

But, as little as I knew, I felt that for a brief moment I had made contact with an elusive reality, a reality that was fast retreating beyond Ik consciousness.

On our descent Atum led the way. It was in direct contrast to the Dodos route, gentle and easy and as much on open land as possible, suited to that long, easy, swinging gait. Atum plunged headlong down the gorge, taking the shortest distance between two points, regardless of what the straight line went through. On the way we heard the peculiar warbling and clucking of the honey guide, and Atum and Lemu both replied with similar cluckings. The bird flew around our heads, then disappeared back into the trees, and Lemu went after it. We watched them both disappear, clucking to each other, as the bird led Lemu to the honey. Atum led me away from it. When we got to the bottom, after a very rough time forcing our way through thorn bushes and thick patches of brier, we found Lemu already there, idly scrubbing his teeth with a stick. He said he had found the honey but could not reach it, Atum would have to send Lomer. As we crossed a corner of Kidepo, heading home, we met the gatherers who had set out with us in the morning, only now there were only two women and the old man. They said the other woman had left them for some *gomoi* berries she thought she saw. The man said she had better hurry back before dark, and showed me the pug marks of a lion. They were going to stay there for the night, and had already gathered some thorn bushes to build a screen around them. Then, they said, they would head on out into Kidepo the next day, over toward Zulia; there might be some food and water over there. I never saw any of them again.

Altogether there was little evidence on Morungole for a Godhead that could serve as the foundation for a unifying belief, a spiritual community, but it was something. There was an undeniable contrast between the reverence shown by the old for tales of long ago, including those of Didigwari, and the total lack of interest among the young. Didigwari had indeed abandoned his people, or else they had abandoned him. Only that peculiar change of mood remained, among both young and old, whenever Morungole was mentioned, as though Didigwari himself had briefly touched the Place of God and left behind a lingering, puzzling recollection of a goodness long since lost.

Sometimes belief, however loosely formulated, none the less may serve a unifying, cohesive function by its manifestation in ritual and, in the absence of a secular law, in the informal do's and don'ts of daily life. But Icien attitudes toward rituals were as ambivalent and indifferent as toward Didigwari. Nobody appeared to place any belief in their efficacy, though on occasions they were deliberately used to achieve certain goals of a very secular nature, but nobody took the trouble to deny their validity. If they could be useful they were valid, and who knew when a use might turn up? One of the main classes of ritual in which we might expect to find belief manifest is that concerned with the life cycle, the business of being born, growing up, marrying and reproducing, growing old and dying. In some societies these various stages are clearly marked and life is punctuated by a series of dramatic *rites de passage* as one progresses from one stage to the next, but with hunters this would not be expected, something less rigid being more usual.

During pregnancy, for instance, intercourse is forbidden (as it is during menstruation) and the woman, before childbirth, is forbidden to lie on her back or look at the apex of the roof inside her house. If she does this the child will be born blind. Then after childbirth the husband is excluded from the house for a whole week. He may sleep in the compound, but if it rains he cannot even enter his house for shelter, he must go to the house of friends or relatives. At the end of the week the paternal grandparents arrive for a visit and are feasted and there is a ceremonial drinking of millet beer, after which they give the child a name. Only then may cohabitation be resumed. The mother is expected to breast-feed the child for at least two years, but after a few months she may start it on solid foods, mixing them with water to soften them, or partially chewing them before giving them to the child. She must call the ritual priest for the proper medicines to ensure its growth, and take note of danger signals such as the lack of a luxurious growth of hair on the child's head, which surely indicates weakness and ill-health to come. Among various herbal remedies supplied, and pro-tective medicines and magic, the priest may divine that certain foods should be tabu to the child, even to the mother.

This would read, to an Ik, like a ludicrously fantastic fairy story, for not only the recommended actions are fantastic, so are the concepts involved. To suggest to a starving people that they should carefully select their foods, rejecting some and limiting the intake of others, is not likely to make much sense. A mother in labor, racked by the additional pains of hunger, thirst and fever, is not going to listen with much sympathy if you tell her not to lie in the one position in which she can get a moment's respite, least of all if you say the consequence is that a child whom she does not particu-larly want and is likely to die soon anyway will be born blind. As for calling in a priest or inviting grandparents to stay, with what are such visitors to be fed and compensated, and for doing what? Yet I not only heard the above list of rituals surrounding pregnancy and birth many times, I even observed them all, at one time or another, being practiced.

When they were practiced, however, it was with ends in
mind quite other than the health of an unborn child, the
selection of a propitious name, the continuity of the family
clan, and so forth. As Yakuma clearly showed, and Matsui,
improper observance of such remembered rituals could be
made an excellent excuse for investing some money in that
old charlatan of a priest and getting it back, magnified, in
the form of a fine. And if money was not available, there
were likely to be pumpkins to be stolen from someone else's
fields, or your husband's tobacco, or your wife's body.

So with the process of growing up and marrying. For boys
the traditional way of proving manhood was success in the
hunt; this was simply and effectively replaced by survival in
the age bands and eventual graduation from the senior band
into the solitariness of adulthood. By then you were
equipped as well as possible to support yourself, and that is
what adulthood is about, for the Ik. Your education included
training in how to use others for your own purposes, toward
your own survival. It was the same for the girls, for they too
had to learn to survive as individuals, but they had an additional chore, childbirth. In the old days it was probably not
considered a chore, but it was nevertheless an additional
problem that men did not have to face, and required ritual
measures to ensure success. When a girl has her first men-
strual period, she must begin to separate herself from her
parents. Under present circumstances that is not difficult, for
she has done it years earlier. Further, she must seek another
girl in a similar condition; there is no urgency, no sense of
dangerous uncleanliness, as there is in some societies, but
the signs of approaching womanhood none the less have to
be met with increasing separation from childhood. When the
girl finds another, or more than one other, they jointly build
a house and live in it, away from their parents, and there

they stay until married. There are none of the elaborate
initiation rites found in more complex societies, none of the
teaching (for the young girls already know all there is to be
known); no old ladies chaperone the budding women. Their
house, however, may not be used to entertain boys; that
must be done off in the woods somewhere.

It is all much the same today, except that entry into adulthood begins rather early, at three years old. Some girls still
build houses together, such as Yakuma's lovely daughters,
Kinimei and Lotuköi, but most are too busy "sleeping out" to
bother. And since the puberty ritual was in any case minimal, its observance or non-observance does not make any
obvious difference. But when a girl has entered her house
and doffed the virgin's bead apron and donned the wide skin
flap of a woman, and when a boy has proven himself as a
hunter, they are expected to marry, and marriage in the past
did not take place with the same relative informality as did
birth and puberty. Ritual for marriage was as important as
ritual for death, and in so far as both involved feasting—
which, translated into the present context, means wastage of
food, a form of suicide—the rituals have been abandoned
except in a much attenuated form. Indeed, marriage and
death themselves have to a large extent been abandoned;
marriage literally and death, since it is less easily avoided,
theoretically. If possible, death is simply ignored.

Death, even in these dire circumstances, must surely
touch the emotions somehow, and if any fragment of religious belief remains, death is likely to revive it. The Ik
remembered well enough, the old ones, what their belief
used to be, and how it used to be manifest in a rather lovely
death ritual. The three old ritual priests, in particular, re-
called with wonder the days in which people had buried
each other with love, and with faith.

The soul, *gor*, is sent by Didigwari to inhabit a female body after a male has copulated with her five times. When she sees that no more blood comes when it should come, she knows that on that day she is with child, she is with soul. A soul is round and red, but it has no arms or legs. It rests somewhere in the vicinity of the stomach, and never leaves the body until Didigwari calls it back. Animals have souls, but rocks and earth do not, and neither do the stars. Lolim, who as a high priest was one of the few people who could see souls, had never seen one in any ordinary tree, though he had seen many trees split open; but he would not swear that they had none. He had once seen a soul inside a special Pirre tree called *mos*. He never saw a man, woman or child who did not have a soul. If a body is mutilated and suffers an open wound, the soul may escape back to Didigwari. In that case, or when Didigwari decides to call it back, the body rots; that is death, the departure of *gor*. It flies past the moon that is good and the sun that is bad, and on to the stars, where the *abang* have their eternal existence, perhaps hunting just as we do on earth; who knows? Not even Lolim, and he knew everything, everything that was knowable.

The burial of the dead was always a ritual for the living, despite the nagging fact that even Lolim did not know just when the soul left the body or how, or whether or not it hovered around before a final leave-taking. The body was buried with due ritual primarily to remind the living of all the good things in life, and of the good way to live that life, but also, by creating goodness in this way, to speed the soul, content, on its journey to the stars of night. The body should rest facing the rising sun, folded up in the fetal position to mark its celestial rebirth; it could even be sitting up, but that meant digging a deep hole, so it was usually buried in a shallow trench, lying down, and covered with rocks and stones. In the old days personal possessions were sometimes buried with it, things the dead person had loved during his life. Today nobody loves, and the corpse is stripped clean of all clothing and ornaments, necklaces and bangles and lip-plugs being snatched away by the eager, joyful hands of the living, the clothing ripped so that only a fragment is left to satisfy the minimal Icien sense of modesty, if the corpse was a woman.

Today the grave is then abandoned and forgotten. But this was not always so. The site chosen used to be a site with a particularly fine and distant view, perhaps a place where the dead person had enjoyed sitting. When the burial was done, a libation of beer was poured over the grave and the rest was drunk by the mourners. This was followed by a whole day of fasting, during which people remembered the dead person and all the good things in his life. Then an old lady from the bereaved clan shaved the heads of all the mourners and ritually broke the fast for each one by placing food in his mouth. Each morsel had to be chewed, then some spat out to the left and some spat out to the right. After that the fast for that person was lifted for that one kind of food. Certain foods were grouped so that any one of each class served to lift the fast from the whole class. Wild fruits, berries, nuts and roots were grouped together in this way, as were meats produced by hunting; another group included all foods that are traded. But water, milk and millet beer were separate items, as were all cultivated foods. If any food was not available that day, the restriction remained until the old lady was able to find some.

That part of the ritual is particularly nonsensical these days, for even if the food were available the notion of getting it as far as the mouth and then spitting it out, however small the quantity, is incomprehensible. It is not surprising that it has been dropped as a superfluous and wasteful act. Its loss struck me as being practical rather than tragic. But the loss of the final rite was more than that, and showed with stark clarity the chill and dreadful emptiness, the emptiness of death itself, that is the life of the Ik. This last rite took place when the next planting time came. Seeds of all the favorite foods were planted over and around the grave, and once again a libation of beer was poured and beer was drunk and food was eaten. Then, as the grave was finally abandoned, the seeds germinated and drew life from the dust of the dead and rooted themselves in what had been man, and anyone passing by during the next harvest season would see crops growing wild, blowing in the wind, the seeds being scattered far and wide to create and maintain still other forms of life. Anyone passing at that next harvest time would know that death is merely life in another form; or so it was.

Death is without such beauty to the Ik today, it is as harsh and ugly as life itself. Parents fight over a child's dead body to decide whether to risk just throwing it out and being accused by someone else of not providing the proper ritual feast, or whether to go to the trouble of scooping out a shallow grave within the compound and telling others that tho child has gone away somewhere and not come back, if anyone asks. Even for an adult nobody was going to cry; still less were they going to waste any food or beer, and by next planting time who remembered? It was this way when Lomeja died. When I finally left his body, I had not even reached the door of the hut when the fighting started, the ripping and tearing at the bandages, the cutting of the thongs that laced the leather shin guards around his legs, the wrenching of the little beads that decorated his ear. My last look at Lomeja, from the door, showed me all the bestiality I ever want to see, and the little boy was fighting to tear the

ivory lip-plug from his father's dead lip, crying because
others were stronger than he.

Even though Lomeja's herd had been stolen, he was still
considered a man of wealth, and relatives flocked to lay
claim to whatever they could. The body was buried in the
boma where he had been shot, in a shallow grave. There was
not a shred of clothing nor one solitary reminder that this
had been a man, young and full of life. The body was
dumped into the grave quickly, folded up on itself, facing
any old way, the eyes looking upward at an uninterested sky.
The legs were bound with thongs to keep the ankles against
the buttocks, and the elbows were also bound so that the
dead clenched fists were tight against the cheeks, as though
Lomeja had been fighting against death even at this last
moment. Vultures were already circling around as earth and
stones were shoveled in, and as though attracted by the
same smell of putrefying meat, the human vultures were not
far behind. They were somewhat disappointed to find that
the burial had already taken place, and asked a few questions, such as whether it had been covered with sticks so
that no earth would touch it, and the answers were always to
the effect that every last ritual injunction had been upheld.
One old lady had actually washed the body, in a perfunctory
way, though she was accused of wasting the drinking water,
and she had even done a lighthearted dance outside, scooping dust over a spot where there had still been some blood
lying on the ground. The feast was held rapidly and directly
on top of the grave site, meat supplied by a Didinga relative
who sat there idly, occasionally spitting on the grave. Lokelatom acted as master of ceremonies and kept the crowd
outside the stockade, where they climbed on rocks so that at
least they could see the food. The select few inside laughed
and chatted and took time off to go inside the house to look

for mementoes, and to flirt with Losealim. The womenfolk were carrying away skin bundles, and by the time the last of the meat had been bolted down the house itself was being dismantled and distributed. The food gone, the fighting about the distribution of the alleged wealth began. Lokeléa was immediately named; he was related to Lomeja's father, and Losealim's father still lived in Lokeléa's village. It was plain the bulk of the wealth had gone there. Lokeléa was urinating at the side of the grave and was knocked down by the sudden rush in his direction. Then he was out through the stockade and half walking, half running over the brow of the hill and down to the sanctuary of his *odok*. The mourners followed like a swarm of termites, and the village was deserted. That night I looked for a new star in the sky, but the sky was overcast and I saw none.

Although the lesser rituals, involving notions of magic and medicine, were in themselves a less promising category than the life-cycle rituals, they were nearly all centered on the person of Lolim, the oldest and greatest of the ritual priests, and the last. He was not much in demand any longer, but he was still greatly held in awe, which means kept at a distance. Whenever he approached a *di*, people cleared a space for him, as far away from themselves as possible. The Ik rarely called on his services, for they had little to pay him with, and he had equally little to offer them. The main things they did try to get out of him were certain forms of medicine, both herbal and magical. Medicines for minor complaints are still known to almost any Ik, though almost certainly they are becoming less and less known. Earache, backache, stomachache and so forth called for Lolim's attention only if they were serious. In that case he either supplied herbs of his own selection, and he was forever wandering off on solitary

gathering expeditions, or else he would say it was a case for
divination. He seldom applied the medicine but just gave
the instructions. If it involved cicatrization he carefully
supervised as the skin was pricked with a thorn and raised,
then slit with a sharp arrow blade before the medicine was
rubbed in, but he never did it himself. The touch of Lolim's
hands was rare. I was told he used it for one of his most
powerful of all medicines, used to make men invisible to
elephants for an elephant hunt.

On other occasions the patient would bring the medicine
himself to Lolim, such as the white clay used to take away
colds. Lolim brought this into his house and warmed it over
his fire, then touched it lightly on the forehead, shoulders
and chest of the sufferer. But while warming it over his fire,
Lolim told me, his *abang* entered his head and spoke to him
about the patient. Since colds were common, Lolim claimed
to know everything about everyone. And while any Ik could
cut a certain kind of wood that in itself is believed to be
powerful and tie it around his neck as a charm or attach it to
his neck-rest, wood cut and touched by Lolim was extra
powerful. So also was his famous anthill medicine. This
was a favorite ingredient in many of Lolim's medicines. He
said that an anthill was like a sick body, with lots of
wounds, yet no matter how often it was laid open, it always
healed itself and grew bigger and stronger. But somehow the
anthill medicine that Lolim touched was more powerful
than any other.

It is often difficult to make a distinction between different
kinds of medicine that we might call effective and magical,
for even the "magical" ones—that is, those which appear to
us to be based on superstition (whatever that is) and to
have no scientific validity—are often effective. The term
"magic" also implies for us the use of the supernatural,

whereas at this level Lolim, for instance, believed that his "magical" substances were actually endowed with power. He, therefore, was still a true doctor, using scientific medicines within the limits of his knowledge. But when it came to a question of his touch, or of his power to talk with the *abang*, Lolim moved from the sphere of science into that of belief. Here Lolim was indisputably a ritual doctor who acted, and whose actions were accepted, in light of a belief. This was seen in every Ik village and in many of the fields, where Lolim's protective medicine was hung to ward off winds and evil spirits, thieves and plagues of locusts. Each village was bisected by a vine run from one side to the other at roof height, from which were hung leaves, special branches, bits of gourd and pierced potsherds. In fields there were similar vines and also twisted sticks which were meant to trap any thief who entered so that he would be paralyzed and unable to move until found by the owners of the field. Again Lolim seldom installed any of this medicine himself, he merely prescribed, like any doctor; but these were medicines that were acknowledged to work through the intervention of spiritual, or supernatural, forces.

The most powerful of all ritual medicines for which the Ik were known was their rain medicine, and ironically it was the very one in which they themselves had no faith at all. Lolim himself used to laugh about it, and seldom had anything to do with it. But the Turkana and Dodos were convinced that the Ik were the only true rainmakers. Lolim showed me one ritual he used to perform in his younger days for the herders. He squatted over some cow dung, saying that nothing worked for the herders unless it had something to do with cattle. He had a gourd full of water nearby, and into this he dipped some leaves, with which he sprinkled the bystanders, then sprinkled up to the sky so that the droplets fell down again like rain. Another version of this was for Ik men and women to come to the sacred tree and perform their "rain dance," which involved dancing in the water and splashing those standing around the edge, then throwing dung on the base of the tree. The water hole was meant never to dry up as long as the tree was covered with dung. Then there were all the various rain trees—nearly every village had one. Sometimes these were little more than stumps with vines growing over them, but that did not matter to the credulous herders. They brought gifts of beer and meat and pots of seeds and placed these all around the rain tree. A goat was sacrificed and eaten, and the horns were placed in the tree. This was always done in the evening, and if in the morning the food was gone it was a sign that the sacrifice had been accepted. Needless to say, it was always gone long before morning. Yet in spite of their neighbors' unshakable belief that the Ik knew the secret of rain and could control it, the Ik claimed no knowledge or power. The rainbow for them meant that the rain was stopped, perhaps by a curse, when it should have continued, and that particular rain would never come back. That is all, or almost all: their name for God is Didiwari, and *didi* means rain.

Nor do the Ik have any knowledge of the abuse of supernatural power; they can neither curse nor bewitch. Even Lolim said he could do neither. But he could divine, and there was nothing mechanical about his divinations, no bags of tricks, no bones to throw, no oracles to consult, just Lolim and the *abang*, the ancestral spirits. During the daytime Lolim needed some help, and his sandals served. When divining he squatted down and carefully placed the sandals sole to sole, running his fingers around the edge to make sure they were fitted neatly together, for he was nearly blind. Then he pinched them between the fingers of one hand and flipped them onto the ground so that one fell on top of the other. The configuration of the throw told him whether or not the *abang* were interested, and whether they were listening. If they were, he talked to the sandals, threw them again, then picked them up and held them to his ear and listened. In fact, he used them much as we do a telephone, and he told what the *abang* told him. He said he used to be able to go into a trance, but it took too much effort now, he could do that only at night. As he lay down on his skin he conjured up the face of his father or mother—sometimes they both appeared—and then he went into a deep sleep and they came to him in reality and talked with him and told him what he wanted to know. They would tell anything, he said, except when it concerned death. About that the *abang* were silent.

Other people threw sandals too, to get answers to simple questions such as in which direction to hunt, but only Lolim could talk to the *abang*. He said they entered his head, and only when they were there did he have any power, for it was their power. When they were not in his head he was just an old man. He said that Didigwari did not give the Ik powers to curse any more than he gave them powers to kill. But with the Dodos it was different. He claimed that they had terrible practices, such as cutting up the flesh of dead people, drying it and using it as charms in cursing others; they could even kill with it.

Lolim said that he had inherited the power from his father. His father had taught him well, but could not give him the power to hear—that had to come from the *abang* themselves. It would be the same with him, he said. He had wanted his oldest son to inherit, and had taught him everything he could. But his son, Longoli, was bad, and the *abang* refused to talk to him. They talked instead to his oldest daughter, bald-headed old Nangoli. He tried teaching his oldest son by his second wife, a good boy, but the *abang* would not enter his head either. Lolim did not quite like the idea of Nangoli inheriting; he had set his heart on its being one of his sons, of whom he was inordinately fond, even the sour-faced Longoli. But he had accepted that Nangoli was to be his successor, and taught her with goodwill. The *abang* impart different levels of power to different people, and they know who is best fitted to inherit such powers.

Lolim was old and wrinkled when I first knew him, but he and his daughter were among the few who always made me feel welcome, even if they did invariably ask for tobacco before I had a chance to greet them. With Nangoli it was a game, and with Lolim it was his due as a ritual priest. But Lolim was a victim of overspecialization, as was Losiké. There soon came the time when all the Ik needed was food in their stomachs, and Lolim could not supply that. People began avoiding him so that he would not be able to ask them for tobacco, for evidently they still felt some kind of obligation to him, amounting to respect, and Lolim managed to survive for a while by virtue of his relations with the herders and with the police at the post, who also made use of his services. But the time came, inevitably, when Lolim was too old and too weak to go out and collect the medicines he needed. He asked his children, one after the other, and they all refused except Nangoli, and then she was put in jail in Kaabong for having been caught gathering in Kidepo Park.

Lolim became ill and had to be protected while eating the food I gave him. Once I caught Lomongin stealing out of Lolim's tin mug while Lolim was eating. Lolim was crying, but did not have the strength to pull the mug away; all he could do was hold on to the mug with one hand and convey as much of the food as possible from mug to mouth with the other. As soon as I appeared Lomongin reversed his actions

and pretended he had been feeding Lolim, saying the old
man was so blind he could not see where his mouth was to
put the food. The old man had enough strength to retort, "At
least I didn't put it in yours!" at which they both rocked
with laughter and held on to each other as though they were
the closest of friends.

On another occasion I watched Lolim leaving my compound with some food and tobacco I had given him. He told
me not to come with him, that he would be all right. He tied
the bundles up and slung them around his neck so that they
hung down his back, under his baboon-skin cape. I watched
him leave and he had not gone ten yards before he was
attacked by Lojieri, who tried to force what he thought was
food or tobacco from one of Lolim's hands. The old man
struggled, then suddenly sat down hard on the stones and
clung to his cape with all his might; Lojieri had found a
bundle of food. I shouted, and Lojieri reluctantly left Lolim,
the way a mosquito is driven away by an angry slap but
prepares to return. He waited until Lolim was out of sight,
and by the time I caught up he had run around another way
and Lolim was sitting on the ground again, huddled into a
protective ball, and Lojieri and one other Ik were pummeling and almost strangling him as they tried to pull the
packets away from his neck. When they saw me they just
stood up, waved and smiled, said "*Ida piaji,*" and walked off.
Lolim remained in a pathetic furry ball, sobbing with weakness, frustration and humiliation.

Then the children began openly ridiculing him and teasing him, dancing in front of him and kneeling down so that
he would trip over them. His grandson, who like all Ik
grandchildren could lawfully joke with and tease his grandparents, stretched his teasing into playful beating, and used
to creep up behind Lolim and with a pair of hard sticks

drum a lively tattoo on the old man's bald head. Once Lolim, trying to cover his poor head with his bony arms, accidentally caught Arawa in the mouth. Instantly Arawa, with the back of his right hand, slapped Lolim as hard as he could on the side of his face, knocking the old man to the ground. There were shrieks of delighted laughter, but as the old man lay still, not moving and not even crying, the fun wore thin, and when I approached, anthropological detachment having long since departed, they lost interest and went away.

I thought Lolim was dead. His eyes were open, he was sprawled as he had fallen, his head resting on a tuft of earth. Then his eyes moved and briefly acknowledged my presence before fading off into the distance again. "The *abang*," he murmured with a quiver of a happy smile, "the *abang* are talking to me." So I too left him ear to ground, and after an hour or two Lolim pulled himself to his feet, groped around for his staff and hobbled off.

I do not remember seeing Lolim talk to anyone after that. He continued hobbling around for a few days, then took to shuffling about while still sitting on his haunches. I fed him whenever I could, but often he did not seem to want more than a bite. Once again I found him with Lokwam and a gang of children dancing around him, shouting and throwing little stones at him, and Lolim was rolled up in his protective ball, crying to himself. He continued crying long after the children had gone, and he clutched at his belly so I thought he might have been hurt. It was much simpler than that. He had had nothing to eat for four days, and the last water he had had was some I had given him about two days earlier. He said he had asked his children and they had all refused and had told him not to come near them.

The next day I saw him leaving Atum's village, where his son Longoli lived. Longoli swore that he had been giving his father food and was looking after him. Lolim was not shuffling away, it was almost a run, the run of a drunken man, staggering from side to side, his hands trailing at his sides, stumbling blindly. I called to him, but he made no sign that he heard, no reply, just a kind of long, continuous and horrible moan, as though it were the last breath he had and it were all running out of him and he were running as though he had to catch up with it. He disappeared over the top of the rise by his old village and descended into the valley below. I did not follow, it was useless; it was all useless. The Ik did not even have the trouble of throwing his body out, they just left it where he fell and died, on a little ridge above the *oror a pirre'l* where it turns to plunge down into Kidepo. He had been to Longoli to beg him to let him into his compound because he knew he was going to die in a few hours, Longoli calmly told me afterward. Now obviously Longoli could not do a thing like that: a man of Lolim's importance would have called for an enormous feast. So he refused. Lolim begged Longoli then at least to open up Nangoli's *asak* for him so that he could crawl there and die in *her* compound, though she was still away in jail for gathering medicines in Kidepo, where only animals have a right to live. But Longoli had driven him out, telling him he, Longoli, was not the old man's son any more than Nangoli was his daughter, and the old man should just go and die outside; there were no *abang* to worry about anyway, they were just the foolish fantasy of an ignorant, senile old man. Longoli asked me if I did not think he was absolutely right.

Atum pulled some stones over the body where it had fallen into a kind of hollow. I saw that the body must have lain parallel with the *oror* and I looked at Atum and he answered without waiting for the question: "He was lying looking up Meraniang." So there he lay, gazing up at Meraniang, over which the sun would continue to rise long after Longoli was cold and dead, and his other children and grandchildren. Every morning Lolim is still the first to greet the new day. And every night as the sun sets behind Morungole its dying rays touch that little pile of rocks; I know because I have been there to watch, and to remember the goodness that was, before all goodness and Godness seemed to retreat in shame from a barren, sterile world.

CHAPTER NINE

Society and Belief

In so far as ritual survived at all, it could hardly be said to be religious, for it did little or nothing to bind Icien society together. But the question still remained, only greatly sharpened: Did this lack of social behavior and of communal ritual or religious expression mean that there was no community of belief? In larger-scale societies we are accustomed to diversity of belief, we even applaud ourselves for our tolerance, not recognizing that a society not bound together by a single powerful belief is not a society at all, but a political association of individuals held together only by the presence of law and force, the very existence of which is a violence. But we have already seen that the Ik had no such law, let alone the means for enforcing conformity to any code of behavior. Such coercion as there was came simply from the circumstances in which they lived and their own will, as individuals, to survive. Their belief, if one existed, was not manifest in any communal practice, ritual or otherwise, and only in a very peculiar sense could one say it was manifest in any common sentiment. Such sentiment at best could hardly be said to be social.

Belief may manifest itself, at either the individual or the communal level, in what we call morality, when we behave according to certain principles supported by our belief even when it seems against our personal interest or not to our personal advantage. When we call ourselves moral, however, we tend to ignore that ultimately our morality benefits us even as individuals, in so far as we are social individuals and live in a society. In the absence of belief, law takes over and morality has little role to play except at a purely individual level, salving individual consciences, acting as a guideline to individual behavior. If there was such a thing as an Icien morality, I had not yet perceived it, though traces of a moral past clearly remained. But it still remained a possibility, as did the existence of an unspoken, unmanifest belief that might yet reveal itself and provide a basis for the reintegration of society. I was somewhat encouraged in this hope by the unexpected flight of the older Nangoli, widow of Amuarkuar, the old man who died of thirst.

When Amuarkuar died he had been collecting grass to make a little shelter in his compound so that when Nangoli came back she would have somewhere to stay since the roof of their old house was falling in and the house had been used as a toilet when he was too weak to go outside. He died, one might say, while performing a social act, even though it contributed directly to his demise. When Nangoli returned and found her husband dead, she did an odd thing, she grieved. She even expended energy to demonstrate her grief; she tore down what was left of their home, for it had been more than a mere house. She uprooted the stockade, she abandoned her little field running into the *oror* feeding the *oror a pirre'i*, tearing up whatever was growing and leaving it to wither still further in the baking sun. But if she cried, I did not see it. Then she fled, the skinny old woman, with a few belongings rolled up and slung across her back, held by a tumpline against her forehead. She did not speak to anyone; she just left, heading for Kidepo.

Some weeks later I heard that she had joined up with others and all had gone over to the Sudan and built a village there. It seemed that the "others" consisted almost exclusively of her family, and this made sense, for, unlike the other Ik villages that I knew, hers at Pirre had been an almost exclusively familial village, with few outsiders. This migration was so unusual that I decided to follow as soon as possible and see if this runaway village was different in any way, as it promised to be. The Uganda-Sudan border in this region is not marked, and since I had no way of knowing which country I was in once I crossed Lomil, I ignored that technicality. It was very likely Kenya.

Lojieri led the way, and Atum came along at his usual sprightly gait. It was not nearly as far as I had thought, and one long day's trek got us there. We crossed over the corner of Kidepo and headed for the middle of Lomil. Although the valley floor looked level enough from above, it too was gouged by ravines, and the heat was stifling. Lojieri nearly trod on a sleeping viper, and shortly afterward a portion of a thorny branch at eye level suddenly detached itself, leaped across the trail and was gone as soon as it touched the ground. Atum, for once quite shaken, said it was a kind of cobra. But of game we saw none. We stopped to pick some bitter yellow fruits, and, bitter though it was, the juice was welcome, for all the way across we saw no signs of water.

My legs were already cut and punctured by thorns, though I was wearing long trousers. Yet Lojieri and Atum seemed unscratched.

Climbing up Lomil was a relatively easy scramble and we reached the top at about four o'clock in the afternoon, having started at dawn. From the other side, looking into the Sudan, we could see the runaway village on the far side of a deep, wide gorge. By now we had to hurry to get there before dark, and Atum and Lojieri scuttled down into the wooded bottom of the gorge without stopping. I was only halfway down when, stopping for a brief rest, I suddenly became aware of the difference between this side of Lomil and the other. From the top I had not even paused to look at the view; the village was pointed out and we were off without wait. But now, still high up, I took a look, and listened. There was no vast expanse as of Kidepo, just a rolling succession of mountains that were green and wooded. Zulia itself, which had always looked isolated and impressive, now looked more friendly, approached by a broad valley. There was a slight breeze blowing, and this carried sounds of birds and animals that suddenly made the world seem alive and worth living in, and it was difficult even to think about the world that we had left behind.

Down in the woods it was cool, and there was a beautiful fresh stream running and jumping over mossy boulders, forming little pools and miniature waterfalls. Lojieri and Atum had both washed and were drinking deep, and I did the same. The climb up to the village was steep, and we were in the woods almost all the way, so as the sun was low it was quite dark, but when we emerged from the woods we were slightly above the village, halfway up the face of the gorge, and the sun was already down behind Lomil. It lay there in the evening light, looking quite unlike an Ik village.

It was open and inviting, with only an outer fence of scrub and brush, the inner compounds left open and clear. The only Ik-like thing about it was that it was empty.

Lojieri pulled part of the brush fence aside and we went in and wandered around. He and Atum looked inside all of the huts, and Lojieri helped himself to tobacco from one and water from another. Surprises were coming so thick and fast I hardly had time to realize that I was still carrying a heavy pack and take it off. That houses should be left open and untended with such wealth inside. . . . That there should have been such wealth even, for as well as tobacco and jars of water there were baskets of food, and meat was drying on racks. . . . The houses were not the Karimojong style with mud walls and conical roofs; they were the *koromot* beehive-shaped huts made of long, dried grass, and they were clean and cool. Logs smoldered, and evidently people gathered around a central fire in the evening, judging by the cleared space around one such hearth. There were half a dozen or so compounds, but they were all open to each other within the outer fence except for two, which were outside and belonged to newcomers. One compound was separated from another, otherwise, only by a short line of sticks and brush which formed a shelter for each kitchen hearth. It was a village, and these were homes, the first and the last I was to see.

The dusk had already fallen and Atum had stoked the central hearth up into a blaze when we heard voices from farther down the valley, with snatches of song. It was the hunt returning, and in five minutes—it was already dark in that short space of time—old Nangoli came in with her sons, Loron, Lodéa and Pedo, and her daughter, Niangorok, with her husband, Teko. Pedo and his wife were the newcomers outside the fence; they had arrived only two days earlier and had not yet bothered moving the fence so as to include

themselves in the village. Pedo had been far off in the Sudan
visiting the relatives of his wife, who was a Topos. They
had heard us, probably long before we heard them, and
came in with warm welcomes, showing no concern at our
presence nor at our having made ourselves so freely at home.
The women and children who followed were the families of
Loron and Pedo, and they carried both meat and berries
from the day's expedition. There was no hunger here, and in
a very short time each kitchen hearth had a fire going and a
pot of food cooking. I was given several different kinds of
food to taste, but out of habit had brought my own. Then we
sat around the central fire and talked until late, and it was
another universe. They were not the least bit interested in
Pirre, nor did they act as though their way of life had
changed in any way. It was just as though this was how they
always had been.

There was no talk of "how much better it is here than
there"; talk revolved around what had happened on the hunt
that day, the way Pedo had saved the situation after Loron
had been even clumsier than usual and let his quiver of
arrows fall over. The quivers are fastened to sticks with
sharp points at the end so that they can be jabbed into the
ground, holding the quiver upright for easy access to the
arrows and without encumbering the bowman. But Loron
was a dreamer rather than a hunter. He loved whittling
wood, and he made the best *karatz*, the little neck-rests that
also serve as seats. He was lying on the ground in front of
the fire as his mother made gentle fun of him, his cheek
resting against his *karatz*. His wife, Kinimei, whom I had
never seen even speak to him at Pirre, put a bowl of fresh-
cooked berries mixed with fruit in front of him. It was all
like a nightmare rather than a fantasy, for it made the reality
of Pirre seem all the more frightening. And Pirre *was* reality.

I felt sure that this was just a game Nangoli and her family were playing, that at any moment they would go back to being Ik. But they did not; we talked and dozed, and when the women and children went inside for the night most of the rest of us stayed and slept around the fire. Lojieri talked in his sleep. Atum snored. Loron always seemed to be sitting up, knees clasped to his chest, gazing at the fire, which reflected something in his eyes that looked strangely like humanity.

I left the next day, before the spell was broken. I wanted to scout out another valley where I thought there might be Ik, though Atum's very willingness to go that way convinced me that there wouldn't be anything, and there wasn't. We kept along the side of the gorge as it rose to meet Lomil at its highest. Then we plunged down a precipitous face into the valley of Nauriendoket. I was wearing sneakers, and for the duration of the descent, something over two hours of nonstop sliding, my feet were angled downward so sharply that my toes were bunched up against the rubber tips. If they hurt, so did the rest of me, and I took no particular notice until I got to the bottom and took the sneakers off to relax. The nails of both big toes were already turning black, and the others looked red and mean. I took some comfort from the fact that Atum was limping too.

Nauriendoket was a small valley that ran up from Kenya and, like Chakolotam, served as one access route for the Turkana. As it rose into Kidepo, however, it became a narrow canyon with vertical sides and occasional overhangs. From the debris that littered the canyon floor it was obvious that the overhangs collapsed from time to time, and although I should have been glad of the shade I found it oppressive. Neither Lojieri nor Atum liked it either, and they said that even the Turkana seldom used Nauriendoket.

It was a relief when after a few miles the canyon opened up and ahead I could see the sweep of Kidepo, with its funny conical hills erupting upward like fish leaping out of the sea. Directly ahead was Kochokomoro, and behind it the more impressive Napuwapet'h. We skirted the base of Kochokomoro and struck out across the Chakolotam entrance, climbing down into the Chakolotam *oror* and up the other side, at the base of Meraniang.

The unpleasantness of returning was somewhat alleviated by Atum's suffering on the way up the stony trail. Several times he slipped, which made Lojieri and me laugh, and he kept stopping to rest, clutching his back with both hands. In spite of the fact that I had already lost both big toenails, it was a pleasure to move rapidly ahead and leave Atum gasping behind so that we could be sitting up on the *di* when he finally appeared and laugh at his discomfort. But I had to forgo the pleasure. On arrival at my own compound I weakened and went right in, heated some water that might have saved someone's life, and stuck my feet in it. Although I knew I had got valuable information from the brief trip, I resented the fact that Nangoli had temporarily softened me and caused me to relax my guard. I had actually shared some of my food with Atum and Lojieri on the other side of Lomil, and now they might expect me to do the same again. I withdrew my feet from the bath and hobbled over to my *odok* and closed it tight, and when I heard Atum wheezing *"Ida piaji"* I kept silent and wondered what I would eat for dinner.

The drought was still severe, and though the Turkana did not occupy Kidepo again, the raids continued. Nights were disturbed by sounds of distant rifle fire and not so distant lowing of cattle being led from one owner to another. This caused more protests from the administration, voiced through the police, for not only were people getting killed, but, due to the movement in cattle, many diseased cattle were entering otherwise clean areas and polluting the rest. All this was aggravated by an increased flux of Didinga refugees from the Sudan, from where we could distinctly hear gunfire and what sounded like bombing. Some came through with cattle and drove them right down to Kaabong, where the administration bought them and sent the Didinga on to Debesien, to join the Didinga settlement there. But then there was the problem of what to do with the cattle; if they were slaughtered at Kaabong it would cause enormous ill-feeling among the herders, who would consider it a great crime and might well take reprisals, even though the cattle were not theirs. So the diseased cattle had to be shipped south for slaughtering, often through a clean area, risking fresh infection.

But none of this bothered the Ik, though they knew all about it and enjoyed the difficulties everyone else was having. Even when they themselves were involved as individuals, it did not seem to worry them. One afternoon an Ik from Nawedo staggered over the top of Meraniang and down into Pirre and came to me for help. Nobody brought him, I just happened to see him sitting on the ground outside my compound. His left arm had been sliced from the shoulder down and under to the elbow, and all sorts of bits and pieces were hanging out even though he had wrapped it up in his dirty old shoulder cloth. He had been guiding some Dodos back from a raid when the Turkana caught up with them, and he had been speared. A few people gathered to watch as I tried to dress the wound, and they laughed at my panic when I took the old cloth off and a large hunk of flesh came with it. He said it had been cut off, and he stuck it back in, thinking it might grow back. I really neither knew

nor cared at that point. I washed the wound as rapidly as I
could, including the hunk of flesh, and wrapped it all up in a
clean bandage and made myself some tea. When I came
back to see about getting the man to Kaabong, he had gone,
nobody knew where.

The lack of any sense of moral responsibility toward each
other, the lack of any sense of belonging to, needing or wanting each other, showed up daily and most clearly in what
otherwise would have passed for familial relationships. The
Ik still recognized them as such, verbally, but the recognition was not matched by any corresponding action. When
Bila was suffering most from her infected breast, which
dripped pus over her nursing child or the food she was
eating, she cared neither about herself nor anyone else. She
acknowledged that it was unclean and unhealthy, and when
told that she could spread illness to others in this way, her
own family, she looked amazed—amazed not that illness
could be spread like this but amazed that anyone should
think she should worry about spreading it. When, at its
height, Bila was in great pain and was sitting outside the
odok crying, holding her breast under which a little puddle
of pus and blood had formed, Atum, her father, took notice
of her only to ask her if she had to sit there—she was blocking the entrance and her crying gave him a headache. In
fact, that was one of the few times he ever bothered to speak
to her. Whenever I mentioned his daughter's illness to him
he just clucked and shook his head and asked what he could
do, he was only her father.

Giriko was even more callous about his son, Lokol, who
developed an intestinal blockage. At first it amused him and
he used to call people to look at the boy's distended belly. It
was a favorite topic for jokes because finally the boy could
neither eat nor drink, since nothing came out that went in.

He even found it difficult to vomit. He was about ten years old, not quite an adult. I tried to persuade Giriko to take Lokol to the hospital in Kaabong; they could have made a litter for him and carried him quite easily. But Giriko said no, he would wait until I had fixed the Land Rover. At that point Lokol could not even sit up, let alone stand, and any food I brought was snatched the moment Lokol rejected it. When he lay down it hurt, so for most of the time he stayed on his hands and knees, even at night, his bloated stomach hanging down and resting on the ground. I finally got the Land Rover fixed and Giriko suddenly became excessively attentive and attached to his son, and announced that he and his two wives were coming with us to Kaabong. I told him that they were not going to do anything of the sort, that there was room only for a few people and there were others who were sick that I had to take. When I went to get Lokol, Giriko had carried him off and hidden him, and said that he would leave the wives and would go in place of the boy, who was miraculously feeling better. When I insisted that it was the boy or nobody, Giriko shrugged, smiled and said he was going back to his field; he would walk to Kaabong the next day and get what he wanted. Shortly afterward Lokol's bowels moved, and for a brief while he was able to eat and drink and seemed to get better. Several times I had to physically force Giriko away to prevent him from stealing the boy's food, and at this point Giriko was by no means starved. But Lokol seemed to have lost any interest in living; he lost that one basic Icien quality, the will to survive. He had one father, two mothers and three sisters, a family of seven including himself, and not one of them had even helped to lift him when he could not move, and when at last he began to defecate they called their friends to see, and the boy was covered in his own mess. When he died I heard about it in

220 THE MOUNTAIN PEOPLE

passing, a casual comment, and my response was "*Yasi-zuuk?*" which at the time I translated as "Really?" but which in fact should be translated as "So what?" for it implies neither surprise nor interest.

The days of drought wore on into weeks and months, and Lokol was not the only casualty, and, like everyone else, I became rather bored with sickness and death. At first I was angry and upset, but then, like the Ik, I found I had to conserve energy. I survived rather as did the young adults, by diligent attention to my own needs while ignoring those of others. And, like the young adults, I was relatively well, though far from plump. I never knew when the road was going to be open or blocked, or when there were going to be raids, or when my food was going to be stolen. On one occasion I found the house stripped of food although the door, which I had specially imported, was as securely locked as ever and undisturbed. It was very simple. With remarkable foresight, when building the house, the house-building team had omitted to secure the roof to the walls in the usual way. It sat on them like a bonnet, and its own weight kept it from blowing off. When there was need all that had to be done was to prop it up on a pole, just as one does the roof of a granary, and climb over the wall. I regretted the loss of food, but noted the technique.

I was not often successful myself in reciprocating, though I did win one or two little trophies: a snuffbox, a comb, a stick from Atum, a neck-rest from Loron. But I derived some pleasure of an Icien kind from extracting information from them which they did not know they were giving and had hoped to withhold so that they could sell it. On one memorable occasion I cooperated with Bila in robbing Atum, whom I had suspected of the major roof-raising theft, which, at the cost of half a sack of sugar and considerable quantities of flour and beans and tea, had at least served as a warning. I should have been grateful, but when Bila came to me and said that her father was going to be away for the night, could I lend her all my keys, I did so with joyful heart. She asked me what I wanted for the loan, and I said nothing, she had already repaid me in full. Shortly thereafter she made me a present of some sugar—mine originally, I am sure— just to be certain that I had nothing over her, and she gave me back the keys. Atum was in a rage when he returned late the next evening, and found his trunk had been opened. He immediately accused his daughter, which showed some family understanding at least. He threatened to call the police and have her locked up, until I asked him where he had got all the sugar he claimed had been stolen, when he was always telling me he had none—at least until my roof had been lifted by someone—and Atum retreated, saying that people with too many keys were dangerous.

It was probably in revenge that Atum arranged that I should awake one morning to find the entire village deserted. It was a great piece of organization, and I still do not know how Atum managed it, but it did not happen by chance. I had made the mistake of stressing how much I wanted to go off with them when the time came to leave the villages and spread out in search of *dang*, termites. No special preparations have to be made, but many people build *tangau,* or termite traps, around and over the termite hills, so that when the termites swarm they all have to leave by one exit and are easily caught in a bag. It requires some cooperation, at least two or three people, and it used to be a family affair, since termite hills, unlike land or hunting territories, are traditionally private property. Anyway, the time had come, and when I got up, feeling that all was too quiet to be normal, every able-bodied person had gone. The few who remained professed ignorance and refused to come with me to look, saying that some termite hills were several days' walk away and who knew where anyone had gone? It was three days before the first came back and a week before Atum appeared. He was as charming as ever, and said they had thought I would not like to go so far, and had not wanted to disturb me to tell me. They had left in the middle of the night.

More and more it was only the young who could go far from the village as hunger became starvation. Yet while others starved, the young remained relatively active. Famine relief had been initiated down at Kasilé and those fit enough to make the trip set off, leaving the others behind. When they came back the contrast between them and the others was that between life and death. At this time people no longer sat on the *di*, they lay there waiting for nothing, the very old and the very young. Youths were too busy at this time to sit on their *di*, for collecting famine relief was virtually a full-time occupation, rather like hunting; it called for cunning and organization. When there was no relief to be had, the people who were well were all off foraging for what food they could find in the mountains or down in Kidepo.

Villages were villages of the dead and dying, and there was little difference between the two. People crawled rather than walked—the very young and the very old all crawled. The usual method was to squat and raise the buttocks off the ground by pressing down on the fists, then swinging the body forward on the arms, like a pendulum, dropping it to the ground again a few inches ahead. After a few feet some would lie down to rest, but they could not be sure of ever being able to sit up again, so they mostly stayed upright until they reached their destination. It was their destination that intrigued me, for really they were going nowhere, these semi-animate bags of skin and bone, they just wanted to be with others, and they stopped whenever they met. Perhaps it was the most important demonstration of sociality I ever saw among the Ik. They just gathered during the morning and stayed until late afternoon. Once together they neither spoke nor did anything together, they were together and that seemed enough. The skin hung from their bones in such wrinkled folds, especially at the joints, that when they raised their backsides off the ground the skin folds that had been buttocks flapped along underneath. In places it was drawn tight, a patchy red, but the overall impression was the blotchy look of a corpse that has been smoked. The fact that these corpses moved and smiled did not make them any easier to live with.

One afternoon I had been trying to feed some of them, in a moment of weakness, when the first of the youths returning from Kasilé arrived, laughing and shouting. One man carried a spear broken off halfway down, for they had been attacked by a buffalo on the way and it had made off with the blade and part of the shaft in its side. Children followed and were promptly sent to get water; they were the older children, almost ready to move into adulthood, and it was yet another contradiction that made no sense to see them fetching water for their "families." They laughed as they splashed in the filthy, muddy pool beneath the sacred tree, and, that done, they set to teasing the old skeletons who by then were dragging their way back to the villages. One girl had fastened a white flower onto a piece of vine, and swung it prettily around her head as she danced around Ngorok and blocked his progress whichever way he turned. Lokwam almost looked attractive; he had adorned himself handsomely with broad bands of grass tied tightly around his calves, his arms and his forehead. But he was more active and liked to push the crawlers lightly so that they teetered and then toppled. It was a time of fun and laughter for all.

In the midst of this conviviality it was mentioned that Jana's wife had not come back. Jana said she had been lagging behind, the fool had been trying to carry some *posho*—much good that would do her if she ever got it as far as Pirre. Someone else said they had seen her fall, but had not bothered to wait and see if she got up again. By then it was getting dark and the high spirits were wearing low, and everyone, including Jana, felt tired and wanted to go to sleep. The next morning this brief surge of good humor had vanished, and children no longer went to fetch water at their elders' behest. Jana announced that he was going up the mountainside to see if there was any of his wife's *posho* left; it was assumed she had died during the night, for she had not come back, and it had been bitterly cold with a strong wind. But someone had been there before him, he angrily told us on his return, and had taken both the *posho* and the skin bag she had been carrying it in. He carried two necklaces his wife had been wearing, one of dark red nuts and the other of bright blue glass beads, and her stick. I wondered why those had not been taken too. She must have died near where Kauar had died, but I could find no mound of stones. Maybe Jana just pushed her over the edge; she would have rolled well out of sight unless the body got stuck in a thorn bush.

Then there was a bad night's raiding in which the police and we were all awakened by shrill ululations and people blowing signal horns as some Dodos pursued Turkana who had stolen their cattle, passing close to Atum's village. Nobody was killed, but there were more injuries, and I for one felt no less unsafe with the police blasting off their rifles in the middle of the night than if they had been Turkana. Even before dawn every single household was at work dismantling what it could, moving possessions down the hillside and choosing new sites for new villages more easily protected by the police and less likely to be in the path of raiders. It was easier for me; all I had to do was to load up the Land Rover and drive back to my old camping site, but the others had to move their belongings and build some sort of shelter for the night. In some cases whole roofs were lifted off and carried, but this required at least four people. More often the thatch was removed and carried in long bundles. Rough shelters were erected of stick frames covered with skins, and thorn scrub served as a temporary outer stockade. In the midst of this hive of activity moved the aged and the crippled, some of whom I had never seen before, like slugs, in danger of being trampled underfoot but seemingly unaware of it, concentrating only on covering the next few feet of ground ahead of them.

It was then that I saw Loiangorok for the first time. He had managed to get out of the ruins of his village by late afternoon, when most of the moving was over for the day, and had started down the hill. But he could not even raise his frail bones off the ground, and was dragging himself along on his side, as though he were swimming. Loiamukat, the *niumpara* of that village, came out with a bundle of sticks and stepped right over the old man and continued down the path. I shouted to him to find out who it was, and he replied, "Loiangorok—don't worry, he's my father." Which, knowing Loiamukat, I thought was the best of reasons for worrying. My nerves were still on edge from the confusion and uncertainty of the night before, and my threats, combined with bribes, were so effective that Loiamukat put down his sticks and returned to pick up his father, who had barely enough strength to put his arms around his son's neck. But when we got in sight of the temporary camp, Niangasir, Loiamukat's younger brother and the old man's youngest son, shrieked with derision to see Loiamukat carrying such a useless bundle. Loiamukat promptly deposited Loiangorok on the ground and told me I could carry him myself, which I did, feeling sick, not at the unkindness, but at the feel of those bones as they wrapped themselves around me.

I carried him past where his sons and daughter were busy setting up their new compounds, to where Atum's village was taking shape. Kinimei and Lotuköi had put up a rough shelter for themselves within what was to be Yakuma's compound, and I paid them to let me use it for the old man. Sensing that food would be in the offing as well as money, they readily agreed and started building another for themselves. Atum had chosen a site closer to the Police Post than any of the others, and I found I could get the Land Rover there without much difficulty. It was there, while I was nursing Loiangorok, that there was a sudden exodus from the village, distant shouts of laughter, and then someone running back to tell me to come quickly. At first I thought it was a trick to get me away from the old man while in the middle of feeding him, so I finished that first and then went to see what the excitement was about. It was someone else whom I had never seen before, dead Lolim's widow, Lo'ono. She too had been abandoned, and had tried to make her way down the mountainside. But she was totally blind and had tripped and rolled to the bottom of the *oror a pirre'i*, and there she lay on her back, her legs and arms thrashing feebly, while a little crowd standing on the edge above looked down at her and laughed at the spectacle.

At this time Joseph Towles was with me and had brought fresh medical supplies. He stayed with her and kept the others away, while I ran back to get medicine and food and water, for Lo'ono was obviously nearly dead from hunger and thirst as well as from the fall. Then a really terrible thing happened. We treated her and fed her, and asked her to come back with us, thinking we might as well start a whole village for the old and abandoned. But she refused, and said she wanted to go on, if we would just point her in the direction of her son's new village. Her son was the same one who had driven old Lolim out so that Lolim died outside, not more than a few yards away. I said I did not think she would get much of a welcome there, and she replied that she knew it but at least she wanted to be near him when she died; perhaps when Longoli saw the food we had given her he might let her into the compound. So we gave her more food and made her eat and drink all she could, put her stick in her hand and pointed her the way she wanted to be pointed, and she suddenly cried. Thinking she was afraid or wanted us to go with her, I asked, and she said no; she was crying, she said, because all of a sudden we had reminded her that there had been a time when people had helped each other, when people had been kind and good. Still crying, she set off.

The Ik up to this point had been tolerant of my activities, but all this was too much, combined with the fact that my colleague established a dispensary where he treated old people as well as young, but gave food only to the old. Openly critical of this waste of effort and food and medicine, the Ik said that what we were doing was wrong. Food and medicine were for the living, not the dead. But the old continued to come, the few who were left, not in the hopes of being kept alive, but so that they could go off quietly and die a little more comfortably. Then I thought of Lo'ono— that incredibly wrinkled old face, the sightless eyes peering as though they could still, with a struggle, see, and then those sudden, frightening tears of anguish at a memory that had been better forgotten. And I thought of other old people who had joined in the merriment when they had been teased, knocked over or had a precious morsel of food taken from their mouths. They knew that it was silly of them to expect to go on living, and, having watched others, they knew that the spectacle really was quite funny. So they joined in the laughter. Perhaps if we had left Lo'ono, she would have died laughing, happy that she was at least providing her children with amusement. But what did we do? We prolonged her misery for no more than a few brief days, for although Longoli did let her into his compound, he took her food and gave her neither food nor water. Even worse, we reminded her of when things had been different, of days when children had cared for parents and parents for children. She was already dead, and we made her unhappy as well. At the time I was sure we were right, doing the only "human" thing. In a way we *were*—we were making life more comfortable for ourselves, confirming our own sense of superiority. But now I wonder. In the end I had a greater respect for the Ik, and I wonder if their way was not right, if I too should not have stood with the little crowd at the top of the *oror* and laughed as Lo'ono flapped about like a withered old tortoise on its back, then left her to die, perhaps laughing at herself, instead of crying.

While I still fought hard to retain some of my old values and principles, others were simply washed away with Lo'ono's tears. I certainly had no illusions about cultural superiority. At the beginning of the famine the local Mission had sent up its Ik catechist, a fifteen-year-old man, with his young ten-year-old assistant. Both wore those indisputable signs of Christianity and progress, pants, and they carried rosaries to show how holy they were. They had been sent to teach for three days, they said, because the missionaries had heard there was hunger and wanted to help. So in three days the missionaries were going to drive up with lots of food and give it to everyone who had learned well. Then they were going to take all the old down to Kasilé and feed and keep them there. There were the equivalent of Icien cheers—hand rubbings and knowing smiles and patting of stomachs. Then everyone turned to with a will and began learning the catechism and how to sing hymns. It was at a time when they were still working in the fields, so the morning session was not well attended. But the young catechist, a horrid pudgy monster so fat that he was bursting through his pants, said he would write down the names of all those who did not come, so all field work was abandoned and the sky echoed to the praises of God.

On the fourth day we were all up early, and a large crowd had gathered to sing and chant so that when the missionaries arrived they would see for themselves how well the Ik had learned their lessons. But just before nine o'clock the singing dwindled away, and the two catechists twirled their rosaries with less enthusiasm. There was talk of going to the fields, but then they might be away when the food—that is, the missionaries—arrived. At noon there was a false alarm and everyone started singing again, looking hopefully at the mountain trail twisting its way crazily down from the summit. Then they began making nasty remarks to the two boys, who were just as anxious as everyone else, and still no food arrived. The fifth day it was the same, only without the singing, and once again the work in the fields was abandoned because of the unfulfilled promise. The missionaries

neither came nor sent word. The whole time I was there the
missionaries never appeared, nor did the local doctor. But
they did occasionally distribute pants and rosaries, with a
crucifix for the very good, who always, I noted, had very full
stomachs.

Considering all this, and my own behavior and attitudes
as well, the quest for morality seemed increasingly pointless.
It was yet another luxury that we find convenient and agreeable and that has become conventional when we can afford
it, but which, in times of stress, can and should be shucked
off, like religion and belief and law and family and all sorts
of other appendages that become hindrances at such times.
If God's own anointed chose not to leave their comfortable
lodgings, their jugs of wine and refrigerated soda pop, to
offer even a word of encouragement, but chose rather to
send a couple of butterballs dressed in pants and rosaries
to tell us all to sing and pray, I felt I could not judge the Ik
harshly for letting the old slip out of such a world just as
quickly and quietly as possible. But it still remained a
mystery to me why any who lacked more than jugs of wine
and refrigerated soda pop should want to stay on in such a
world, as the younger Ik mostly did.

Ngorok was a man at barely twelve. Lomer, his older
brother, at fifteen was showing signs of strain and when he
was working in a field or carrying any load his face wrinkled
and took on a curious expression of pain that was no physical pain. Giriko at twenty-five was forty, Atum at forty was
sixty-five, and the very oldest, perhaps a bare fifty, were
centenarians. And I, at forty, was younger than any of them,
for I still enjoyed life, which they learned was not the adult
attitude when they were as young as three. But they retained their will to survive, and so offered grudging respect
to those who had survived for long. In this respect for the

aged I saw a last flicker of hope, though watching the way
the old were treated physically made the vision more than
blurred. "Old people," they said, "have no eyes or legs.
Young people are people who do have eyes and legs." I wondered why arms seemed unimportant, but in Ik life the main
problems, of course, are to be the first to see food and to
get to it before anyone else. It was probably as simple as
that, for the Ik are not given to subtleties. And the young got
upset when famine struck and the old began to get moody
and bad-tempered, though bad temper is not really an Icien
trait at all. Bad temper, after all, connotes its opposite, good
temper, and such a thing is inconceivable to the younger Ik,
who are temperless, cold-bloodedly surviving without wishing anyone else any harm or good.

Why bother surviving to grow old so quickly? For few
reached Atum's age, or retained his health. For most the
plump years, the stomach-filled years, the good years, were
between about fifteen and nineteen; by twenty-five, like
Giriko, you were well on your way out or, like Kauar and
Lokol and Adupa and so many others younger still, already
under a careless pile of stones. But even in the teasing of the
old there was a glimmer of hope, shining in both directions.
It denoted a certain intimacy, a special relationship, that did
not exist between adjacent generations. This is quite common in small-scale societies, and in many, perhaps most,
others as well. Grandparents are often much more intimate
with their grandchildren than the parents are. They are not
the disciplinarians, for one thing, but still other things, more
important, are involved. Each looks at the other as representing, in a way, the future and the past. To the child, the
aged represent ancient history, a world that existed long
before their own birth, other ways of living and thinking;
and the aged also represent an awful and dread unknown

world to come, a world of which they will soon be a part, and where in due time they will be joined by their grand-children: the world of death. It has already touched the old, perhaps they have already visited it, for something shows in their faces that is not in the faces of the young; above all, it shows in the eyes.

And the old, looking at the young, see the future, they see themselves perhaps reborn, their name continued as well as their line, they see their unfulfilled dreams as having fulfill-ment; and they see the past, their own past and that of their grandparents and so on back to the beginning of time. In this way the very old and the very young share one great belief in common, a belief in continuity, and a hope that is a hope for the past just as it is a hope for the future. It is a belief that is rudely shattered by every violation that is felt when another body dies, though each time, sooner or later, another star is seen in the skies and hope is reborn. It is a belief that surely is equally rudely shattered for the Icien old when they look at the very young and see the emptiness that has taken the place of the life *they* knew. That is why the Icien old now look only at the very, very young, for only with them can they retain any belief, any hope. The urge to survive in such circumstances must in itself indicate a belief in some kind of continuity, some kind of future, though whether or not that indicates some kind of hope which would make life more bearable I do not know. And now that all the old are dead, what is left? The newly old no longer remember, as Lo'ono did, that there was a time when people were kind, when parents looked after their children and children looked after their parents. Every one of the Ik who are old today was thrown out at three, and has survived in consequence, and in consequence has thrown his own chil-dren out and knows full well that they will not help him in his old age any more than he helped his parents, the Lolims and Lomeraniangs, the Losikés and Lo'onos of the past. The system has turned one full cycle and is now self-perpetuating; it has eradicated what we know as "humanity" and has turned the world into a chilly void where man does not even seem to care for himself, but survives. Yet into this hideous world, from that other world on the far side of Lomil, Nangoli and her family unexpectedly returned, quietly and unobtrusively, because they could not bear to be alone.

CHAPTER TEN

The Loveless People

FOR THE moment abandoning the very old and the very, very young and the rather bleak future they hold in their hands, the Ik as a whole must be searched for one last lingering trace of humanity as we like to think of it, as being so far different from and elevated above the rest of animality. And right there we should pause and take a look at the Ik, if not at ourselves, and ask just what *is* the difference. The Ik appear to have disposed of virtually all the qualities that we normally consider are just those qualities that differentiate us from other primates, and yet they survive without seeming, if we are honest, to be greatly different from ourselves in terms of behavior; their behavior is more extreme, for we do not start throwing our children out until kindergarten, the beginning of a training period also, reaching on through school and summer camps, all things that effectively divorce us from them. We have shifted the responsibility from family to state, the Ik have shifted it to the individual. But each of us can best make the comparison for himself; for me the main difference seems to be that the Ik are perfectly honest about what they do and are rather more consistent, having abandoned any beliefs that might conflict with behavior necessary for survival.

Many of those who have studied animal behavior in depth, and not necessarily only the primates, come to rather similar conclusions about our place in the animal world: there is not all that much difference. Technologically we are superior in some respects—that is, we have developed some abilities and lost others, but we do seem to have developed the art of verbal communication to a point that gives us an enormous potential advantage over other animals. We do not always make the best use of it, however, and it can readily be shown that both speech and writing, misused, have led to many of the disasters peculiar to humanity. We have, indeed, developed to perfection the ability to destroy ourselves, if that can be cited to show our superiority over animals who lack this ability. Others point, rather than to speech and writing, to the belief that we are created in superior form by God. With belief, of course, one cannot argue in so far as it rests on faith, for when it runs counter to all rational evidence, final refuge is always taken in the unknowability of God's ways. But a major claim has been that human beings are capable of love and, indeed, are dependent upon it for survival and sanity. This at one time was held to differentiate us from other animals, until animal studies showed that other animals too are not only capable of love but dependent upon it. Having raised, as well as the more common domestic animals, a pair of baby leopards that the Ik were about to consume, and a baboon similarly destined for the pot, and a chimpanzee, I can attest to the fact

that there is little difference between them and us in their
need for "love," but here the word has to go into quotes, for
while other animal lovers will tend to agree, and even prima-
tologists and others similarly qualified will assert that animals
can die through lack of love just as easily as human beings,
there will be those who will assert that there is a difference
in the *quality* of love. Again it is an issue difficult to argue
beyond a point, since we have not developed any very satisfactory method of communication with species other than
our own, and even there much remains to be achieved. But
the Ik offer us an opportunity for testing this cherished
notion that love is essential to survival. If it is, the Ik should
have it. Whether that makes them or us any different from
other animals is a matter of opinion, but I must confess that
early during my field work I wrote back that I could not
believe I was studying a human society; it was rather like
looking at a singularly well-ordered community of baboons.
This was meant to be insulting neither to the Ik nor to
baboons; it was a sober, unhumorous expression of my dis-
belief that human beings *could* behave like this, no matter
how severe the circumstances. Even in the concentration
camps during the Second World War, where conditions
were in some ways comparable (except that there was the
knowledge, among those suffering, that their plight was
deliberately and willfully conceived by other human beings,
and was dependent upon the continued power of that segment of humanity), it was rare for man to shed so much of
his "humanity," though it happened, at Treblinka and elsewhere.

Seeing the more obvious human traits shed so lightly,
especially those associated with social organization, including religious belief and practice, and not seeing any outward
manifestation of love, I searched for evidence of love almost

from the beginning. I found more of it in those two baby leopards than I did among the Ik. I was under no illusions about the nature of that leopard love: the poor creatures, eyes just opening, needed warmth and food; to say that they needed love is to say the same thing, or is that the difference that we would like to maintain exists between us and them? Forgetting the fact, then, that in nearly two years I received more love from those leopards and was able to give more than with the Ik, what took its place among the Ik? Love, however defined, implies duality of some kind, it has to be reciprocated or it dies, it cannot feed on itself. In extreme cases love may feed on an image, a concept, a belief, without human mediation; in others, far less satisfactory, animal substitutes are found, and one might suppose that the keeping of pets, which is one of the characteristics special to civilization, indicates a deterioration in human relationships. But love in human relationships implies mutuality, a willingness to sacrifice the self that springs from a consciousness of identity. This almost seems to bring us back to the Ik, for it implies that the giving of love, like other giving, is self-oriented, that even the supreme sacrifice of one's life for one's beloved is no more than selfishness, however beautifully conceived, and that the victim feels amply rewarded by the pleasure and happiness and satisfaction he feels in making the sacrifice for some other. The Ik, however, do not value emotion above survival, and they are without love.

But I kept looking, for it was the one thing that could fill the void their survival tactics had created around each one of them, and if love was not there in some form, it meant that for all humanity love is not a necessity at all, but a luxury, or an illusion. And if it was not among the Ik, it meant that, be it luxury or illusion, mankind can lose it, and that the very conditions pertaining in the Western world

today are those that might make such a loss not only possible but inevitable; the process has already begun. I found
it difficult, living among the Ik, to remember what love was
like, to define it even for myself. It had to be something
different from need, beyond need and beyond mere desire; it
had to be a fulfillment, a completion and a burning, consum-
ing realization of the truth of that fulfillment. This was how
I could remember love, as something that filled life and gave
it meaning; something that could not be desired because it
had significance only in being.

The question as to whether or not the Ik had this kind of
relationship with the natural world around them, rather as
the Mbuti Pygmies do with their forest world, and many
other peoples similarly, or whether they were imbued with
any spiritual love deriving from religious belief, was a question that demanded a measure of philosophical discussion
and could not be answered purely from observation. Observation in no way indicated any such relationship, nor did the
limited conversations I was able to stimulate on the topic.
Their own conversation never once revealed a hint of interest in this direction. The only possibility for any discovery of
love lay in the realm of inter-personal relationships. Here the
outlook was far from bright, for the excessive individualism
of the Ik, coupled with the solitude and boredom of daily
life, did not make for many significant relationships of any
kind. Even boredom is not the right word, so difficult is their
life to describe, for if they had been bored they might have
done something about it. They were, each one, simply alone,
and seemingly content to be alone. It was this very accep-
tance of individual isolation that made love almost impossible. Contact, when made, was usually for a very specific
and practical purpose having to do with food and the filling
of a stomach, a single stomach. Such contacts were tempo-

rary and contextual, and did not have anything like the permanence or duration required to develop a situation in which love was possible. The last possibility was affection, which may be a forerunner to love, and which requires perhaps less contact. I did not preclude the possibility of some form of spontaneous, intuitional love at first sight, though it was one of the few notions that ever made me smile in those days.

If people went off in hunting or gathering parties, for the mutual protection of numbers or for necessary cooperation, such goodwill as might have been engendered by the companionship and cooperation was quickly dispelled by the acrimony involved in division of the spoils, if they were communally acquired, or by the sheer envy of seeing anyone else eating food even if it was acquired by his own solitary effort. And if, inconceivably, there was neither acrimony nor envy, then there would be suspicion that during the cooperative effort one might have laid oneself open to a subsequent charge of indebtedness. More often all three forces were at work—acrimony, envy and suspicion—and that was not fertile ground for the seeds of affection. I suppose I should emphasize that this is not mere opinion, but merely a summary of hundreds of pages of notes detailing incident after tedious incident, enough examples of which, I feel, have already been cited. Here just a few examples of a rather different nature should suffice to corroborate what might otherwise be dismissed as the product of a warped mind. Instead of looking at the more dramatic non-social actions, such as chortling at Lo'ono lying on her back and flailing like a tortoise, or using Lolim's head as a toy drum, or playing "just before she swallows" with Adupa, or Humpty Dumpty with squatting skeletons, let us look at seemingly ordinary, harmless everyday activities which in themselves at least seemed to be devoid of ill-will and without hurt to anyone.

One of the major needs in Icien technology was vine from which cord and twine could be made and which was also used untwined, merely slit into strips, for binding house and roof frames, stockades, panniers, baskets and other things in daily use. There were different kinds, but the most common *sim* was taken from what were small trees rather than vines. It was an activity that really required only one person, but in this, as in other such activities, the Ik sometimes went in company, though not a word might be exchanged. They merely could be seen to look at each other from time to time. It was those looks that were significant. *Sim* trees could be found in clusters, and it was the bark that was used. To remove it a wedge-shaped stone tool was used, cutting the bark around the base about twelve inches from the ground, then up on two sides to a height of about five or six feet. The flat side of the stone, or any other suitably shaped stone around, was then used to pummel the bark, all branches first having been cut off as close as possible. This pummeling loosened the bark so that to remove it all you had to do was to pry out a flap on one side, at the bottom and, putting your foot on the base of the tree, pull upward, ending with a strong jerk that ripped the strip of bark clean away from the tree as high as the branches had been cut. It was in the upward ripping that disaster was likely to occur, and it was then that the other Ik would stop their own work and look, with hope and anticipation. If the rip was clean, work was resumed, but if the bark tore at a knot or where a branch had been cut too close or not close enough, there were howls of laughter. In the cold, sober light of reappraisal some years later, it seems that the only motive for working in company on this activity, and many others like it, was the pleasurable prospect of being able to enjoy someone else's misfortune. Back on the *di*, where the finer and much more interesting work of making twine is done, people do not look at each other, though they may look at the work in the hope of being able to criticize. But during the bark cutting, eyes flick hungrily from the ripping bark to the face, so as to be able to detect the first sign of splitting and the subsequent expression of anger or frustration.

So it was with many *di* activities, where people did not consciously set out to accompany each other on any specific task, but gathered to be in company. Among the more common *di* activities, other than just staring into the distance (which was the most common), were spear making and *karatz* making. Spear making involved a little cooperation, as not everyone had or could be bothered to make the stone tools used, but it also offered endless opportunity for criticism and ridicule. *Karatz* making was highly individual, even to the cutting of the forked branch that eventually would become a neck-rest (but which, like bark cutting, was sometimes done in company), but it was accompanied by the danger of calamity almost to the end, as the legs grew more and more delicate. One badly judged chip with the blade and a leg could be split right off. Some *karatz* makers reacted by being content with chunky legs, though they were then ridiculed for poor workmanship. The only exception, really, was Loron, old Nangoli's oldest son. And he was so skilled that nobody bothered to watch him working since they knew there would be no disaster. Oddly, Loron never bothered looking at others, though at the time I put this down simply to his excessive individualism and isolation. In view of the episode of the runaway village, however, it is worth noting.

On one occasion and one only I saw something take place

at a *di* which made me feel that all might not be lost, though I think I was overeager. A number of youths were sitting around, doing nothing, just looking into space, waiting for something to happen. One of the youths picked up a sliver of wood left by a *karatz* maker and, after holding it for some minutes, began whittling at it with one of the stone flakes used for shaping and smoothing a neck-rest when it is all but finished. He whittled idly, and the piece of wood turned into a long wooden needle. Another youth was lying beside him, his head propped up on a *karatz*, and, reaching down, the first youth started teasing his hair. After a few minutes the second youth shifted and propped himself up in the first youth's lap so that his hair could be worked more easily. By afternoon other teasing needles had been made, and other couples formed spontaneously, nestling in each other's laps, teasing each other's hair. It continued for the next day, some being content with an overall fuzzy surface, a few wanting the hair braided into patterns.

That is all—a simple activity, but unusual in the extreme because it involved no danger of disaster, no chance for ridicule or criticism, it was not necessary, nor in any way connected with food, yet somehow it seemed to give mutual satisfaction. Each got exactly what he gave, which is not the Icien notion of a bargain at all. But I began to see that, whether or not there had been any pleasure in the physical proximity, the affectionate (as I had hopefully construed it) reclining in each other's laps was merely a means to an end: personal adornment that could not be achieved by oneself. Further, the motive for this vanity was not even to attract a wife or a girl friend, merely to *be* attractive. No one youth looked at another, none of them looked at passing girls any more than passing girls looked at the youths, but when mirrors were produced each youth looked at himself with satisfaction, smiled and nodded at his image, tossed his head a couple of times and then lost interest even in himself.

For the moment—delaying the issue of sexual interest, which normally (but by no means always, for the Ik) involves rather close cooperation and a degree of at least temporary affection, if only of an animal nature—the kind of scene on the *di* when the boys teased each other's hair raised the question as to whether there were any special friendships, bond or otherwise, that led to repeated patterns of cooperation in activities of this kind. All I can say is that in this case I noted who was cooperating with whom, as I did every time there was the faintest excuse for noting such a phenomenon, and it was not part of any pattern denoting a relation of friendship, though it was the closest I ever saw the Ik come to affection. I have seen a team of people working to help Atum in his field on the far side of Meraniang, but every one of those "friends" was a debtor, and gave that as his reason, at least in part, for working for Atum. No one was a bond friend, not one even acknowledged friendship. All, however, had received honey from Atum the year before, and he had chosen this time to claim repayment. He in turn, it might be noted, had received the honey from Lomer, who had been helped in the gathering of honey by others, so we should not be quick to dismiss this kind of gift giving; it achieves important and practical goals and establishes a chain of mutual dependency which is one of the very few things, if not the only thing, that hold the Ik together and prevent anarchy. The attitude toward each other even when so involved with each other was nicely expressed by Lomongin when referring to his bond friend Lokeléa. He said that he was Lokeléa's bond friend because Lokeléa was not an Ik and was wealthy with cattle and goats and Lokeléa had everything to lose whereas Lomongin could only gain. He pointed to the scar on the side of Kalimon where Lokeléa had his farthest, highest and steepest field, so steep I could not even stand upright in it. He said, "Lokeléa thinks that will stop anyone from stealing from it; show me the field that can be planted that can not be stolen from"; he spoke, unselfconsciously, openly, honestly, from personal experience.

It is significant that most Ik friendships which can be recognized and described as such are bond friendships, and nearly all of these are formed with non-Ik, for obvious reasons of economic gain. In general, the Ik claim both the Dodos and the Turkana as their *bam*, their friends. They form individual friendships with both, but toward neither, as groups or as individuals, is there any of the affection that we associate with the term "friendship." In fact, they display open contempt for them, especially the Dodos. Both are ridiculed for being "stealable"; any gift that is brought by an expectant herder is mentioned as further evidence of their stupidity. Nor do they escape in more personal terms. The Dodos are frequently mocked, even to their faces, for their manner of hair styling. The traditional form for a young man as yet to enter full manhood is a tall basketry cone caked with ocher-colored mud. The adult lets his hair grow long, mats it into hair he has saved from previous cuttings, gathers it all in a bundle as it hangs behind his neck and secures it in a kind of net. This the Ik find both ridiculous and impractical, and ask how you can run with either. . . . The tall one gets caught in thorny branches, and the other, under which all sorts of valuables including coins are kept, bounces up and down if you do more than walk gently, and when running the Dodos have to tie it down with a vine around the neck. To the Ik, survival often depends on mobility, and anything that impedes it is foolish. The Turkana hair styles are mud packs that lie close to the head, handsome and uncumbersome. Some Ik even imitate them, such as the Mkungu's old father at Loitanet. But the Turkana are far more generous than the Dodos, having rather more to give, and are ridiculed for that.

Since they ridicule their bond friends for trusting them, it is not surprising that the Ik do not trust their bond friends and that mutual mistrust becomes one of the characteristics of the relationship. The rules of bond friendship are observed only as long as observance is compelled, as in the case of the reluctant freedom given to one's bond friend to take snuff if he can find it on you. But any successful way of avoiding an obligation is allowable. There was nearly a serious fight once when Yakuma was visited by his Dodos bond friend. A number of us were sitting under the shade tree that marked the *di* of Atum's new village, and the Dodos ambled slowly in and stood alone for a few minutes before sitting down or speaking. His stance was the easy, graceful stance of the herder, all the weight on one leg, the other bent lazily, the cattle stick behind the neck with both arms draped over it. Finally he sat down and said to Yakuma that he had come for some tobacco. He added that he wanted to buy it, for tobacco is such a valuable commodity that it is not sold to just anyone, and even bond friends expect to pay for it. Yakuma asked him what he had brought. The Dodos said that unfortunately he had nothing with him but the five shillings to pay for the tobacco. Yakuma could see he had nothing else. Naked as he was, that was plain enough. There was some haggling about how much tobacco he could get for the money, and when he put his hand into his hair flap to get out the five shillings every neck craned to see what else was hidden there. But only the five promised shillings came out, and with a final bicker the deal was completed. Lomongin stood up and stretched and wandered off, as did a couple of others, then the Dodos. Immediately two of those who had left approached him and demanded that he give them some of the tobacco, which he refused to do although they pursued him for some way. Then he shook them off and disappeared from sight.

In a couple of minutes Lomongin came flying past the *di*, ran to his *odok* and called to Lokwam to come out. He whispered some instructions and Lokwam took off at speed, in the direction taken by the Dodos. Yakuma, who had been pretending to doze, suddenly sat up and demanded of his brother-in-law and fellow *odok* member what was going on. Lomongin said that he had just happened to be watching the Dodos and saw, from some way off, that he had not been alone at all, but had been joined by a boy with two bags, whom he had left hiding in the bush before he came to the *di*. Lomongin had sent Lokwam to find out what was in those bags, for the Dodos had asserted he had nothing but the five shillings. Yakuma was furious, and said that if there was anything there it belonged to him, not Lomongin; the Dodos was *his* bond friend. None the less, he stood up expectantly and waited, with Lomongin, for Lokwam's return. Lokwam came back after ten minutes or so, and said the bags had contained only *posho*, no meat or real food. Yakuma now flew into a real rage, and said he was hungry and *posho* was the one thing he wanted. He went off himself, as fast as he could, but when he caught up with the Dodos there was no boy and no bags of *posho*. What had happened was that Lomongin, ever the schemer, had merely told Lokwam to warn the Dodos that his bond brother had seen him go off with the boy he had left guarding the bags, and to get what he could for his services. Lokwam brought back some of the tobacco Yakuma had just sold the man. As predicted, Yakuma pursued his bond brother and found nothing, but knew he had been tricked. He did not, however, know by whom.

On the other hand, there was Pedo, younger brother to Loron the *karatz* maker, third son to Nangoli and Amuarkuar, who had died for want of water. Pedo's wife was a Topos woman, and Pedo had formed a bond friendship with her brother. When his father died Pedo was away on the far side of Zulia, well into the Sudan, helping his bond friend to escape with his family and at least some of their cattle. It was a risky business, and Pedo could easily have lost his life. Of course he was paid, but the payment was only some goat meat, for the cattle were all captured by the police at Opotipot. Even so, Pedo helped his friend to get away, and led him all the way to Kaabong before returning to join the rest of his family in that strange little village on the far side of Lomil.

It seemed that Nangoli's family was exceptional in more ways than one, for her married daughter, Niangorok, persuaded her husband to join the old lady in the runaway village and help her survive. That it was they who, in turn, persuaded the old lady to return to Pirre is immaterial, for Nangoli herself told me it was persuasion, not compulsion. Most families I could observe only rather haphazardly, as they were so seldom together as a unit, and since visits to the family compounds were discouraged even with the bribe of tobacco and food held in the offing. But since in two successive villages my own compound was adjacent to those of Atum, Yakuma and Longoli, especially that of Atum, I came to learn some of the more intimate details of family life that would otherwise have been denied me. Proximity was such, for instance, that with the nightly flapping of sleeping skins to get rid of bugs and lice, I could tell that whereas the adults flapped their skins outside the hut, the children, perhaps in retaliation for having to sleep outside, always did their best to dispose of their lice *inside* the hut. This was a cause for much glee on one side and anger on the other. That, I think, illustrates the parent-child relationship at its happiest, for the anger was mingled with respect for the child who had managed to do it again.

Atum's oldest daughter, Nachapio, was married to a policeman at Moroto. There was tremendous excitement when she announced that she was returning to visit her father, after repeated requests and bribes. She finally arrived at Kaabong, but, to Atum's distress, sent word that she could not come to Pirre because she had too much luggage to carry. Now, the luggage was Atum's whole objective in inviting his daughter to return and in investing some capital in the bribes. He did not boast, as others might have been content to do, that his daughter had so much luggage that she could not carry it, and use this as proof of her self-advancement and thus add to his own status. He was not concerned with such trivialities as status; he wanted that luggage. So he set off for Kaabong on foot, having failed to get me to take him in the Land Rover. In three days he was back with the police vehicle, his daughter and all her luggage, which he hastily installed in his own house, though of course Nachapio was to sleep outside.

Nachapio brought many things, though I managed to trace only a few of them; the more readily consumable goods Atum kept for himself. But she wore a bright blue dress with a floral print when she arrived, and after her one night in the compound with Kinimei and Lotuköi the dress was split and somehow Lojieri, her brother-in-law, had got half of it and was wearing it like a robe over one shoulder. It had been a jolly night, to start with, and from my own compound I

could with ease listen to Nachapio telling stories of her
thievish exploits at Moroto, and how she fooled her husband
much of the time as well as stealing from him, all of which
brought exclamations of praise and envy from her young
cousins. Then there were sounds of *asak* being moved and
giggles of a different nature ensued, and finally a mild scuffle
and fight, which was explained by Lojieri's appearing in half
of Nachapio's dress the next morning.

Mostly, however, Nachapio slept where it paid, and that
was not with her family, but at the Police Post. That was
another part of Atum's master plan, and it was through
Nachapio's flirtations, coupled with the fact that her husband was a policeman and Atum himself had been a police
porter, that he hoped to get permission to use the police bore
hole. He even made arrangements for Nachapio's nocturnal
occupation, and if they did not coincide with her own
arrangements she usually managed to handle both. But
when he wanted her also to sleep with Lokeléa, so as to get
at some of those cattle, she refused. Lokeléa's bad breath
came up for discussion again, and Nachapio had a stormy
interview within her father's *asak* in which she demanded to
be paid, as promised, two hundred shillings—a considerable
sum, but one which Atum could easily afford. (For comparison, however, Ik were at that time being paid three shillings
per day for full-time work on the road or for part-time work
for the police.) Atum raised his voice so that all could judge
and said that she had not yet got him invitations to the
Police Post beer-drinking parties, and now she refused him
access to Lokeléa's cattle. Nachapio politely told her father
that he could go and sleep with Lokeléa himself. He called
her an adulteress, *bukoniam,* and she called him *ko 'onam,* a
committer of incest. There was then a ripping sound and
Nachapio emerged with her yellow dress torn from top to

bottom and a necklace she had just won from the Police Post broken. She was pursued by Atum, who stopped only to pick up some of the beads from the broken necklace, but this gave Nachapio time to flee. The police came down to retrieve such of her belongings as were left, and that very afternoon she left for Kasilé, with police porters carrying her two tin trunks and two enormous skin bags full of something that she had not had when she came.

Bukoniam was not an accusation heard often, for adultery was everyday practice and was not in any way considered reprehensible. In using it as he did, and I asked him why, Atum explained that he had been pointing out that she had slept well but not wisely; she had in fact been wasteful, there had been no profit. I mentioned the bulging skin bags with which she had left. Atum said that he had told one of the porters, Amoiché, to find out what was in them and if possible to bring some of it back. He said those were for the sleeping she did on her own behalf, and he was talking about what he had paid her to do.

Atum's relations with his other daughter, Bila, were better only in that they did not constantly fight, and they knew each other well enough not to try to exploit each other unduly. Bila and Matsui, her sister-in-law, often used to go off together, with their soft skin bags folded up and balanced on their heads, looking like bundles of cloth. But they were strong, voluminous skins, and the two women sometimes came back with them full as the result of what seemed to be a form of joint adultery. I wondered if, like the bark strippers, they enjoyed such calamities as befell the other. They too mainly patronized the police, but also the Dodos. The police had the pick of the younger girls, and what Matsui and Bila had to offer, other than every known disease, I cannot guess. Nor did they have the energy to offer it as

frequently as the younger ones, but when they did sally
forth they always returned in high good humor, so there was
something to be said for it, as well as the bulging skin bags.
It would be tedious to go through all the various possible
familial relationships that should have been marked by
affection, if not love; what was true for parent-child was true
for husband-wife or brother-sister. Losiké stole a pumpkin
from the field of her brother Lemu, who announced the theft
from his *odok* early one morning. Losiké, already starving,
did not have the strength to shout her response, but croaked
it none the less. I was too far away to hear her, but I was
told that she asked how could one steal from a brother, did
her brother want her to starve and contribute to her funeral
feast? Lemu, whose reply was strong and clear in the cold
morning air, said she should have asked him before she stole
(he used the verb *duués*, "to steal," rather than *goétés*, "to
take"). Losiké said if she had asked, Lemu would of course
have refused, which put her brother in a better mood; he
laughed loudly and said, "Yes, I would have refused, and
then I would have lain in wait for you and beaten you with
thorns as a man beats his wife." And, still chuckling, he left
it at that. The verdict arrived at by Atum's *di* was that Lemu
was right, it was all right for a woman to try to take (but
they used *goétés*) from her brother, but she should ask him
first so as to give him a chance to stop her. There was no
agreement when I suggested that Lemu should have given
his sister food in the first place, even though by then they
knew that this was the kind of behavior I considered right.

Relationships between grandparent and grandchild, between alternate generations, were better. They were marked
by what was at one time a formal joking relationship, which
implied freedom to take certain liberties, obligation to take
others, and generally a rather friendly and companionable

coexistence. Children were frequently named after their grandparents, as my genealogies showed, but the same tables showed a sharp decrease in such namings with the contemporary generation, and this was accompanied by a corresponding deterioration in the alternate-generation relationship. Joking became something rather more serious, as though the grandchildren took the liberty of doing what should have been done by someone else and were disposing of their grandparents. Without killing, it is difficult to get closer to disposal than by taking the food out of an old person's mouth, and this was primarily an adjacent-generational occupation, as were tripping and pushing off balance. However, I confess that they never expressed any *intent* to kill; it was all good clean fun.

But most of the old were completely abandoned, as much by their grandchildren (except for a few fond practical jokes) as by their children. Little wisps of smoke in the middle of a parched field often indicated where some old person was struggling to make a little charcoal, a lengthy and tedious process, to sell at the Police Post for a bowl of food, after approximately three days' work. Never did I see a family member helping, even offering a word of encouragement. The only exception, again, was Nangoli, for she was always with her family; and, perhaps significantly, she was never with anyone else. I met and knew most Ik families, for by the end their numbers had been drastically reduced, but Nangoli's was the only family, without exception, to which the term could be applied in any but the crudest biological sense. Even Lolim and Lo'ono had virtually been forced apart, each having to survive separately as best he or she could, not through any fault of their own but through that of their children and grandchildren and the world around them. Yet Nangoli lived in the same world, but still managed to make something different of it. It was even unique to her family that sex should be an occasion for pleasure, for it was more commonly and openly referred to as a necessary chore, and mildly pleasurable, like defecation.

Defecation was not considered an unclean thing, as evidenced by the openness with which it was performed; it was a natural function, comparable to a sexual orgasm, in which, similarly, waste matter is excreted. *Edziaagés* and *butaanés*, "to defecate" and "to copulate," were similarly compared in what to me was a much more distressing manner, however, than by reference to their excretory functions; for when I said that copulation, as opposed to masturbation, gave pleasure to two whereas defecation gave pleasure, if at all, to only one, I got the bland reply: "Who knows what the other is feeling? In each you only know your own feeling."

Lodéa, Nangoli's only unmarried son, was a happy exception. He claimed that he enjoyed sex, and that was why he was not married.

The same lassitude and inertia that pervaded the rest of life for the Ik characterized their sexual life, particularly for the men; they had better uses for their energy. The occasional flirtations were nearly all adulterous, and seemed to have been performed for the sake of stirring up some excitement or out of a typically Icien desire to gain at another's expense. But when a man felt that the need for sexual relief was irresistible, there were still two major factors against it, no matter how much he might enjoy the fun of cuckolding his brother, say; both reasons were economic. A woman required a gift of food at least, and possibly food and money, and most Ik had neither. For the girls it was their major asset, and they were not going to dispose of it wastefully. The second factor was the expenditure of energy involved, and the young men, the only ones smitten by this ridiculous

urge, pointed out that it required much less energy to mastur-
bate. Also, they said, it was unfair to have to pay a girl when
she enjoyed what she was doing. On one occasion I saw two
youths on a ridge high up on Kalimon masturbating each
other. It showed some degree of conviviality, but not much,
for there was no affection in their mutuality; each was
gazing in a different direction, looking for signs of food; they
were not, so far as I knew, even friends, and were no more
frequently seen with each other than with anyone else. One
of them was Lomongin's only son.

But for the girls and even some of the younger women it
was different; this was their major source of goodness, food,
and they went to it with a will. A good example was Koko,
whose father's brother was Lomongin's son-in-law. Lomongin made that an excuse for inviting Koko to stay in his compound, and though he never got as fat as Koko he certainly
derived some material benefit. Koko was the plumpest Ik I
ever saw, and the best adorned with precious necklaces of
ostrich eggshell, stone, seed and bead. She was the most
smiling and laughing Ik, and seemingly the happiest. She
and Nachapio, Lomongin's eldest daughter by his third wife,
used to go courting, if that is the word, together. Never with
Ik, for they had no wealth, but with the police, the Turkana,
the Dodos, the Didinga, and the Topos. They particularly
favored the Turkana, who were a high-spirited lot and gave
them all they wanted. Their method of approach was to
advance hand in hand, dancing in a way that left nothing to
doubt, beads swinging and aprons flapping and breasts
bouncing. They gave little yodels in harmony as they
danced, getting more and more suggestive as they neared
their victim. Then just as he reached out to them they
turned and bent down, knees straight, swung up their apron
flaps and presented their backsides to the laughing man.

Everyone enjoyed the act, and the game was for the man not to show any interest until the moment when, instead of presenting their backsides, the girls suddenly reached out and seized the man, rather like a couple of spiders working in unison. Another example of Icien cooperativeness, I suppose.

The reason these girls preferred the Turkana was simple: only the Turkana, as far as my observations went, might produce such a one as could stand impassively picking his teeth or switching himself with a fly-whisk, then all at once grab them by the waist and carry them both off to the bush, from which they would all emerge in due course smiling and giggling. But they were smiling at different things, I fear, for Koko was not shy of boasting how well she could fool her men into thinking she was giving her all whereas she was hard put to it to remember when she had ever given it. She claimed that if she did, it was by mistake, for it would spoil her ability to fool the next. Koko's plumpness lasted a whole year, and when her charms began to wane with the onset of disease, Lomongin turned her out.

Acute hunger and the physical hardship of the food quest obviously weakened the sexual appetite of the Ik, and in so doing, it deprived them of a major drive toward sociality and confirmed them in their solitariness. It was not immediately discernible, for on occasion the men would primp and preen, as they did during that hair-styling session. While the women were openly flirting, though with more than usual commercial concern, the men often seemed to be preparing to flirt. They did not generally go to such lengths as a complete hair style, but they might take a flower and stick it in their hair, or strip the leaves of the *adokana* palm, whose fruit the elephants love to eat, and make gleaming white bands with which to adorn their arms and legs and foreheads. A few, like Longoli, young brother to Bila's husband, affected the hide shin guards worn by the Turkana for protection against thorns. Youths in this way fairly often seemed to be preparing for some amorous expedition. But when the primping was done they would get a bit of broken mirror and gaze at themselves with pleasure, then wander off to some solitary spot with a good view and become more solitary than ever. If there was any love in their sexual life, it was only for themselves.

It is understandable that the Ik have lost whatever love they might once have had for their mountain world, but that love is not transformed into hate or despair, but once again into a boredom relieved, if anything, by a moody mistrust and skepticism. At Pirre, as at Nawedo, heavy rain clouds frequently blew overhead and on out into the park without shedding a drop; Morungole was often shrouded in swirling mists; but nobody really even looked for signs of rain, though sometimes they went through the motions for the sake of a discussion when they felt sociable. And when rain did come, the loud cry of *"Aats a didi!"* was no cry of joy, but of mild anger, for rain meant coldness and wetness, two things the Ik loathe. At the slightest hint of either, no matter what they were doing, they would stop and with exasperation make up a fire and huddle around. If there was more than a passing hint of rain, if the signs really were indisputable, exasperation became anger. There would be arguments as to why it had to come now, as though any time could be a bad time in that parched, thirsty land. One day when they were all ready to go to Kasilé for some special famine relief that had arrived there for them, they started arguing about rain and the fact that it had not come, which of course they allowed to annoy them almost as much as when it did come. They fell into such ill humor that out of sheer self-spite, which for the Ik is much the same as self-love, they decided not to go to Kasilé. I did not understand at the time and asked why, when so much *ngag* was waiting for them, and I pointed out that if they did not go the Ik from the escarpment would get it all. They said that there was to be a big Dodos feast that afternoon and they were going to stay for that. Of course there was nothing of the sort and they knew it, but they felt obliged to explain their behavior to me, though it needed no such rationale for them. They not only rejected the food that the government had sent for them, they started in on all manner of utterly useless energy-consuming activities such as sweeping aimlessly outside the village, leaving the compounds as unswept as ever. Others walked from *di* to *di*. Some went and cut lots of *sim*, then left it all lying in the sun, where it dried out and became useless within a couple of hours. The less energetic just sat and whittled aimlessly at pieces of wood, whittling them into nothing but useless shavings on the ground.

The cutting of *sim* always had the effect of making an Ik village look abandoned and desolate even before it was built, since the trees nearest to the village were naturally cut first. In this way the surrounding countryside was studded with dead trees, the bark ripped off, sometimes uselessly just for something to do. When rain threatened and there were no more *sim* trees left to destroy, the Ik would idly tear up bushes or other greenery, saying they got in the way, or cut down a whole tree for no immediate purpose, particularly if it was one they otherwise used for shade. It was a kind of self-destruction, and at first it seemed ironical that the possibility of rain, which they needed so desperately, should be the cause. But when I saw my first rain, during my second year, I understood; it only served to increase frustration by its utter unpredictability, and to make life still more bitter by its destructiveness. Sometimes there were violent thunderstorms that lasted for whole nights without shedding a single drop of rain. For want of something to do, I used to measure the amount of rain that fell, not exactly by the drop, but at least in terms of the number of seconds the rainfall lasted. One particularly good night my notes tell of two rainfalls during such a storm; the first was of large, heavy drops and lasted ten seconds; the second, at 2:40 A.M., half an hour later, was of lighter droplets and lasted thirty-two seconds. The exactness of detail was no measure of my academic zeal, simply of my own frustration and boredom. I tried recording the peculiarly loud splashes made by that first kind of rain, the rain that comes in extraordinarily large, heavy drops, each of which bursts into a miniature pool when it hits the ground. But when real rain came, there was no time for such frivolities. It was on you within half a minute, the only warning being a sinister, sharp hissing sound growing louder and louder as it swept up the other side of the mountain. Then it burst in a deluge that within a very few minutes turned the parched *oror* into raging torrents, and if you were caught in one you were killed. Again you had about half a minute of warning, a deep rumbling sound from higher up. It was not only a tidal wave, a wall of water all the more vicious for being so confined, it was also a cascade of tumbling rocks and boulders swept along with the water. And all the while the water was pouring over the fields, which were baked so dry that nothing could penetrate, so the water just swept everything with it, terraces and dykes and crops and all.

Such storms were over within ten minutes, usually, subsiding with a roaring of wind that might follow in the form of a tornado to complete the devastation. A tornado could come as suddenly as rain, the first warning in the midst of utter stillness being the halfhearted twitch of a dead leaf lying at your feet. Then it would twitch again, and you took shelter before you were knocked over. The lighter rains, which were even more rare, had their drawbacks too, though they did less damage. There was little greenery to freshen at this time, though what there was took on a brilliant hue as though it had suddenly sprung to life whereas in fact the dust of the months past had merely been washed off. But there were those Icien feces, which in the sun baked dry and were relatively inoffensive. After a light rain, however, even the Ik wrinkled their noses while they continued defecating on their doorsteps.

Yet the world itself was beautiful, as beautiful as it had always been. It had lost its beauty for the Ik because they had lost their freedom to be one with it, moving according to its own known rhythm and free to escape its whims and move elsewhere. It was easy to sense what the beauty must once have meant, and to believe that there had been a love for that world. Morungole was always beautiful, with the moving clouds changing the shadows and hues on its side just as they made patches of sunlight sweep rapidly across the valleys and park below. The mists that swirled around the mountain on those cold, damp mornings constantly changed the shape of its summit; it was never the same mountain, but it was always beautiful—if you had the time and stomach for beauty when you were not free to respond and be a part of it. The Ik, like all hunters, must have been as much a part of their natural world as the mountains and winds and rains and the very game they hunted and wild fruits they gathered. Wherever they went there was beauty, for, as Didigwari had told them, there would always be enough. But when they were imprisoned in one tiny corner, the world became something cruel and hostile, and in their lives cruelty took the place of love.

It was there in their laughter, in all the things that gave them pleasure, in the way they communicated with each other, the way they lived and the way they died. Misfortune of others was their greatest joy, and I wondered whether in their minds it lessened the probability of misfortune visiting them or increased it. But personal misfortune was really beyond the realm of probability, it was a certainty. So cruelty was with them, in their humor, in their interpersonal relations, in their thoughts and reflections. Yet, so utter was their isolation, as individuals, that I do not think they thought of their cruelty as affecting others.

Even when it appeared mild it was not. A group of men sitting on a *di* would start teasing any women who had the temerity to sit nearby. They assumed a high falsetto and feminine gesticulations and referred to their sexual affairs, misfortunes and inabilities, to their sores and their syphilis, to all that lay below those dirty aprons. But for them it was a play with words, and the women retaliated in kind.

Lokeléa came in for more than the usual amount of teasing because, not being an Ik, he was more readily tricked and made into a buffoon. In particular he was mocked for his kindness, for Lokeléa *was* kind and generous and was surprised rather than hurt when the people he had adopted as his own did not respond. I only once saw him really upset, and then he turned his goats loose into Lomongin's one field that was producing anything. Everyone sat around and watched the destruction, occasionally pointing out this goat or that, and finally they awakened Lomongin so that they could enjoy his discomfiture while the very last of the damage was being done, his hunger for another year assured, his starvation probable.

The Ik had a nice sense of timing in such matters, and the joking relationship between alternate generations made

good use of it. It was rather commonplace, during the
second year's drought, to see the very young prying open the
mouths of the very old and pulling out food they had been
chewing and had not had time to swallow. But it called for
delicate timing. It was the same game they had played with
Adupa, and the fun was to play on the uncertainty the old
person felt, not knowing whether the food would be
snatched before he got it to his mouth or after. And sometimes, to really torment him, they would make as if to take
the food and then not take it, so the victim swallowed in
haste and surprise and choked on it.

Only with the children was there real physical violence
and cruelty, but even then it was not without refinement and
was not violence for its sake alone. Nine-year-old Lokwam,
for instance, watched six-year-old Naduie, his sister, spend
two days making a little charcoal, like the very old people,
to sell to the police for some food. She was too young, still,
to sell herself. I saw her when she was making the pit the
first day, in which to lay and burn the wood. Lokwam was
watching from a distance. I saw her on the afternoon of the
second day, near dusk, with a little skin bag of charcoal
clutched in her two hands, making her way across the fields
to the Police Post, and I saw Lokwam follow her slowly,
letting her take fright, then more swiftly, to give her time to
begin to cry with the pain of hopelessness, and only then did
he commit the physical violence of leaping on her, beating
her savagely to the ground, then pummeling her further
before even trying to get the charcoal, which Naduié had
clutched as she fell; she was protecting it by lying on top of
it, as a mother who was not an Ik might protect her child,
her life. That made it fun for Lokwam, who was full of
energy. When he could not tug it away he just stood up
suddenly and jumped on Naduié's back, forcing the bag of

charcoal into her belly so that she screamed with pain and rolled over, clutching her injured stomach. Lokwam looked at her idly for a moment, but seeing no further amusement, he casually picked up the bag of charcoal and continued up to the Police Post.

These were observable realities, and so they were graspable and comprehensible, however disconcerting. But the intangible realm of the mind I could not fathom. Atum once pointed out a twisting spiral of pale blue smoke rising from a wooded face high up on Morungole. He came to me specially to show it to me, so I asked what it was, since he still said nothing beyond telling me to look. He looked me straight in the eye as he carefully said, "They are burning a man for incest." I think he was looking for some kind of reaction that he could exploit, but I merely felt a mild interest and asked if they would burn him dead. Atum said he would have to wait and watch the smoke, you could sometimes tell by that, and again he looked at me quizzically. But when he saw I was looking at him with the same kind of interest, and finding no pleasure in any game that two can play, he just shrugged his shoulders and ambled back to the *di*. But he continued looking at that spiral of smoke, and whether his story was fact or fancy made little difference, for I felt he was seeing it all and imagining, perhaps, my discomfort if I too could have been made to see it.

The isolation that made love impossible, however, was not completely proof against loneliness. I no longer noticed normal behavior, such as the way people ate when they got food, gobbling it like hungry old hens, running as they gobbled, often, so as to escape others and have it all for themselves. But I did notice how, on any *di* where people were sitting together and someone was making a *karatz* or twine or straightening a spear shaft, the focus of attention for the spectators was not the person but the action. They watched only the hands at work; there was no interest in the person. But if they were caught watching by the one being watched and their eyes met, the reaction was a sharp retreat on both sides, as though they had been caught in an unforgivable act of personal, mutual interest.

The older people, while the young were working in this way nearby, often took pains to remove themselves, perhaps as much as fifteen feet, to make it plain that they had no such interest in anyone else. They closed their eyes and pretended to sleep, but every now and then I could see them with eyes wide open, staring at what was going on, as though they wished things were other than they were and there was some real excuse for doing something, for doing it together, instead of this futile masquerade.

Only Nangoli did not feel lonely, I think, for she always had her family, and she seemed to have retained her love for the world around her. At least she still understood it and tried to respond with understanding even to its harshness. She was too old to work herself, but she advised her children on how to choose sites that would not be swept by sheets of water, and how to dam up *oror* where the dam would not be swept away, and where the pent-up waters would escape gently to flood a carefully terraced little field. And she understood her fellow Ik, and herself sat guard over her field.

And only Lokeléa *did* feel lonely, for although I detected signs, symptoms of loneliness, I think the others really felt nothing; though perhaps in reality that is the greatest loneliness of all. But Lokeléa felt deeply. I remember one night that really moved me with its beauty. There was a full moon and shortly after dark it rose above Meraniang and touched

the summit of Morungole, already silhouetted by a burning
bush fire on the far side. Slowly and peacefully that special
silvery gleam spread down the side, leaving a shadow in the
shape of the hills behind me. Over the glimmering stretch of
park, at the base of Lotuköi, a tiny red glow told of a camp.
I knew it was Lomer, gathering honey out in that vast expanse, and alone. I stayed awake a long time, and when I
went to sleep it seemed only a few minutes before I heard
Lokeléa. But it was half-past four in the morning, and the
moonlight was gone and the beauty was gone, and outside
was nothing but blackness of night and soul, cold and
blustery. Lokeléa had wakened to find his wife and children
were already awake with cold and hunger and were huddled
over a fire. He gave out a cry of despair that, being Lokeléa,
he turned to poetry and to song, asking how God could
allow such unhappiness and misery to those he had let down
from the sky; asking why he had retreated beyond their
reach, leaving them without hope. He sang to himself and
his wife and children for half an hour, and then fell into a
silence that was even more bitter than the song.

For all around were others who also were cold and
hungry, but who had lost all trust in the world, lost all love
and all hope, who merely accepted life's brutality and
cruelty because it was empty of all else. They had no love
left that could be tortured and compelled to express itself as
grief, and no God to sing to, for they were Ik.

CHAPTER ELEVEN

The End of Goodness

W HEN THE RAINS failed for the second year running I knew that the Ik as a society were almost certainly finished, and that the monster they had created in its place, that passionless, feelingless association of individuals, would continue, spreading like a fungus, contaminating all it touched. When I left I too had been contaminated, I knew, by the lack of feeling as the house that I had tried to make a home was invaded, the stockade was broken down, and the things I had left to be shared were despoiled by avarice. I was not surprised, nor did it upset me. And it did not upset me when I said goodbye to old Loiangorok, who by now had been nursed back to some semblance of life, though his face was unhealthily puffy. He had been frightened during the night by a prowling leopard, for the girls had never finished his shelter and it was doorless. He had cried out and people around had laughed. But in the morning I told him I had left a sack of *posho* with the police for him to get enough for his needs every day, and I told him I would send money for more sacks when that ran out. He had spent the morning talking to himself about all the food he was going to eat from now on: *posho*, corn, beans, pumpkins, rice, tea and sugar. He was now able to drag himself slowly toward the *di* every day, though he sometimes got only part of the way, and as he did so he always clutched a knife. When he got there, or as far as he could, he squatted down and whittled at some wood, thus proving to himself and others that he was still alive and able to do things, even if useless. After all, any one action is as useless as another, unless directly related to the stomach. The *posho* would have been enough to last him for months, but I felt no particular emotion when I estimated that he would last one month, even with the *posho* in the hands of the police. I underestimated his son Loiamukat, who within two days had persuaded the police that it would save them a lot of bother if he looked after the *posho;* as much as the police knew of the Ik, they always felt, as loyal Africans, that I exaggerated and that no human, least of all one with an African's highly developed sense of family, would allow a father to starve. Loiamukat kept his father alive just long enough to allay suspicions, but not long enough to let him make any inroads into the *posho*. I heard, later, that Loiangorok died of starvation within two weeks.

So I departed with a kind of forced gaiety, feeling I should be glad to be gone, but having forgotten how to be glad. I certainly was not thinking of returning within a year, but I did. The following spring I heard from the Police Post that rains had come at last, and that the fields of the Ik had never looked so prosperous, nor the country so green and fertile, nor the cattle so well fed. There had been little raiding, just a few youthful escapades of junior *moran* displaying their bravery and proving their fitness as adults. Atum, the letter said, was well. That I could have guessed—and as warm, woolly and cuddly as ever. However, a few months away had refreshed me, and I wondered if my gloomy conclusions had not been excessively pessimistic. Under conditions of plenty, surely, the Ik would be a different people, and life would return to their world and to them. So, early that summer I set off once more so as to be present for the first harvests in three years. This time there were no misconceptions, except the basic one that the Ik might have changed with the weather, and I felt ready for almost anything.

So I was not surprised too much when two days after my arrival and installation at the Police Post I found Logwara, the blind man, lying on the roadside bruised and bleeding, while a hundred yards up, at the post, other Ik were squabbling over the body of a hyena that had fallen into a leopard trap. Logwara had tried to get there ahead of the others, and had simply been trampled on. Much the same thing had happened to him once before, but then he had been stronger and had scrambled to his feet and fought his way into the mob. This time he just lay there, waiting until he could find enough strength to return to his house.

For this trip I brought young Gabriel Loyola, the Dodos youth, with me. It was partly for company, knowing that I would need it, but mainly so that he would be able to translate for me whenever the Ik tried to fool me by breaking into one of the Karimojong dialects, for Gabriel knew them all. It was altogether a different experience, for, knowing that I had only the summer, I did not wait for things to happen. There were specific things I wanted to discover, others that I wanted to see, and my mildly aggressive mood seemed to make for much better relations all around; it certainly made me feel better. So did the lush greenery which was now deep and fresh where before there had been only baked earth and rock. Arriving at Pirre, we had to splash through the stream of clean water that flowed from the water hole, and the villages of the Ik themselves looked fresh. They were actually the same villages, but tomatoes and pumpkins had grown up over the outer stockades and covered them, even extending into the inner compounds. My old house was now occuped by Atum, who prized it for its size and fortress-like construction, but he had paid the price of leaving the village, for although he had extended the stockade to incorporate the house, it had its own *odok* within which his was the solitary *asak*. Lomongin was again in the ascendant. I was given a house at the Police Post, and Atum presented himself for work within minutes of my arrival, as though I had never left, or as though he had been fully aware of my plans. Instantly aware that the Iciebam was in a more aggressive mood, he responded with excessive servility, promising to show me all sorts of things that he had been afraid to show me before, and to do whatever I wanted.

First we looked at the villages. On closer inspection they showed that the lush outer covering concealed an inner decay. Giriko's village, which had swelled to such large proportions during the flight from Meraniang when all the other villages moved, had shrunk as his guests, who were mostly old, died off. The old houses had simply crumbled and fallen in the midst of those still lived in. All the villages were like this to some extent, except for Lokeléa's, which was solid and prosperous. There I noticed that the tomatoes and pumpkins which twined around his outer stockade were carefully pruned and cleaned, so that the fruits were larger and healthier, whereas in the other villages they were allowed to run wild and the tomatoes were the size of small marbles. In what had been my own compound the shade tree had been cut down for firewood, and the lovely hanging nests of the weaver birds everywhere were gone—the moment the eggs were ready to hatch, they were taken and eaten, unborn weaver and all. Despite the overall greenery outside, the desolation was still there, for even more trees had been destroyed for *sim*, and everywhere the green undergrowth was broken by the gaunt gray branches of trees that had been killed.

The fields, which at first promised to be so encouraging, were even more desolate. They were full enough, both those on the steep slopes and those on the lesser slopes. Every field without exception had yielded in abundance and it was a new sensation to have vision cut off by thick crops that waved all around me, with maize reaching far above my head. The reason for the desolation in the midst of this abundance was that every crop, in every field, was rotting through sheer neglect. Birds scarcely eyed us as we beat our way through the tangled wastes of what should have been food for the Ik; grubs and caterpillars were everywhere, and some fields had been destroyed by baboons. I came across a number of three-year-old field shelters, collapsed in ruins, but none that had been built or used since to help guard this bumper crop. One or two watchtowers still stood, though most had collapsed, and on one of these boys stood idly flicking mud pellets at some of the nearer birds. I remembered the fields Gabriel had showed me, where each field had a central shelter with a reinforced roof for standing on, as well as other shelters and towers: he had said it needed ten people to watch one field properly. There were not as many as half a dozen in the whole length of the *oror a pirre'i.* Pumpkins rotted on the ground, and I thought of all those whom I had known who had died, such a short time before, of want.

The Ik themselves were as open as ever, and said that they had no need to bother guarding the fields. There was so much food they could never eat it all, so why not let the birds and baboons take some? They went out each day and cut what they wanted for the day, whether it was ripe or not. If you can eat bark and uncooked grass seed, and swallow nicely rounded pebbles and earth, it is of no importance whether maize, millet or sorghum is ripe or not, and if the fruit is full of grubs, so much the better. The Ik had full bellies; they were good. It was a good year. The *di* at Atum's village was much the same as usual, people sitting or lying about doing nothing very much, but forever scanning the horizon, and every now and then wandering off on some errand, followed by inquisitive eyes. Everyone still ate by himself, though now not so afraid to do so with others around, as there was plenty for all. The main trouble was that there was too much and although each person had all he could eat, he was still unwilling to see others eat what he could not. People were still stealing from each other's fields, though this only added to the problem of how to dispose of the food in their own fields. Certainly nobody thought of saving for any future day, let alone for next year's sowing. The granaries, which were few, were empty. After the last move nobody had built any new granaries, and most people had not bothered to move their old ones.

Up on Meraniang my first house site could still be clearly seen. The house was gone and the ground was cleared, but parts of the old stockade still stood, termite-eaten and not worth moving, and tomatoes, a leafy vegetable and tobacco had been carefully planted and tended there by someone, and some wild blue flowers where I had once tried to make a garden. Atum told me it was Nangoli, Lolim's daughter, who had gone mad. He said she heard voices in her head and claimed to see visions and talk to the *abang,* and she was always off on her own, tending gardens that required care and hard work while everywhere else food grew wild. I thought of Nangoli fondly, but learned that once more she was in jail. There had been a big fight when she had accused someone of stealing her tobacco, and the police had had to intervene. Everyone blamed Nangoli for starting it, and since she refused to defend herself the police had sent her to Kaabong. To keep her there the Ik added accusations that she was a witch and was cursing them and their fields so that they would all die. Atum thought that was particularly funny, given the lack of belief in such fantasies among the Ik. I got permission to see Nangoli, but she said she did not want to see anyone, she would rather stay where she was. When she was let out some time later she immediately attacked a policeman simply to be put back inside, away from a world that had grown, if possible, even more unbearable. Nangoli, I think, was the last Ik who was human.

I do not know what happened to the other Nangoli, widow of Amuarkuai; she and her family had taken off again for the Sudan after some halfhearted attempt to move the Ik close to the Napore, away from Morungole. She might just possibly have survived; otherwise Atum was the only old person left alive, and he was not all that old. However, if he remembered days when things were better, he chose to ignore them; like everyone else, he accepted things as they were and played the game that way. I could see that, despite his protestations of help, what he intended was to stick as close to me as possible, yet it did not seem to be for material gain alone, which was puzzling; it certainly was not out of affection. I voiced an interest in visiting the hidden granaries along the escarpment, which I had heard about on my previous trip but had never been able to see because nobody would ever take me there. At that time I had not wanted to be overly aggressive, but this time I said that I would go by myself if nobody else would come. Atum volunteered without hesitation. But first I made a few shorter trips, to get back into shape for climbing and scrambling, and I made the mistake of going without Gabriel, who was not used to the Ik and did not enjoy their company very much.

I went on one trip with Atum, Lokbo'ok and Lojieri, Bila's husband. Lojieri led, then Atum, and Lokbo'ok brought up the rear. We climbed up Meraniang and on over to the other side, from where one could look across a sharp angle in the escarpment to near where Nawedo lay, in the far distance. The grass was so high that often I could not see over it and tracks indicated that buffalo had been all around. Even Atum carried a spear this time, instead of his stick, and I too was given one. Then the first of several incidents happened. Once again I was led across a narrow ledge with a dangerous drop on one side when, it turned out, there was no need for it at all; in fact, a detour had been made specially to go that way. It did not worry me overly, but the next incident did. We were moving very fast along fairly level ground, and Lojieri suddenly dashed off into the tall grass, far above his head, saying something about a buffalo. Buffaloes are nasty creatures at the best of times, and I did not slacken pace when Atum stopped to urinate, nodding with his head for me to continue down the path, which was beginning to slope at a steeper angle. I still could see nothing ahead but the tall grass until the path suddenly turned and dipped so violently that I slipped and almost fell. Then I had all the view I wanted; the grass fell away in front of me just as the land fell away, and I was on the edge of the escarpment with fifteen hundred feet between me and Kenya below, the path becoming a tiny ledge that would have made even an Ik hesitate.

When I turned to go back, having recovered from the fright at so nearly going right over the edge, I found that the path was not easy to see—I might have followed a turning that was an animal trail rather than a foot trail and come to the escarpment that way. . . . Anyway, there was no sign of Lokbo'ok, who had been close behind me, I thought, nor any sign of Atum. Although the grass was dense as well as tall, I did not see how they could have missed me or be far away, but when I called out there was no answer. I sat down and waited for half an hour, and finally Lokbo'ok came ambling down the trail followed by Lojieri, and going on about a hundred yards we found Atum, picking some berries. "You took the wrong turning," said Atum, "you could have fallen over." For a moment his face was serious, almost cross, and I was warmed at his concern. Then I heard a muffled snort behind me and found Lojieri doubled up with laughter, at which Atum could control himself no longer, and laughed and slapped his side until his eyes just streamed with tears. "You don't like heights, do you?" he asked and, leaving the question unanswered, continued ahead, now leading the procession, still laughing. It is difficult to tell whether they would have laughed harder if I had fallen, or would have felt deprived of future possibilities for fun.

On another occasion that same day they managed to lose me for nearly two hours, though there was no immediate danger that I know of and it seemed rather pointless. It was funny to me because it was so obvious and charmingly open and neat. As if by prearrangement, and it may well have been, they all three said, simultaneously, the equivalent of "Excuse me a minute," "*Kwesida kwatz*," and took off in different directions and were quickly lost to sight in the grass and euphorbia. By the time I had tried to make up my mind which one to follow, all had gone. With the long grass blocking familiar views, I could easily get lost, so I just lay down in the shade of a large acacia tree and dozed until they came back, offering not the slightest explanation. That one day made it quite clear that they were doing their best to gently discourage me from roaming about, and the long grass changed the countryside so much that except for a few trails where I had a clear view or where paths were well marked it would be impossible to go without a guide. I felt that the discouragement had something to do with my desire to see the hidden granaries.

Before, my curiosity had been idle—there was not likely to be much of interest in an empty granary, hidden or otherwise—but when Gabriel told me that the Dodos said that the Ik hid things in caves on the face of the escarpment no amount of discouragement would keep me away. The granaries had been moved, said Atum. After all, there was plenty of food now, so why hide them? Very well, I would go to see the full granaries. Well, that would not be possible either because the Ik had either eaten or given all their food away, so there was no need for any granaries. Then I would simply go and see the caves. That was just a Dodos story, there were no caves; besides, they were halfway down the escarpment and I didn't like heights. We got back to my threat to go with the police, and I showed my letter of authorization from the government. Atum grumbled, but finally agreed that we would go to Nawedo and ask the villagers if they knew anything about granaries or caves. He grumbled even more when I said just he and I would go, with Gabriel.

At Nawedo there was even stronger resistance, and the

closest I got to cooperation was when one man offered to sell me his secret granary for five hundred shillings, not expecting me to agree. I agreed, intending not to pay nor even to bargain but just to see what he would do; he held a hurried consultation in Didinga right in front of me, then said he had only been joking, he had no granary, there were none, nor were there any caves. Gabriel gave me a prearranged signal telling me that I was being fooled, and told me later that they had discussed my governmental letter of authorization and had said I must be kept away at all costs. While I continued arguing, he was scouting around, and in half an hour he was back and told me in English that he had found a path down the escarpment.

The Ik were as surprised as I was when I followed Gabriel over the edge and started scrambling and sliding and edging my way down. The first cave I came to was not more than a couple of hundred feet below the top, and though it was little more than a rocky overhang, it had traces of recent chalk drawings of animals and people. During the whole of my previous trip I had heard stories that this had been done in the past, but that no drawings were left and nobody did them now, and though I examined every rocky overhang and cave I could find I had never come across any traces. While looking at the drawings we were joined by a frightened-looking Atum and a couple of very angry Ik from Nawedo. They calmed down when they saw my interest in the drawings and started pouring out information—which may or may not have been true—about the significance; they claimed that children amused themselves this way and sometimes old people taught children, through drawings, how they used to hunt. I also detected traces of what I thought had been outlines of mountains, but was told that they were just empty lines without significance.

Coming back out to the face of the escarpment, I found Atum was already scrambling up, expecting me to follow, but Gabriel, who seemed almost as surefooted as the Ik, beckoned me on down, pointing to where he said he could see another cave opening, a hundred feet or so down. This time there were loud cries of protest and accusations that I was not Iciebam at all but a government agent; then Atum added that the cliff face was dangerous and that I would fall, which was expressed not so much as a threat or a warning as a hope. Gabriel helped me around a nasty boulder, and on reaching the cave I found it to be about ten feet deep, but with ample room to stand up, even to walk around, and I sat down to catch my breath. I had already seen that the back of the cave was filled with gourds and other objects, and from where I sat I could see a cleft in the face of the rock, near the entrance, which also looked promising. The cave filled up with the others and still more who had appeared from nowhere on hearing the alarm, and we settled the matter of my status. I said I was not a government agent; I was expected to submit a report to the government just as I had done the last time, but I would not say anything that would harm the Ik, any more than I had done before, and would only try to help them. Atum said that this was so, that no harm had come to them before from my report.

They were somewhat appeased, and no longer blocked my way when I tried to get to the back of the cave to see what was hidden there. There were no granaries and no grain: a few skin bags, empty and folded neatly, some hides, a pot filled with ostrich-eggshell necklaces and beads, and a rack, carefully made of sticks lashed together with *sim*, holding a number of gourds of different sizes and shapes, and every one of them was etched with an intricate design picked out

with a black dye. That interested me more than all the granaries in Karimoja, and the Ik were obviously relieved to see
my genuine interest. They said that there were caves like
this all along the face of the escarpment, mostly a few
hundred feet lower than this one. Each cave was sacred to a
family, and each contained these gourds, which belonged to
the *abang;* the designs on them were again special to each
family. I disbelieved every word of this on principle, but it
was an interesting story, and there was very likely some
truth in it which under normal conditions could have been
checked in the course of the field study. But these were not
normal conditions, and I had to be content with what frag-
ments came my way. I remembered Kila carving just such a
gourd and even giving me the story associated with the
carving I had taken the gourd and showed it to someone
else, who looked at the carving and gave the same story, so
there evidently was still an art form with a possibly rich
symbolism amounting to a pictorial language. It was frus-
trating at this late stage to come across something of such
vital importance and know that there was absolutely nothing
I could do about it, short of spending another two years at
least; but then frustration had become a way of life.

I did my best with sketches of the gourds, then as I left I
went to the crack in the rock face and on tiptoe tried to peer
in. The protests did not deter me, and still less Gabriel, who
climbed up and reached in, shoulders and all; he emerged
with two soft skin bags full of tobacco, and said there were
lots more there too. Tobacco is the main wealth of the Ik,
and in normal times was their major medium of exchange
with the herders, who gave them milk and blood in return,
or luxury items such as bead necklaces or ivory or brass lip-
plugs. In another cave nearby were the same things: the
carved gourds, the skins and the tobacco, and a metal trunk

with a padlock which Aperit, from Nawedo, said was full of money. That was as likely a possibility as any, and so bold a statement as to be quite possibly true. Anyway, I had found what I had wanted and was more than content to leave and to start the upward climb. I was told that formerly grain too had been hidden in the caves, but that that was no longer necessary, which I took to refer to the present glut in the fields. But the Ik here too, just as at Pirre, could see no point in saving even enough to plant, let alone enough to see them through the leaner months ahead or against the possibility of another famine. They shrugged and said, "Only the old die." According to them, children did not die; maybe the escarpment Ik had additional resources for the children, but I doubted it; their only advantage over Pirre was their proximity to the Turkana, who seemed to be more generous toward the Ik than the Dodos. There was still some missing link somewhere.

It was again thanks to Gabriel that I came to hear of the cattle camp on the steep eastern slopes of Lotim, between Pirre and Nawedo. As a Dodos, he knew that such a camp always existed, though it was moved from time to time; he found out where it was right now, and told me. Apart from acting as spies and guides, he said, the Ik often kept stolen herds for the victors in these remote, inaccessible cattle camps until the hue and cry was over and both the victims and the police had given up the chase. I told Atum that I knew where it was and was going to see it to collect genealogies, and promised not to divulge its whereabouts until well after it had been moved, which he said would be in less than a year. With some further financial inducement he agreed to make it easier by guiding us. The journey was much of the same, only more so; access was extremely difficult and dangerous from the west, which is the way the police would

have to come, using the trail on the far side of Lotim, and
though it was easier from the east it was by no means easy,
and was much longer and would have given ample time for
escape had the cattle keepers been discovered. There was no
chance of surprise attack from any direction. We approached from the west and finally reached a canyon that
was about seven hundred feet deep, maybe a little more, yet
seemed to be only a hundred yards across. I suppose it must
have been wider, but none the less it was steep and treacherous both going down and climbing up. On the far side was
the cattle camp, with no cattle but with a fair-sized village
of Ik and a number of guest compounds outside in which the
victorious herders, or some of them, stayed. The head of the
village explained that for some reason the herders did not
trust the Ik and always insisted on leaving *moran* to protect
the cattle they had just stolen. He said he did not know
when the next raid would be, but it would be soon. Apparently he got a sizable commission according to the number
of cattle that finally arrived at their new home. This was
paid in milk and blood, for the herders knew that if they
gave cattle they would be slaughtered, and never did so
except in extreme circumstances. But they did sometimes
give goats, and on the far side of the village was a small
enclosure for them.

The camp was strategically located, and I began to appreciate that the Ik were no amateurs in their position as
middlemen between the herders, and that the administration
had an even bigger problem on its hands than it thought.
The camp was placed so that it could receive cattle and
disperse them from and to north, east or south, the major
barrier being between it and the only road by which police
or troops could be brought in, to the west. Lookout shelters
covered all approaches, with horns hanging ready to sound

alarms. The headman said they accepted cattle from any client, with no tribal discrimination, and that his village alone would profit. But because of the need to maintain communications in all directions he said that he always had people from just about every Ik village. He was almost right—every clan but one was represented, and almost every village. There were three families I had known at Pirre, and two more besides, plus a similar coverage from the escarpment side. Only Naputiro was not represented, and it was not far away and apparently served as a kind of "front"; in case the police heard there was a "secret village" in this direction, they could always be told it was just Naputiro. I do not think the police were as easily fooled as that, but Naputiro itself served as a communication center between the two major blocks of Ik, and its proximity to the cattle camp was certainly convenient. In this way, indirectly, all the other villages also benefited.

I learned a few other new things, but the main objective was accomplished far more readily, for it was obvious from the outset that nothing had really changed due to the sudden glut of food, except to cause inter-personal relationships to deteriorate still further if possible, and heighten Icien individualism beyond what I would have thought even Ik to be capable of. If they had been mean and greedy and selfish before with nothing to be mean and greedy and selfish over, now that they had something they really excelled themselves in what would be an insult to animals to call bestiality.

The Ik had faced a conscious choice between being humans and being parasites, and of course had chosen the latter. When they saw their fields come alive, even those which had not been planted but in which seed had lain dormant and never germinated, they were confronted with a problem. If they reaped the harvest, they would then be courting disaster for the following year, which might be another famine year, for they would have to store grain for eating and planting, and every Ik knew that trying to store anything was a waste of time. Further, if they made their fields look too promising, by cultivating them and keeping them free of insect and bird damage, the government would stop famine relief, and famine relief had shown itself to be a far easier way of getting food than farming. So the Ik let their fields rot, just eating what they wanted when they wanted, if it was still there, and continued to draw famine relief, which only confirmed them in their parasitic tendencies.

The relief was offered by the government against genuine emergency, but it was offered by the local authorities with all the blind paternalism of a British colonial government, blind to the point of being arrogant. Had it been in the hands of Africans alone, it might have been different, but the old paternalistic influence was there still, with its urge to do the right thing, to do good, but without stopping to consider what it meant by good. Ironically, the expatriate famine-relief officer evidently had the same concept of goodness as the Ik, and saw his duty as being the filling of stomachs without inquiry into whether this was really necessary, whether it would really help the people, and without any adequate supervision of how it was done. Perhaps there was not adequate personnel for supervision, but the famine relief was a good example of good intent gone very wrong.

The Ik were not starving any longer; the old and infirm had all died the previous year, and between the rotting crops and the rakeoff from their various subsidiary economies the younger survivors were doing quite well. But, as in the previous year, the famine relief was administered in a way that was little short of criminal. It was not only a waste of good government money, but it spelled the end of the Ik. It was delivered to Kasilé and left there for the Jakite and the *mkungu* to distribute according to the records they kept, so much per man, woman and child. Apart from the usual amount of loss in any such scheme, I estimated that the records indicated a population about twenty percent in excess of the surviving population. Even the most cursory check revealed names of people who, like Atum's wife, had been dead for two years. It did not take much inquiry, either, to find that in all likelihood many of these had been allowed to die so as to effectively double the ration of the next of kin. Further still, as before, and as reported, only the young and well were able to get down from Pirre to collect the relief, and they were given relief for the others who could not come, and told to take it back. But naturally they never did. So those who were in no real need got the relief intended for themselves as well as that intended for all their truly needy kin. They grew fat on stupidity, while others died.

Not more than a few miles from Kasilé, well out of sight and reach, was a stopping place where the Ik, one might think rather prematurely, sat down to rest on their way back from a famine-relief expedition, laden with *posho* for the dying and dead. But it was not to rest that they halted, it was to gobble and gorge themselves until they were bloated and had to vomit before they could finally dispose of the last traces of the do-gooder's bounty. I had seen this during the previous year, accompanied by Kauar. Kauar was carrying home his relief as well as that for his wife and child, who were sick at the time. When we reached the stopping place, we too stopped as the orgy began, but Kauar looked off in another direction. The others mocked him for his weakness and said he should not carry the load on his head, better to carry it in his stomach. They said, jokingly, that he would die. Only a few reserved their food for farther along the trail where they could eat it at greater leisure.

When asked for advice on relocation, I had to give advice that I knew could never be accepted, even if the government believed the situation to be as extreme as I painted it. But Karimoja is a vast territory to administer, and the whole time I was at Pirre the administrator was able to get up only once, and stayed a couple of hours. He could have stayed a couple of days, weeks or months and still not been convinced that the degeneration of society was as complete as it was. The surface looked bad enough, the hunger could be seen and the trickery perceived, and the political games were well enough known, but one had to live among the Ik and see them day in and day out and watch them defecating on each other's doorsteps, and taking food out of each other's mouths, and vomiting so as to finish what belonged to the starving, to begin to know what had happened to them.

My suggestion was simple enough. It recognized that physical coercion would be necessary to relocate them, for they would never move of their own accord. They would have to be rounded up in something approaching a military operation. The terrain, although difficult, was not spacious, and a well-organized operation could have enclosed them and caught most of them before they could flee. Then they would have to be taken to parts of Uganda sufficiently remote for them not to be able to return to northern Karimoja, for as long as they were within reach they would always try to return. The territory for relocation would have to be mountainous and capable of being worked productively. All this might have been acceptable except for the use of force, which would have put the government in a bad light if misreported, as it almost certainly would have been by the international press. But my last stipulation was doomed to rejection. In discussing the use of force I said that men, women and children could be rounded up at random and should be dispersed throughout the country, in its mountainous regions, in small units of about ten. Age, sex or kinship was immaterial. Such random grouping would do no violence to the family structure, but would, if anything, be beneficial, for it would complete the fragmentation already complete in all but their continued localization, and would compel their integration into the life of the communities to which they would be allocated. If kept in larger units, they might well be able to band together to work their magic around them wherever they went, perpetuating their survival system and perhaps corrupting still others. Whereas if dispersed in small groups, they would be forced to find their own individual ways, which would suit them temperamentally, and would quickly lose their language and with it their last sense of belonging to a world long gone beyond recall.

I could see no other solution. If moved to areas where there were others somewhat akin to them, like the Napore and the Niangea, they would be able to go right back to their old ways whenever they wanted to, and would in all likelihood quickly reduce their neighbors to similar straits. They were beyond saving as a society, the family clearly held no emotional value for them at all and virtually no economic value, they had cultivated individualism to its apex, so why not accept that and try to reintroduce them as individuals into a world where human beings are also social and care about each other, rather as other animals seem to do?

I was told, frankly enough, that my report seemed extreme

and seemed to exaggerate the situation somewhat: Africans were known for their devotion to family, and even under the worst circumstances . . . and so forth and so forth. I was also told, with equal frankness, that even if the situation *was* as bad as I said, it was unlikely that the government could take such extreme measures. I believe there was an attempt to move the Ik to Napore, and they all simply allowed themselves to be moved, then turned around and walked back.

Luckily the Ik are not numerous—about two thousand— and those two years reduced their numbers greatly. So I am hopeful that their isolation will remain as complete as in the past, until they die out completely. I am only sorry that so many individuals will have to die, slowly and painfully, until the end comes to them all. For the individuals one can only feel infinite sorrow at what they have lost; hatred must be reserved for the so-called society they live in, the machine they have constructed to enable them to survive. They have not created it willingly or consciously; it has created itself through their biological need for survival, out of the only materials available, and in the only possible form. It is that survival machine that is the monster, not the Atums and Lojieris and Lokbo'oks, not even the Lomongins and Loi-amukats. They had a simple choice of living or dying; they had already lost the rest—family, friendship, hope, love— and they made the same choice that most of us, I believe, would make. The only hope now is the unborn or the unweaned, and had they been rounded up and carted off like cattle, they might have grown up as human beings. No, one can be far more certain, they *would* have grown up as human beings, loved by their foster parents with all the intense love that is so truly a part of ordinary African life, and loving in return. But because of sensitivity to foreign opinion, and other political considerations, and heaven knows what else that goes into administration and govern-mental decision, they were condemned to grow up like their parents and, if they survived, to spawn more of the same. And somewhere, without doubt, someone made a final deci-sion thinking that he was doing so "for their own good."

There is no goodness left for the Ik, only a full stomach, and that only for those whose stomachs are already full. But if there is no goodness, stop to think, there is no badness, and if there is no love, neither is there any hate. Perhaps that, after all, is progress; but it is also emptiness.

CHAPTER TWELVE

The World That Is

IT IS, of course, guesswork when we try to say what the Ik
were like before all this happened, for there are no records.
However, the guesswork is not entirely without foundation,
for we can use our knowledge of other hunting peoples for
comparison, and we have the remnants of past traditions,
customs and beliefs, and something of their own oral tradition, all of which indicate that they were, much like other
hunters and gatherers, an easy-going, loosely organized people whose fluid organization enabled them to respond with
sensitivity to the ever changing demands of their environment. There is ample evidence in their language that they
once held values which they no longer hold, that they understood by "goodness" and "happiness" something very different from what those words have come to mean now. It is
reasonable to suppose that the Ik were much like any other
human society in terms of how firmly they held to their

values and put their beliefs into practice, and it is by no
means unreasonable, by comparison with other hunting societies, to suppose that very likely they were rather more
faithful to their stated beliefs than we have become. Fidelity
was possible for them; it is becoming impossible for us. And
now, in one dramatic generation, they have leaped ahead
and given us a taste of things to come.

In evidence, too, of how recently the Ik knew goodness,
and of how rapidly we could lose it, are not only the stories
told by the old who remembered it, but their lives. There
was Nangoli and her family, who still wanted to be a family,
yet who also still wanted to be part of the larger family of
mountain people, the *kwarikik*. And Lolim, who wanted to
die as a father should, in what should have been his *asak*
shared with his son, but had become his son's *asak* from
which he was turned away. Lomeraniang, Amuarkuar,
Loiangorok—they all died without complaint, long before
their time, because of the end of goodness; and goodness
died with them. They died without complaint because the
chill dispassion that is the Ik's new weapon against the
world, their world, had touched them. Only Lo'ono remembered in full, when we reminded her, and made her cry and
die in grief. And Adupa, who died because she was mad—or
perhaps because she was kind and wanted her parents to be
kind, for that, among the Ik, is a sure madness.

The facts are there, though heaven knows those which can
be read here form but a fraction of what one person was able
to gather in under two years. If others can interpret them
differently—more charitably perhaps they would like to
say—then they are lucky, for they have neither lived among
the Ik and lived those facts every minute of every day, nor
have they gathered, through the medium of nice clean pages
read with a full stomach, anything of what I have tried to

convey. And if any persist in feeling that I am overly pessimistic or extreme in my interpretation of the facts, there can
be no mistaking the direction in which those facts point, and
that is the most important thing of all, for it may affect the
rest of mankind as it has affected the Ik. The Ik have "progressed," one might say, since the change that has come to
them has come with the advent of civilization to Africa and
is therefore a part of that phenomenon we so blandly and
unthinkingly refer to as progress. They have made of a
world that was alive a world that is dead, a cold, dispas-
sionate world that is without ugliness because it is without
beauty, without hate because it is without love, and is
without any realization of truth even, because it simply is.
And the symptoms of change in our own society indicate
that we are heading in precisely the same direction.

If we grant, as the evidence indicates we should, that the
Ik were not always as they are, and that they once possessed
in full measure those values that we all hold to be basic to
humanity, indispensable for both survival and sanity, then
what the Ik are telling us is that these qualities are not
inherent in humanity at all, they are not a necessary part of
human nature. Those values which we cherish so highly and
which some use to point to our infinite superiority over other
forms of animal life may indeed be basic to human society,
but not to humanity, and that means that the Ik clearly show
that society itself is not indispensable for man's survival, that
man is not the social animal he has always thought himself
to be, and that he is perfectly capable of associating for
purposes of survival without being social. The Ik have successfully abandoned useless appendages, by which I refer to
those "basic" qualities such as family, cooperative sociality,
belief, love, hope and so forth, for the very good reason that
in their context these militated against survival. By showing

that man can do without these appendages the Ik show that man can do without society in the sense we mostly mean by the word (implying those qualities), for they have replaced human society with a mere survival system that does not take human emotion into account. As yet the system is imperfect, for although survival is assured, it is at a minimal level and there is still competition between the individuals within the system. With our intellectual sophistication and with our advanced technology we should be able to perfect the system and eliminate competition, guaranteeing survival for a given number of years for all, reducing the demands made upon us by a social system with all its necessary structural oppositions and inherent conflicts, abolishing desire and consequently that ever present and vital gap between desire and achievement, treating us, in a word, as individuals with one basic individual right, the right to survive, so that man becomes the perfect vegetable, no longer an animal, human or otherwise.

Such interaction as there is within this system is one of mutual exploitation. That is the relationship between all, old and young, parent and child, brother and sister, husband and wife, friend and friend. That is how it already is with the Ik. They are brought together by self-interest alone, and the system takes care that such association is of a temporary nature and cannot flourish into anything as dysfunctional as affection or trust. Does that sound so very different from our own society? In our own world the very mainstays of a society based on a truly social sense of mutuality are breaking down, indicating that perhaps society itself as we know it has outworn its usefulness, and that by clinging to an outworn system more proper to the neolithic age we are bringing about our own destruction. We have tinkered with society, patching it up to cope with two thousand years of change, but it shows signs of collapse almost everywhere, and the signs are the more violent where the society is more "advanced." It is only to the "backward societies" that this new violence has not yet come. Family, economy, government and religion, the basic categories of social activity and behavior, despite our tinkering, are no longer structured in a way that makes them compatible with each other or with us, for they are no longer structured in such a way as to create any sense of social unity involving a shared and mutual responsibility between all members of our society. At the best they are structured so as to enable the individual to survive as an individual, with as little demand as possible that any vestigial remains of mutual responsibility should be expressed in mutuality of action. It is the world of the individual, as is the world of the Ik.

What has become of the Western family? The very old and the very young are separated, but we dispose of them in homes for the aged or in day schools and summer camps instead of on the slopes of Meraniang. Marital relations are barely even fodder for comedians, and responsibility for health, education and welfare has been gladly abandoned to the state. That is where we have a technological advantage over the Ik, for they have had to abandon such responsibility to the three-year-olds; it is difficult to say which of us is more advanced in this respect. The individualism that is preached with a curious fanaticism, heightened by our ever growing emphasis on competitive sports, the more violent the better, and suicidal recreations, is of course at direct variance with our still proclaimed social ideals, but we ignore that, for we are already individuals at heart and society has become a game that we play in our old age, to remind us of our childhood. It is reflected in our cutthroat economics, where almost any kind of exploitation and degra-

dation of others, impoverishment and ruin, is justified in
terms of an expanding economy and the consequent confine-
ment of the world's riches in the pockets of the few. The rot
is in all of us, for how many of us would be willing to divide
our riches among our own family, let alone the poor or
needy, beyond of course what we can easily afford—for if
we were willing, why have we not done it? Each of us gives
according to his conscience, and the amount that is given is
a nice measure of today's sociality, just as the amount taken
is a good measure of man's individuality.

The great religions which arose as if in an effort to provide
some means for uniting the ever expanding and increasingly
diverse societies brought about by the agricultural revolu-
tion seem on the verge of defeat. They still unite large
blocks, but with less and less efficiency, and all are increasingly rent with internal schism. This has nothing to do with
their impact on any individual, or perhaps in a way it has,
for that is now apparently the growing role of religion, to
provide some kind of anesthesia for those unable to face the
world as it is. Another, even less laudable (in terms of its
own professed beliefs) role played by formal religion is to
lend support to the state, even when this is in direct conflict
with its own principles. The state itself, resting ever more on
both intellectual and physical violence to assert itself, is
where the nucleus of the new system is forming, it seems,
and the loud-mouthed anti-intellectual blabberings of heads
of state and their assistants show as well as anything that we
are well along on the Icien road, where man must not only
not believe or trust or love or hope, but must not think. The
job of government seems to be regarded more and more as
simply to *govern,* to conform to the self-creating system, and
to enforce conformity on the governed. As yet the word
"democracy" still has some soporific value, lulling the un-

thinking but nicely filled stomachs into a sense of security, but good government regards those with minds and with the will to express themselves as a nuisance, to be destroyed if they cannot be made to conform. It is worth noting, too, that high places in government are not conspicuously occupied by men with minds, merely by men with certain political (and not necessarily social) abilities.

The sorry state of society in the civilized world today, which contrasts so strongly with the still social society of the "primitive," is in large measure due to the simple fact that social change has not kept up with technological change, which has not only been almost inconceivably rapid but has been accelerating with even greater rapidity, carrying us with it in an unknown direction, leaving our old form of society behind but, the signs seem to indicate, holding in store for us the future already tasted by the Ik. It is this mad, senseless, unthinking commitment to technological change that we call progress, despite the grim trail of disaster it is wreaking all around us, including overpopulation and pollution, either of which may be sufficient to exterminate the human race in a very short time even without the assistance of other technological benefits such as nuclear warfare. But since we have already become individualized and desocialized we say to ourselves that extermination will not come in our time, which shows about as much sense of family devotion as one might expect from the Ik, and as little sense of social responsibility.

Even supposing we can avert the disaster of nuclear holocaust or that of the almost universal famine that may be expected by the middle of the next century if population keeps expanding and pollution remains unchecked, what will be the cost, if not the same already paid by the Ik? They too were driven by the need to survive against seemingly invincible odds, and they succeeded, at the cost of their humanity. We are already beginning to pay the same price, but the difference is that we not only still have the choice (though we may not have the will or courage to make it), we also have the intellectual and technological ability to avert an Icien end. Many will say, are already saying, that it is too late—by which they mean it is too late for the change to benefit them. Any change as radical as that likely to be necessary, certainly, is not likely to bring material benefits to the present generation, though for those with a belief in the future, and an interest in it, there will be ample compensation, for only then *will* there be a future. And naturally it is the young—whose future, even as individuals, stretches beyond that of the ruling generation—who are most concerned, and in whose hands, perhaps, society and humanity lie. But it is difficult to predict their feelings, however bold their demand for change may be now, when in a few short years they too begin to think of their old age and personal security. It is also difficult to say how long the choice will be open to us before we are irrevocably committed.

The Ik teach us that our much vaunted human values are not inherent in humanity at all, but are associated only with a particular form of survival called society, and that all, even society itself, are luxuries that can be dispensed with. That does not make them any the less wonderful or desirable, and if man has any greatness it is surely in his ability to maintain these values, clinging to them to an often very bitter end, even shortening an already pitifully short life rather than sacrificing his humanity. But that too involves choice, and the Ik teach us that man can lose the will to make it. That is the point at which there is an end to truth, to goodness and to beauty; an end to the struggle for their achievement, which gives life to the individual while at the same time giving strength and meaning to society. The Ik have relinquished all luxury in the name of individual survival, and the result is that they live on as a people without life, without passion, beyond humanity. We pursue those trivial, idiotic technological encumbrances and imagine *them* to be the luxuries that make life worth living, and all the time we are losing our potential for social rather than individual survival, for hating as well as loving, losing perhaps our last chance to enjoy life with all the passion that is our nature and being.

Glossary

(The singular form is given; in most words, however, the same form is used for the plural.)

ASAK: Door or gateway, especially that leading into the family compound, as distinct from *odok* (see)

ASKARI: Soldier, or armed guard

AO: Village, a number of family compounds, all divided from each other by inner stockades, but all contained within a single outer stockade

ANAZÉ: An elder

ABANG: An ancestor

ADOKANA: A palm tree providing fruit eaten by elephant

BOMA: A cattle compound

BONIT: A clan

BUTAANÉS: To copulate

BADIAM: A sorcerer

BEDES: To want or need

BAM: A friend
BUKONIAM: An adulterer

DI: A sitting place, often open, sometimes sheltered
DZUUAM: A thief
DIDI: Rain
DANG: A termite
DUUES: To steal

EDZIAAGES: To defecate

GOMOI: A bitter but edible berry
GOR: A soul
GOETES: To take

IAKW: A man (*iakw anamarang*—a good man)
ICIEBAM (Icie-bam): Friend of the Ik

KWARIKIK: Mountain people
KARATZ: A small carved wooden neck rest also used as a seat
KOROMOT: The traditional beehive-shaped hut the Ik used to make
   of grass
KO'ONAM: A person who commits incest

LOTOP: Tobacco

MENYATTA: The village of cattle herders
MKUNGU: Chief, ruler
MARANG: Good
MARANGIK: Goodness
MORAN: An initiated youth among the herders, charged with the
   defense of his people and their cattle
MOS: A special kind of Pirre tree

NGAG: Food
NIECHAI: Tea

NYOT: Bond brotherhood, a bond brother
NAKUT: A digging stick
NYEG: Hunger

OROR: A ravine or gulley; a watercourse
ODOK: The gateway through the outer stockade of a village

POSHO: Ground corn (maize) meal, or the porridge made from it

SANZA: The Swahili term for a musical instrument widespread throughout Africa, played by plucking metal or bamboo strips fitted like keys on a wooden resonator
SIM: Cord made from the bark of vines or trees

TANGAU: A termite trap, built around a termite hill to enable Ik to catch the termites when they swarm

YASIZUUK: Really, truly

COMMON PHRASES
Ida piaji. This is the common, everyday greeting.
Brinji lotop. Give me tobacco.
Brinji ngag. Give me food.
Bera ngag. There is no food.
Itelida korobo jiig baraz, baraz. You will see everything, tomorrow, tomorrow.
Bedia inaares abi. I want (need) to help you.
Aats a didi! Rain is coming!
Kwesida kwatz. Wait a moment; excuse me a moment.

Guide to Pronunciation
of African Words

Consonants have approximately the same sound as in English, with the exception of *c*, as in Acoli, which is pronounced as *ch* in "church," so "Acoli" would be pronounced "Acholi."

Vowels are pronounced as follows:

a   as in   father
e   as in   met, perhaps a little closer to the *a* in make.
i   as in   mill, perhaps a little longer, as the "ee" in been.
o   as in   fold.
u   as in   rude.

It is important that every vowel be pronounced separately, so that "Lokcléa" is pronounced something like *loh-kay-lay-ah;* and "Kokoi" as *koh-koh-ee*. This guide is only approximate, but will help give a reasonable idea of how most of the words and names sound.

An accent has been placed over some vowels to emphasize the need to pronounce them distinctly; sometimes double vowels are separated by an apostrophe to indicate that each must be uttered separately. Thus "Lo'ono" is made to sound *Loh-oh-noh*.

Index

303

About the Author

Colin M. Turnbull was born in London, and now lives in Connecticut. He was educated at Westminster School and Magdalen College, Oxford, where he studied philosophy and politics. After serving in the Royal Naval Volunteer Reserve during World War II, he held a research grant for two years in the Department of Indian Religion and Philosophy at Banaras Hindu University, in India, and then returned to Oxford, where he studied anthropology, specializing in the African field.

He has made five extended field trips to Africa, the last of which was spent mainly in the Republic of Zaïre. From these trips he drew the material for his first book, *The Forest People*, an account of the three years he spent with the Pygmies of Zaïre.

Mr. Turnbull was a Professor of Anthropology at George Washington University in Washington, D.C. He is a Research Associate at the American Museum of Natural History in New York, and a Corresponding Member of Le Musée Royal d'Afrique Centrale.